I0084717

LEARNING RELIGION

Methodology and History in Anthropology

General Editor: David Parkin, Director of the Institute of Social and Cultural Anthropology, University of Oxford

Volume 1
Marcel Mauss: A Centenary Tribute
Edited by Wendy James and N.J. Allen

Volume 2
*Franz Baerman Steiner: Selected Writings Volume I: Taboo, Truth and Religion.
Franz B. Steiner*
Edited by Jeremy Adler and Richard Fardon

Volume 3
Franz Baerman Steiner. Selected Writings Volume II: Orientalism, Value, and Civilisation. Franz B. Steiner
Edited by Jeremy Adler and Richard Fardon

Volume 4
The Problem of Context
Edited by Roy Dilley

Volume 5
Religion in English Everyday Life
By Timothy Jenkins

Volume 6
Hunting the Gatherers: Ethnographic Collectors, Agents and Agency in Melanesia, 1870s–1930s
Edited by Michael O'Hanlon and Robert L. Welsch

Volume 7
Anthropologists in a Wider World: Essays on Field Research
Edited by Paul Dresch, Wendy James and David Parkin

Volume 8
Categories and Classifications: Maussian Reflections on the Social
By N.J. Allen

Volume 9
Louis Dumont and Hierarchical Opposition
By Robert Parkin

Volume 10
Categories of Self: Louis Dumont's Theory of the Individual
By André Celtel

Volume 11
Existential Anthropology: Events, Exigencies and Effects
By Michael Jackson

Volume 12
An Introduction to Two Theories of Social Anthropology: Descent Groups and Marriage Alliance. Louis Dumont
Edited and Translated by Robert Parkin

Volume 13
Navigating Terrains of War: Youth and Soldering in Guinea-Bissau
By Henrik Vigh

Volume 14
The Politics of Egalitarianism: Theory and Practice
Edited by Jacqueline Solway

Volume 15
A History of Oxford Anthropology
Edited by Peter Rivière

Volume 16
Holistic Anthropology: Emergence and Convergence
Edited by David Parkin and Stanley Ulijaszek

Volume 17
Learning Religion: Anthropological Approaches
Edited by David Berliner and Ramon Sarró

Volume 18
Ways of Knowing: Anthropological Approaches to Crafting Experience and Knowledge
Edited by Mark Harris

LEARNING RELIGION

Anthropological Approaches

Edited by

David Berliner and Ramon Sarró

Berghahn Books
New York • Oxford

First published in 2007 by

Berghahn Books

www.berghahnbooks.com

©2007, 2009 David Berliner and Ramon Sarró
First paperback edition published in 2009

All rights reserved.
Except for the quotation of short passages for the purpose of criticism and review, no part of this book may be reproduced in any form or by any means, electronic or mechanical, including photocopying, recording, or any information storage and retrieval system now known or to be invented, without written permission of the publisher.

Library of Congress Cataloging-in-Publication Data

Learning religion : anthropological approaches / edited by David Berliner and Ramon Sarró.
    p. cm. -- (Methodology and history in anthropology)
Includes bibliographical references and index.
 ISBN: 978-1-84545-374-9 (hardback : alk. paper)-- ISBN: 978-1-84545-594-1 (paperback : alk. paper)
 1. Ethnology--Religious aspects. 2. Religion. I. Berliner, David C. II. Sarró, Ramon.
BL256.L385 2007
207'.5--dc22

2007035361

British Library Cataloguing in Publication Data

A catalogue record for this book is available from the British Library

Printed on acid-free paper

ISBN 978-1-84545-374-9 (hbk)
ISBN 978-1-84545-594-1 (pbk)

CONTENTS

Acknowledgements   vii

1. On Learning Religion: An Introduction   1
    David Berliner and Ramon Sarró

2. Learning to Believe: A Preliminary Approach   21
    Carlo Severi

3. Menstrual Slaps and First Blood Celebrations: Inference,
    Simulation and the Learning of Ritual   31
    Michael Houseman

4. The Accidental in Religious Instruction: Ideas and
    Convictions   49
    David Parkin

5. On Catching Up With Oneself: Learning to Know That One
    Means What One Does   65
    Michael Lambek

6. How Do You Learn to Know That it is God Who Speaks?   83
    T.M. Luhrmann

7. How to Learn in an Afro-Brazilian Spirit Possession
    Religion: Ontology and Multiplicity in Candomblé   103
    Marcio Goldman

8. Learning to be a Proper Medium: Middle-Class
    Womanhood and Spirit Mediumship at Christian
    Rationalist Séances in Cape Verde   121
    João Vasconcelos

9. Copyright and Authorship: Ritual Speech and the New
    Market of Words in Toraja   141
    Aurora Donzelli

10. Learning Faith: Young Christians and Catechism   161
        Laurence Hérault

11. What is Interesting about Chinese Religion   177
        Charles Stafford

12. The Sound of Witchcraft: Noise as Mediation in
      Religious Transmission   191
        Michael Rowlands

Bibliography   209

Notes on Contributors   229

Index   233

ACKNOWLEDGEMENTS

This volume is the product of a conference held at the Institute of Social Sciences, University of Lisbon, on 8–11 September 2005. We would like to express our gratitude first and foremost to Christina Toren and to João Pina-Cabral for having encouraged us to organize it and to the Institute of Social Sciences for having offered such a wonderful venue for it, as well as to the many institutions that funded it: The Wennegren Foundation for Anthropological Research was our main sponsor, but we would also like to remember here the significant contributions of the Gulbenkian Foundation, the Luso-American Foundation, the British Council, the Foundation for Science and Technology (Portugal) and, last but not least, the Institute itself, not only for the financial help but also for the efficiency with which it dealt with the organization of the event.

Special thanks are, of course, due to the guests to the conference who made it an unforgettable meeting. Our paper givers Rita Astuti, Ruy Blanes, Aurora Donzelli, Carlos Fausto, Anna Fedele, Marcio Goldman, Peter Gow, Arnauld Halloy, Laurence Hérault, Charles Hirschkind, Michael Houseman, Michael Lambek, Tanya Luhrmann, José Mapril, Adeline Masquelier, David Parkin, Michael Rowlands, Carlo Severi, Sónia Silva, Benjamin Soares, Charles Stafford, Marina P. Temudo, Christina Toren, and João Vasconcelos; as well as our chairs/discussants: Catarina A. Costa, Cristiana Bastos, Joan Bestard, Stephen Dix, Antónia P. de Lima, João Pina-Cabral, Nuno Porto, Gonçalo D. dos Santos, Nina C. Tiesler, Wilson Trajano F. and Susana M. Viegas.

Finally, we would also like to express here our deepest gratitude to David Parkin who engineered the book with us and invited us to submit it to the collection he edits for Berghahn Books and for his instrumental help in putting it together.

Chapter 1

ON LEARNING RELIGION: AN INTRODUCTION

David Berliner and Ramon Sarró

Religion, Recollection and Learning

A Biblical text (*Acts of the Apostles*, 8: 31–32) tells us that immediately after Pentecost, when the Holy Ghost inspired Jesus' disciples to spread the good news, Philip, one of the apostles, saw the eunuch of the queen of the Ethiopians reading the Book of Isaiah. 'Do you understand what you are reading?' asked Philip. 'How can I, unless someone instructs me?' replied the eunuch. Then Philip carefully read the text with him and explained that what they were reading was in fact the announcement of the coming of Jesus. The eunuch not only understood then what he had been reading (*and* told), but also asked to be baptized with water. Something somewhat similar happened two thousand years later when a Russian woman we met told us she used to read the Bible a lot, but had not understood it. She only understood it when her boyfriend, a Jehovah's Witness, explained the meaning of the texts to her. Not only did she then 'understand' the Bible, but she also converted from the Orthodox Church to the Jehovah's Witnesses' religion.

These relatively simple occurrences could exemplify some of the aspects we wanted to explore when in September 2005, under the aegis of the Wennergen Foundation for Anthropological Research, we organized a symposium, rather intriguingly called 'learning religion', at the Institute of Social Sciences, Lisbon. We have here a man and a woman who respectively celebrate a religious action routinely (reading a holy text without 'understanding' it) and an instructor who fills this ritual action with 'meaning', which then leads to their finally experiencing a transformation we would normally refer to as 'conversion'. Of course both the eunuch and the Russian woman had already had some instruction, otherwise they would not have spent their time reading such solemn texts. Yet, the experience of suddenly 'understanding' something when someone else brings an explanation from outside and forces a new reading of one's routine is not only a characteristic of conversion narratives, but in many ways it may be essential to religion itself.

Already in the first century BC, the Roman thinker Cicero in his *De Natura Deorum* (II: 72) had established a solid distinction between those who conducted a religious ritual routinely just because they were asked or instructed to do so but paid no attention to it (Cicero called them 'superstitious', a word whose meaning has changed enormously) and those who followed it attentively and consciously. These were called 'religious' – or so Cicero claimed – because they did what in Latin was called *relego*: to do something in full consciousness ('observing' a cult, as the English has it), a concept sometimes translated as 're-reading' and sometimes, probably more accurately, as 'recollecting'.[1] For Cicero, a religious person was one who not only performed a rite, but also conducted it carefully. As some contemporary colleagues would put it, 'orthopraxis' is for many religious people more important than orthodoxy, but it must be taken into account that Cicero's suggestion was that this 'orthopraxis' should not become mechanical but remain conscious, otherwise it would then be mere *superstitio*. So one had to conduct rites with full attention and with full intention.

Some readers could disagree and insist that the two cases in point do not exemplify Cicero's *relego* but rather give it a 'serendipitous' twist: it is when re-reading the texts with the (should we say misleading?) help from Philip or a boyfriend that our protagonists suddenly 'understood' what they had been reading and entered a different religion to that in which they had been socialized. However, if we follow Emile Benveniste (1969), who for many years has provided the most reliable hermeneutic of these Ciceronian concepts, the disagreement would be ironed out. For him, the idea that *relego* implied a new rendering of an old practice (be it a rite or a text) was implicit in the concept. He translated *relego* by the obsolete French verb *recollecter* and glossed it as 'going back to a previous synthesis in order to recompose it' (Benveniste 1969, Vol. 2: 271; our translation). A religious person should constantly read the foundations of his or her beliefs and apply them to new situations, always revisiting, like a chameleon, the trodden path with renewed intent to move forward. The basic foundations of a religious system may be very solid, but they can be 'observed' in very different ways by different actors or even by the same actor at different times, as Clifford Geertz proved in his classic comparison of two Muslim settings (Geertz 1971). Of course, the fact that *relego* implied some re-reading does not solve the problem of conversion (which in any case is not the problem this volume addresses), but we think that in many cases even conversion could be more fruitfully seen as a process of recollection and reinterpretation of one's past than as a biographical 'rupture'.

As is well known, Cicero's etymological exploration (probably whimsical) of 'religion' was later contested by Christian apologetics, most notably Lactantius (third century) and later Augustine (fourth century), for whom the Latin word *religio* stemmed (probably whimsically too) from the verb religo (to re-bind), because religion means binding someone to the divinity (for further reading on these etymologies, see Meslin 1988: 24–42; Smith 1998: 269–70). This set a characteristically theological (Christian) way of thinking about religion that has been a problem not only for theologians, but also for historians of religion, anthropologists and other social scientists (Asad 1993). Indeed we cannot reduce religion to inner devotion (although this should not be neglected either) and, to our understanding, Cicero's exploration seems much more descriptive and open to other religions than Lactantius' or Augustine's inner re-binding. In any case, the most interesting thing about these two etymologies may be that they both coincide on one thing: the reiterative aspect of religion. Whether we recollect or we re-bind, whether the etymology of religion is *relego* or *religio*, we are fundamentally talking about some kind of repetitive action (Latour 2002). No matter how it is defined, religion has to do with reiteration: of words, actions, intentions or memories. How it repeats and replicates itself over time and space is what we ethnographers are here to find out.

However, finding out about this is not an obvious matter either at the theoretical or methodological level. In many ways this volume, just as the 2005 Lisbon conference on which it is based, is the direct outcome of this difficulty and the concomitant need to start clearing up the path. Both of us have done fieldwork and have written about roughly the same area (coastal Guinea), enveloped in the same environment marked by strong secrecy, legacies of iconoclastic Muslim movements and socialist 'campaigns of demystification' and by the pervading presence of spiritual agencies despite the absence of formal institutions of religious learning (Berliner 2005b, 2005c; Sarró 2002, 2007b). It may not come as a surprise that Guinea also offered a field site for Christian Højbjerg, who has also worked on transmission of religious knowledge and has developed a theory of the 'robustness' of religious notions to explain the tenacity of religious representations even when religious institutions are officially banned (Højbjerg

2002b), as well as for Michael McGovern, author of a PhD dissertation on the impact of anti-ritualist policies in the making of contemporary Guinean subjectivities (McGovern 2004). Richard Fardon (1990) once wrote that anthropological paradigms are often inscribed in regional areas. Without claiming to have invented a new paradigm in Guinea, there is no doubt that the specific religious history in this country led us to think through issues of learning and transmission in religion and to discover, alas, that despite anthropologists' long-standing interest in religion, we still lacked the methodological tools to start tackling the topic of its learning. We thought that organizing a conference with some of the best specialists in religious knowledge would be a good way to make a start. It was a good idea.

Anthropologists have defined 'religion' in many ways, and although we do not want to convert this introductory chapter into a list of definitions, it may be useful to recollect some trends that have accompanied our discipline since the nineteenth century. Edward Tylor's classic and succinct definition of religion as 'belief in spiritual beings' has been a powerful one and although today it may sound slightly too obvious, we must keep in mind that in its days it was meant as a provocation against a legion of scholars who argued that unless you had a temple, a holy scripture, a priestly class and (only) one high god, you could not really claim you had 'religion' (Tylor 1903 [1871], Vol. 1: 424; for a contextualization of Tylor's definition, see Pals 1996: 16–29 and Stringer 1999). Despite its own inner problems (what exactly is a 'belief'? what kind of being is a 'spiritual' one?), Tylor's definition, together with its concomitant concepts of 'animism' and 'intellectualism' proved to be sufficiently thought-provoking tools for anthropology. Not only did they give rise to much debate and research about what makes religion something different from any other human activity, but in fact today they are also coming back and articulating fresh research on why and how it is possible for people to believe in non-sensorial entities that, for the lack of a better word, we might as well call 'spiritual', although 'supernatural' would probably be a more neutral term (for contemporary cognitive approaches to 'animism', see Guthrie 1993, Boyer 1996, and much of the cognitive approaches to religion reviewed in the next section).

Another angle that has proved quite consistent is one that views religion as a sentiment of dependence from – or of belonging to – a superior force. This idea was very dear to German Protestant thinkers, from Schleiermacher (1994 [1799]) to the founders of modern comparative history of religions such as Friedrich Max Müller (1878) and a little later Rudolf Otto (1956 [1918]), but it had its clearly non-religious variant in the Durkheiman line of analysis (Durkheim 1995 [1912]). The approach is still being fruitfully explored by contemporary authors who see religion as, among other things, a system of subordination to both superhuman entities and an encompassing ideological system (for a paradigmatic example, see Bloch 1992). Symbolic anthropology of the 1960s, which was probably more strongly influenced by Weber than Durkheim, gave rise to new definitions of religion, such as that of Clifford Geertz (1969; see his recent reappraisal in Geertz 2005). That religion was a system of symbols through which people constructed a meaningful world also had its imprint on the history of religions, especially in the anthropologically-oriented version of Jonathan Z. Smith and his followers, a school that has learnt to use anthropology in very enriching ways (Smith 1976, 1989, 2002) and has in turn given feedback to anthropological analyses of ritual and religion (see, for example, Ray 2000).[2] There are undoubtedly many other approaches that should be taken into account. We might as well decide that the exercise of trying to define 'religion' is futile and should be given up, as seem inclined Talal Asad (1983), William Arnal (Arnal 2000) and other contemporary scholars of religion. There are indeed many things one can say about religion. One can even deny its existence as a 'thing' to be studied[3] or, more intriguingly, that it exists for other people, as in the case of an Orthodox Christian who said he could not discuss religion with Protestants because, according to him, they did *not* have religion (Sarró 2007a). But one thing we definitely cannot do is claim that whatever it is that we, or the people we have mentioned, call 'religion' (be it their inner convictions or their social institutions) is something that just came 'out of the blue'. People live in society, and it is in society they are socialized and learn to be grown-ups – *religious* grown-ups, sometimes.

There is little doubt then that no matter how well- or ill-defined they are, religious dynamics have been a profusely explored area in the history of anthropology. Religion, beliefs and rituals have been a cherished area of anthropological analysis and reflection even since the days of Frazer's and Tylor's insistence on the explanatory role of beliefs; ever since Durkheim's seminal influence on British functionalism and French structuralism when he showed that religion is fundamental in creating a sense of coherence and belonging to a social group; ever since Evans-Pritchard's study on the Azande showed that 'witchcraft' was not a string of irrational ideas but rather a system of logically coherent beliefs and practices[4] and ever since anthropologists realized that in colonial situations people often went to religion in order to recreate their sense of cosmos and their dignity either in Melanesian 'cargo cults' or in African and American prophetic movements.[5] Religion has grown up with anthropology, and in fact it would require 'bad faith' to claim that the connection between religion and education has been completely neglected. Durkheim, for a start, saw religion as fundamentally a mechanism to enable social agents to become well adapted to social groups and he even wrote that the kind of transformation achieved by religion, i.e. 'conversion', is – or should be at any rate – similar to the transformation all educators try to effect upon their pupils (Durkheim 1938, quoted in Giddens 1972: 205–15). Durkheim's major study on religion (Durkheim 1995 [1912]) was based on Australian societies where initiation played a significant role in education and processes of coming of age, and together with the parallel influence of Arnold van Gennep's work on rites of passage (van Gennep 1960 [1909]), they triggered an anthropological interest in initiations that eventually yielded such extraordinary results as Audrey Richards' study on female initiation among the Bemba (Richards 1956) and Victor Turner's study on boy's initiation among the Ndembu (Turner 1967), to mention just two exemplary analyses of the interface between religion and the making of moral agents in a community. The same interface, of course, has been analysed by anthropologists working on literate societies, and here we should mention the names of Eickelman (1974) and Brenner (2000) as two very important contributors to the study of religious education in Muslim societies.

In the last few years studies of memory and the transmission of the past have blossomed in anthropology (for a critical review, see Berliner 2005a). These studies focus on history as it is lived, on how remembrances shared and transmitted by social groups cling to our past and how we are shaped by it. Some of these recent works have concentrated on the study of 'collective religious memory' (in the sense first given by Halbwachs 1994 [1925]: 243–300). This is particularly clear in the powerful study by Jun Jing (Jing 1996), in which he describes memories from the Chinese communist persecution era and the contemporary 'resurgence of popular religion' by a people 'trying to rebuild their life after grievous assaults on their cultural identity, sense of history, and religious faith' (Jing 1996: 22). This may be a paradigmatic case, but there are other detailed ethnographies testifying to how religious practices can be treated as sites of memory to be transmitted. Without making an exhaustive list, we could here remember, as token examples, the detailed accounts of Maurice Bloch in Madagascar (1998), Paul Stoller in Niger (1995) and Marianne Ferme and Rosalind Shaw in Sierra Leone (Ferme 2001; Shaw 2002).

However, despite the laudable efforts and ethnographic accounts on the interface between religion, transmission and learning, there has been in anthropology, as David Parkin (pers. comm.) has put it: 'the assumption that religion just happens to people' and to forget that much time and effort is invested in instructing people. In 1938, Meyer Fortes insightfully noted that 'a great deal of information has been accumulated about what is transmitted from one generation to the next ... Of the process of education – how one generation is "moulded" by the superior generation, how it assimilates and perpetuates its cultural heritage – much less is known' (1970: 14). Since he wrote this, numerous authors have been interested in the diversity of knowledge systems and in the processes of transmission of knowledge, especially in the field of the anthropology of education (Middleton [ed.] 1970; Spindler 1997). Their works, which are too numerous to mention in detail here, deal with the transmission of historical knowledge (Borofsky 1987; Crook 1996; Price 1983; Stobart and Howard 2002), apprenticeship and the transmission of *savoirs faires* (for a comprehensive bibliography, see Herzfeld 2004), as well as the role of schooling in the transmission of literary knowledge (Bloch 1998; Spindler 1997). However, at least until recently, not many anthropologists were interested in the construction of religious knowledge though there were some well-known exceptions such as the innovative studies of transmission of knowledge in initiatory rituals in Papua New Guinea by F. Barth (1975, 1987) or, more recently, Danièle Hervieu-Léger's work on transmission (Hervieu-Léger 1997). But apart from these, most contemporary studies of resurgent and syncretistic religions usually take for granted, or give only secondary importance to, the processes of transmission and learning. The precise way religious concepts about supernatural beings are acquired and practices linked to them are learnt has remained largely understudied by anthropologists, despite the above-mentioned anthropologies of learning, education and apprenticeship. Only recently have anthropologists started to think seriously about how the acquisition of religion happens in people's mind. This has been possible thanks to the progress of a rather new discipline: the cognitive approaches to religion, a field in expansion to which we now turn our attention.

Explaining Religious Transmission

In recent years, issues of learning and transmission of religious ideas and rituals have received considerable attention in the burgeoning field of cognitive studies. Still marginalized and of little importance for many anthropologists, these cognitive perspectives on religion are nowadays getting an increasing amount of attention in European and American anthropological circles. Indeed, some anthropologists such as Atran (2002), Bloch (1998, 2005), Hirschfeld (1996) and many others have highlighted the crucial role of cognitive psychology in providing new concepts and methods for our discipline, and not only for religion. French anthropologist Dan Sperber is considered by many to be the father of the cognitive explanatory programme in anthropology, mainly because of his epidemiological model of cultural transmission (Sperber 1996).

Most cognition-oriented anthropologists of today are interested in religion, i.e. in making use of relevant findings of cognitive sciences to illuminate the field of anthropology of religious representations and practices (Boyer 1994, 2001a, 2001b; Højbjerg 2002b; Whitehouse 2001, 2004, 2005). Allied with philosophers such as Lawson, religionists such as McCauley (Lawson and McCauley 1990; McCauley and Lawson 2002) and psychologists such as Barrett (2004), they propose to 'formulate new theories about a wide range of religious materials' (McCauley and Whitehouse 2005: 2) by borrowing data from cognitive linguistics, evolutionary psychology and cognitive psychology. Although each of these scholars has his or her own perspective, most of them react against what they call 'the methodological sloppiness of interpretivism and, more generally, of the postmodern critique' (Whitehouse 2005: 25), calling for an epistemological return to the general and the explanatory in religious studies (Boyer 1994; Lawson and McCauley 1990; McCauley and Lawson 2002). They see themselves as theorists about patterns rather than 'interpreters of meanings' of religion – more to do with *explaining* than *interpreting* religion (McCauley 2003; see also Lawson and McCauley 1990: 12–31). Rather than engaging with anthropologists, they seem in general to be more willing to enter into dialogue with cognitive sciences, a discipline that by and large has not been interested in religious issues (McCauley and Whitehouse 2005: 3).

Reading Boyer, Whitehouse or McCauley and Lawson, the emphasis is clearly placed on the cognitive mechanisms of *transmission*, i.e. how cognitive properties constrain the formation and transmission of religious representations and practices. As Tanya Luhrmann (this volume) correctly observes, for most of these scholars 'the problem of religion is the problem of transmission'. In particular, knowing the workings of our mental machinery better can help towards explaining the intricacies of how people acquire religious concepts and practices. Pascal Boyer, for instance, has shown how human 'cognitive architecture' plays a crucial causal role in the generation, spread and especially the *acquisition* of religious ideas. His model attempts to explain why certain religious representations are more attention-grabbing, more catchy and 'yummy' (writes McCauley) and, thus, more transmissible than others (Boyer 2001b). Boyer finds that religious ideas are those representations that are optimally counter-intuitive, entailing breaches of our intuitive knowledge (for instance, intuitive physics) in such a way that they are attention-grabbing, easily remembered and communicable. Not only do odd, religious supernatural agents such as witches, ghosts, gods or ancestors subtly violate intuitive ontological expectations about physics and the world but this also explains, according to Boyer, why they persist and get transmitted more easily to other representations.

In the same vein, McCauley and Lawson propose to investigate the intrinsic cognitive properties of religious rituals in order to explain why and how ritual transmission operates. For them, some rites are more transmissible than others, in particular those that 'pack enough emotional wallop to convince them [participants] that they have dealt with the divine' (McCauley and Lawson 2002: 211). In fact, to explain the persistence of ritual through time, one has to take into account not only mnemonic issues, but also the motivation of participants to transmit. Some rites 'contain extensive sensory pageantry that produces elevated levels of emotion' (ibid.: 112), aimed at persuading participants of the divine importance of these rites and at arousing their motivation to transmit them.

These two authors refer to Harvey Whitehouse's modes of religiosity theory (Whitehouse 2000, 2002, 2004, 2005) and attempt to complicate it. In comparison with his cognition-oriented colleagues, Whitehouse proposes a somehow softer cognitive version of religious transmission. While Boyer claims that what people think and say has little impact on our understanding of religious transmission and that we should search outside conscious awareness, Whitehouse claims that his approach is 'more flexible, conscious, and context sensitive' (Whitehouse 2005: 216). He considers people's statements on religious transmission seriously and sees cognition as something that does not 'take place exclusively in the brain/mind' (ibid.: 221) and he seems to keep his distance from an only cognitive form of explanation:

> Only some aspects of cultural learning can be understood in terms of cognitive 'hardware'. [...] To understand religious transmission at any depth, we must envisage the mind not as a fixed generic device, such as a computer, but as a constantly developing organic structure ... (Whitehouse 2004: 27).

However, Whitehouse bases his theory of the two modes of religiosity 'on two distinct mechanisms of long-term memory, founded in the material conditions of the brain' (Whitehouse and Laidlaw 2004: 6). For him, these forms of memory, the semantic and the episodic, correspond to two different styles of religious life: the 'doctrinal' mode (sober, organized, and verbal) and the 'imagistic' mode (emotional, personal and non-verbal). Accordingly, all religious traditions, from initiation ceremonies in Papua New Guinea to Christian rituals, can be looked at through the lens of this psychological memory-based dichotomy. While the doctrinal mode is characterized by highly repetitive, routinized forms of religious activities, the imaginistic mode presents very emotionally-loaded religious practices. As for religious transmission, the two modes are also distinct: in the first case, the transmission of religious practice is frequently repeated, standardized and relies on a great deal of explicit verbal knowledge stored in semantic memory (sermon type).[6] In the second case, the imaginistic mode, learning strategies imply infrequent repetitions and often traumatic experiences (such as bush initiations) involving highly emotional arousal that activates episodic or flashbulb memories.

These psychologically inspired models are refreshing for anthropologists, as they shed a different explanatory light on questions of religious transmission and learning. They use what neurologists and psychologists know about the brain and its cognitive constraints and properties and, armed with this knowledge, they attempt to explain how and why religion is transmitted and persists through time. However, some of these authors also recognize the limitations of their cognitive approaches, which may help to explain certain aspects of religious thinking, but leave 'largely undiscussed many features of religious experience [...]' (McCauley and Whitehouse 2005: 4–5). And indeed, the gap between the social and the cognitive can become too wide.

Religious Learning as a Social Process

This volume emerges from an endeavour to fill this gap. We are familiar with these cognitive approaches to religion and, in our view, the cognitivist move toward describing the psychological operations at play in religious thinking and modelling rituals, while helping to explain some specific aspects of religious thinking also risks ignoring the social complexity of religious transmission and learning. There has to be more to the story if one is to understand the *experience* of transmitting/learning religion. 'Acquiring religion' is not merely a cold-blooded technical process of cognitive downloading. It takes place in a specific interactive social and cultural environment, and one must, therefore, also examine it as a 'dimension of social practice' (Lave and Wenger 1991: 47). As French sociologist Bernard Lahire (2005) reminds us, in a pamphlet denouncing the risk of naturalizing learning, one still has to develop a genetic and disposition-oriented sociology of socialization, which he sees as a description of the concrete, contextual, social conditions of learning and transmission. Indeed, these new cognitive developments 'à la Boyer' obfuscate the foundational idea that 'cognition, emotion, motivation, perception, imagination, memory ... are social affairs' (Geertz 1983: 153). By focusing primarily on the kind of cognitive processes and structures involved, they seem to forget that the 'mind is a function of the whole person that is constituted over time in intersubjective relations with others in the environing world' (Toren 1999: 21), and they ignore the entire spectrum of how religious practices, representations and emotions are socially transmitted and learned.

The cognitive study of religion is not, however, the only development in the recent past to have created useful tools to investigate how religion is replicated. Another area that has been crucial in this domain has been that of the anthropology of learning. Indeed, paying special attention to what Jean Lave called 'situated learning', authors such as Jean Lave (Lave and Wenger 1991; Lave and Chaiklin (eds) 1996), Harry Wolcott (1982), Christina Toren (1998, 1999, 2001, 2004), Charles Stafford (1995), Carlo Severi (Severi 2002, 2004), Michael Houseman (2005; Houseman and Severi 1998), Maurice Bloch (1998, 2005), Rita Astuti (1995, 2001) and other anthropologists, together with fine-grained studies about children and socialization (Briggs 1998, Gottlieb 2004, Morton 1996, Thorne 1993), have created a corpus on learning processes that, in some cases, also looks at religious learning. This is seen by these authors as dynamically constituted not by passive 'recipients' but by agents actively engaged in acquisition processes. This is not to deny the importance of cognition (in fact, all these authors are very interested in cognitive issues), but their works show – as do the case studies in this volume – that processes of religious learning and transmission often happen in the interstices of social interaction and not only in the cognitive capacities of people's minds (and, incidentally, not always in the institutional sites where they are supposed to take place either). Thanks to these new approaches emphasizing the interactive and situated dimension of learning and transmission, combined with the cognitive findings of authors such as Sperber, Boyer and Whitehouse, we are becoming increasingly capable of accounting for the ways individuals arrive at religious concepts and practices. By learning religion, we want to understand how people learn religious concepts, values, emotions, attitudes and practices in the very texture of social life and from their own standpoint.

So, how are religious concepts, practices, interactions, and emotions acquired? What are the sites of religious learning (body, language, the media, etc.)? Who are the different agents at stake (teachers, religious experts, elites, women, children)? What are the roles of narratives, objects, places and times in religious learning? How is religious learning seen and verbalized by the actors themselves? What are the connections between politics, ideologies and religious learning? The papers gathered in this volume, as well as those that unfortunately could not make it into the volume but interacted with them at our meeting in Lisbon, are ethnographic attempts at addressing these questions.

In our eyes, the richness of the papers resides in the fact that their authors are not subscribing to one particular 'school' or another, but that they all combine different anthropological and philosophical approaches, traditions, sources and methods to reveal the social logics of learning and transmitting religious knowledge and behaviour in several settings, including Europe, East Africa and the Indic Ocean, West Africa and the Atlantic, China, North America, South America and Indonesia. Despite each author's singularity and focus, there is an overlapping of themes. They all show the complexity of learning religion that cannot be understood as a monolithic process or just as the reproduction of some immutable knowledge of practices from one generation to another, or from one person to another. It is a rather complex process that involves - apart from repetition and memorization - creativity, interpretation, accident, and concepts that need to be discussed and clarified such as 'belief', 'doubt', 'certainty', 'scepticism', 'conviction', 'possession' and 'participation' (cf. the vindication of doubt and reflexivity in Højbjerg 2002a). It is also a process that involves a multiplicity of agents in interaction, mostly, of course, between adults and children – although this is by no means the only interaction to be taken into account.

Carlo Severi starts the volume with a study of the processes of memorization and recollection involved in what he terms 'learning to believe'. His chapter is a valiant attempt to bring back to the scene the concept of 'belief', which ever since its deconstruction by Rodney Needham (Needham 1972) has found it difficult to find a place in anthropological scrutiny. Today, it is true, many cognitive anthropologists use the concept, but they do so without a great deal of analysis, as Maurice Bloch has already pointed out (Bloch 2002). For Severi, the problem is that too many of us accepted Needham's views according to which the concept was Eurocentric and not translatable into non-Western languages, and therefore did not consider that it might relate to learning processes and states of mind that are to be found cross-culturally. In this preliminary paper, Severi wants to take the issue up where Wittgenstein and Needham left it and continue a philosophical investigation into what exactly a religious belief is and its relationship with faith, certainty and, last but not least, doubt. In order to understand how this state of mind is created, Severi suggests we study the interface between two kinds of memory: a semantic, mechanic memory that transmits fixed content (here exemplified with the transmission of the Christian *Pater Noster* prayer) and a pragmatic memory whose function is not to transmit content but context, and which is fundamental in the transmission of more abstract beliefs, based, as

Severi puts it, 'on the re-elaboration of hints, through inference and imagination'. The functioning of this latter memory is here exemplified with an intriguing case: the presence in people's imagination, still in the late twentieth century, of roughly the same belief in the 'monstrous wolf' that Robert Louis Stevenson found in Lozère when he did his celebrated travels with a donkey around that French region back in 1878.

Michael Houseman proposes a theoretical approach to learning that, much like Severi's, insists on transmission of ritual context and social relations. Against the intuitive inclination to see learning as acquisition of content, Houseman shows that in order to understand how rituals are transmitted, looking at ideas and concepts may be much less useful than looking at the very relationships that are played out and reproduced in these rituals. Houseman explores this line of research in two different female rituals of menstruation, one of them being the 'menstrual slap' (when a woman slaps her daughter upon finding out the latter has had her first menstruation, thereby creating a flashbulb memory of the event with little semantic content and limited interpretation) and the other a new age rite of coming of age also performed at the first menstruation, much softer and much more semantically elaborated than the menstrual slap. The two cases are very different, but in the performance of both of them a general set of relations are transmitted and womanhood thus constructed in such a way that present iterations relate to past performances. Both achieve this through a combination of what Houseman calls the principles of 'inferential interpretation' and that of 'empathic simulation', which open up two different ways of transmitting and learning ritual. While the former impels performers to repeat the action that was imposed on them in their inchoate attempt at capturing its meaning, in the latter they are lead to act in a stereotyped fashion that agents very self-consciously reproduce in order to act as they think someone else did in a distant, imaginary past.

David Parkin explores the making of a multifaceted religious culture on the East African Swahili coast and Zanzibar, where orthodox Islam meets with both local non-Muslim traditions and with Sufism. It is subsequently where different systems of learning are at play: one based on centripetal notions of knowledge to be kept secret by elders, such as the initiatic traditions, others based on centripetal notions of knowledge to be spread by any knowledgeable person despite their age, such as the Wahabbi reformers, and still others somewhere in the middle, such as the learning traditions of Sufi orders. Parkin's chapter invites us to see these traditions not as separate modes of learning, each one pitted against the other, but rather as making a continuum with multiple feedbacks among them, with learning persons having to interpret and incorporate into their knowledge bits and pieces they gather, sometimes accidentally, from everywhere else – a bit like the eunuch with whom we started this introduction, who learned to incorporate the message brought by Philip with his own religious biography and by so doing learned another religion. Following the ideas of Whitehouse, Parkin claims that there is a difference between doctrinal modes based on semantic memory and imaginistic modes of religiosity based on episodic memory, but he suggests that they are not to be seen as opposed modes of religiosity but as mutually enriching ones, for the episodic can (and often does) become part of the doctrine and thus modify it.

In a deeply philosophical text, Michael Lambek reconstructs a long path that goes from mimetic behaviour to the acquisition of religious conviction in the process of learning to be possessed by spirits. After a philosophical survey that takes us from Kierkagaard to Austin in order to explore what it means to be 'serious' and to have religious conviction, a problem which Lambek links to the performative power of ritual and religious iteration, he takes us farther away to East Africa (nor too far from Parkin's field site and an equally multifaceted one) to discuss the life-story of a woman and her process from being possessed to becoming a *fundi* (master, curer). Following this case study, we observe her becoming possessed by spirits and more importantly, growing more and more possessed by, and convinced of, her own abilities. The possessed person, Lambek concludes, is not an immutable, subjacent subject (with apologies for the pleonasm) who makes iterations, but is also the result of these iterations. Learning religion is, one could say, a process of making oneself or, as Kierkegaard put it thereby providing an optimal title for Lambek, of 'catching up with oneself'.

The issue of possession and of how it makes us re-evaluate our thinking of religious learning reappears in chapters by Tanya Luhrmann, Marcio Goldman, and, to a certain extent, João Vasconcelos (although whether the séances he describes belong to the category of 'possession' is, in fact, a matter of contention). All of them would agree with Lambek's methodological invitation (this volume) that looking at possession from a learning angle may yield many more challenging fruits than following the old epidemiological paradigms.

Tanya Luhrmann's chapter on evangelical movements in the US has a double agenda: on the one hand, to illustrate how the knowledge of what it means to be in close touch with God is constructed through a consistent feedback between Bible reading, attending meetings and performing rituals. The process of acquiring religious conviction and firm attitudes is discussed along lines that make her chapter a good companion to that of Lambek. On the other hand, the relevance of Luhrmann's chapter in this collection is her resolve to establish a dialogue between cognitive studies of religion such as those of Boyer, Dennett or Whitehouse and other cultural psychological approaches. Her feeling, shared by many of our contributors, is that cognitive aspects must be studied but that religion is not something that happens only in cogitations, and that therefore cognitive approaches have their own internal constrictions and limitations. In order to understand the feelings and bodily experiences of those who are learning to be possessed by religious truth, Luhrmann goes back to one of the most problematic thinkers in the history of anthropology: Lucien Lévy-Bruhl (1857–1939). Lévy-Bruhl, a poorly studied and often misrepresented scholar, introduced in anthropology a concept with a long history in Western philosophy: that of 'participation' (*methexis*, in Platonic usage) which, unlike its far too frequently used and even abused twin sibling *mimesis*, has kept a rather low profile in our discipline. Luhrmann convincingly argues that the concept is still useful to help understand the kind of experiences of those who suddenly feel part of something larger than themselves. Other than a vindication of a forgotten author, Luhrmann's chapter and exploration of participative thinking and learning offers a good model to acknowledge that while cognition is important in learning there are also aspects that involve vivid experiences rather than the acquisition of concepts or the application of templates and that consequently need other models, concepts and paradigms to account for them.

To many a reader, the mention of Lévy-Bruhl will immediately bring to mind the name of Marcio Goldman, the Brazilian author of a monograph on the French philosopher (Goldman 1994). In his contribution to this volume, Goldman, also a specialist in Candomblé and in the historiography of Afro-Brazilian cults, explores how one learns to be possessed in Candomblé and, much like Lurhmann, he finds that exploring philosophical thought may be a more fruitful avenue than exploring mental processes. Candomblé is a religion with very little explicit doctrine or theology. As with many other religions across cultures, there have been, of course, efforts at systematizing a 'Candomblé cosmology', but what really is at the core of this cult is a vivid experience of becoming. Following Bastide, Goldman prefers to talk about 'ontology' (a very fluid one at that) rather than a fixed cosmology, and in order to explore the central importance of becoming in this fluid ontology, he looks for a hermeneutical tool in the philosophy of Deleuze and Guattari. Goldman also finishes his chapter with a re-examination of Lévy-Bruhl's notion of participation and of the hot debate it gave rise to among such funding scholars as Marcel Mauss and Roger Bastide.

João Vasconcelos follows a similar path to that of Goldman and, to a certain extent, Lurhmann as well. In his study of Christian Rationalism, a spiritual movement quite popular in Cape Verde today but originally an offshoot of Brazilian forms of Kardecism, Vasconcelos shows how middle-aged women learn to interpret their unusual experiences as spiritual presences and thus become mediums. Like Luhrmann, Vasconcelos finds cognitive approaches useful to explore the kind of concepts we normally consider part of religion, but limited when it comes to explaining how the acquisition of religious ideas or, as he prefers to put it, spiritual knowledge, is related to past lived-through experiences and to the non-representational aspects of this spiritual knowledge. Following Max Weber's distinction between an experienced or, in Weber's own terms, 'possessed' faith and a 'rationalized' theology, Vasconcelos attempts to grasp the former – much like Goldman does in his work on Candomblé – by analysing the ethnographic material and the life stories of Christian Rationalist female mediums through the philosophical lens of Deleuzian notions of 'becoming' and the philosopher's distinctions between 'affects' and 'precepts'. Beyond the depth of the analysis, the chapter should also become a useful methodological tool for anthropologists of religion as it illustrates a characteristic dilemma of the discipline: while having to explain how people incorporate new ideas and experiences in their biographies and societies, anthropologists – who ideally ought to remain as 'musically unreligious' as possible in keeping with Weber's concepts – must incorporate their findings into a body of literature and social scientific paradigms that risks taking them far away from people's lived world, and thereby making the analyses irrelevant, in order to assess the importance of religious ideas in people's lives. Vasconcelos offers a good model of how to explain religious ideas scientifically *and* still get hold of their fundamental importance for those who live with them.

Ethnolinguist Aurora Donzelli explores how the new commodification of ritual speech affects the nature of both religious transmission and the ideology of transmission. In her study we can see how pervading notions of 'development' and 'modernization', introduced in Indonesia by colonizers, Calvinist missionaries and post-colonial discourses entangle with the practice of learning ritual speech. Until recently, traditional Toraja ritual speech was considered the outcome of passivity on the part of the learner, and its transmission as the passing down of fixed notions and formulae. People did not acknowledge human agency: it was as though in order to become a good orator the word had to descend upon you rather than you train for its usage. Today it is increasingly perceived as the outcome of a training in which the role of the performer is not only acknowledged, but proudly vindicated and even protected both by a shared understanding of 'copyright' and by secrecy – and in this respect the new ritual speech meets the old one, equally enveloped in secrecy, although the reasons for secrecy are different. This shift in the ideology of ritual learning from passive recipient to active searcher and writer has to do with global shifts in Indonesian societies, with the role of objectified notions of 'tradition' and of 'religion' in the public sphere and in political discourses and with the development of a new, 'modernizing' subjectivity.

Laurence Hérault's chapter explores how the meaning of communion is constructed in Protestant and Catholic catechisms in Europe. She starts by tracing some recent changes in the very ideology of Christian teaching. In the past, catechism was based on the rigid model of transmission (the 'mechanic memory', to use Severi's concept), the catechised being obliged to memorize a series of mysterious, unintelligible information entirely by heart. Nowadays, catechism (or at least this is what their practitioners say) is not based on mechanic memorization but on acquiring the basic competences upon which the boy or girl will build some knowledge about faith and freely choose to be a Christian (or not). Hérault looks at the performance of the teaching in the two churches and in particular at how children learn to believe in the solemnity of the act of communion. Despite the fact that one of the most important bones of contention between Catholicism and Protestantism is that according to Catholicism the host is the body of Christ while for Calvinists it is a sign but no 'real presence', what Hérault observed in her fieldwork was that such theological nuances were played down in catechesis. However, she observed some fundamental differences; thus, while for Catholic youths the communion is taught as a 'mystery' about which nothing other is to be sought, Protestant children are not told much about its nature, mysterious or not, but instead are instructed to pay attention to (and try to reproduce as closely as possible) the ritual performance and the distribution and relations among participants.

Charles Stafford has written a thought-provoking chapter on the ways religious practices in China create a setting for children to fully develop cognitive competences necessary to think about gods and about other people's inner intentions and to start growing up as religious people. Stafford argues that while much religious discourse (things said during rituals by ritual specialists) is meant to transmit a message, in fact folks attending the ritual are very often not only not listening to it but also doing other things, or at least focusing their attention on something else. Stafford's ethnography suggests that what attracts people *about* religion (and *towards* religion), i.e., what makes it *interesting*, is precisely those aspects that make it easier for people to connect spirits and extraordinary beliefs to ordinary life: religion becomes real and ordinary because it has so many things in common with everyday reality. While Stafford acknowledges that much of religion is transmitted by people just being there, looking around and

absorbing attitudes from their environment, his chapter warns against
the abuse of such notions as 'habitus', 'embodied' memories or
'unconscious' learning with which anthropologists have been explaining cultural transmission over the last twenty years but that get little
support from psychologists (and sometimes their explicit questioning).
In order to explain the kind of religious socialization that children are
subjected to he invites us instead to do what so far only few anthropologists are willing – and able – to do: to look at the psychology of learning, to investigate actors as they activate their faculties in order to pay
attention to and grasp the world around them and the thoughts of
those who surround them. After a description of China and Taiwan
and an exploration of people's theories of spirits and of minds, Stafford
ends his paper encouraging anthropologists to dialogue more openly
with Paul Harris (2000), undoubtedly the one psychologist who over
the last years has done most original research on children's minds and
religious imaginations.

The volume closes with Michael Rowlands inviting us to look at
what some would wrongly consider merely peripheral aspects of religious transmission, such as sound, music and noise. Rowlands claims
that noise and music are crucial for the establishment of certain kinds
of emotional states and assumptions about social relations. It is not
that music *transmits* these messages, but rather that it *is* the message:
in their immediacy, sounds can provide a sense of living in a harmonious world or in a disordered hell. When talking about cognition we
should be looking not only at concepts and logical inferences, but also
at the kind of 'envelope' (in particular 'sound envelope') in which cogitations happen and in which we feel socially included. Rowlands'
ethnographic case study from the Grassfields (Cameroon), which is
accompanied by a theoretical discussion on the political economy of
noise, shows the social relevance of the 'sonoric baths' surrounding
and reinforcing notions of ancestors, secrets, well-being, fear, witches
and contact with the invisible realm. In this part of Africa, sound is
very important in ritual masquerades and cementing a structural
dichotomy between village and forest, day and night, ambivalent
forces that may work towards group cohesion (and individual excellence within the group) or against the group or particular individuals,
in which case they are 'unblocked' through ritual and sound. Rowlands discusses how these notions at the village level play an unheard-
of (with apologies for the pun) relevance among 'new born'
(Pentecostal) converts, for whom learning about spirits, God, ancestors, witches, 'the devil' and more petrified notions of good and evil
through sounds and noise is inscribed in a path towards self-realiza-
tion, although one leading to somewhat new forms of wealth and success. New they are indeed, but the social logics that articulate them are

as old as they are unexplored unfortunately if looked at from the angle of sound envelopes and of their potential for inclusion and exclusion.

Without learning, without transmission, there is no such thing as religion. All in all, this fine collection of essays should help the reader, as they did the organizers of the colloquium and the authors themselves, to continue this line of research and encourage further discussion on the subtle realities of learning religion. Nothing is set in stone in such a complex area as the anthropological study of religion, and whatever is set in stone is subject to new interpretations. We will be happy if even the issues upon which there may be disagreement should give rise to further debate, interdisciplinary dialogues and research.

Notes

1. In a detailed study of notions of 'tradition' and 'passing down' from a semiological point of view, Peter Jackson (2004) has written one of the most thorough revisions of Cicero's *relego*. Without ruling out 'recollection' as a translation he goes beyond it in order to capture the complexity of the Latin verb and glosses it as 'to pick up again, to go back over, retrace (a path), to transverse an area again' (Jackson 2004: 2).
2. Many of the short essays collected in two companion volumes to religion (Taylor (ed.) 1998, Braun and McCutcheon (eds) 2000) also show a strong influence of J. Z. Smith upon their respective authors and therefore a spirit, rare until now in both the history of religions and the anthropology of religion, to listen to each other.
3. As Maurice Bloch (2002: 239) succinctly put it: 'there is no such *thing* as religion, other than the somewhat, but only somewhat, similar phenomena one finds in different places, and which remind the observer, in a theoretically insignificant way, therefore, of what we have been brought up to understand by the term'.
4. It is worth noting that Zande witchcraft has become a paradigm of African religions and systematically used by anthropologists and philosophers to exemplify the kind of notions and beliefs we call 'religious' (for instance by Pascal Boyer 2001b: 14, 20) while, in fact, Evans-Pritchard himself did *not* consider it part of Zande 'religion' (Evans-Pritchard 1937: 3). This poses interesting questions about who decides what 'religion' is and supports Maurice Bloch's caution (see note 3) that maybe one of the problems of contemporary cognitive anthropologists is that they have found the 'object' of the study of religion a bit to hastily and uncritically.
5. So far we have only knitted together a few elements of the very complex history of anthropology of religion to tune the reader into the theme of this volume. The most erudite, succinct and up-to-date history of this discipline we can think of as a companion to this introduction is the overview provided by Wendy James in chapter 5 ('Ritual, Memory, and Religion') of her latest book *The Ceremonial Animal: A New Portrait of Anthropology* (James 2003: 100–136).
6. Without delving into a complete analysis, we note that, following cognitive psychologist Alan Baddeley, Whitehouse distinguishes between 'semantic memory' (mental representations of a general, propositional nature, such as the knowledge one has concerning road signs or how to behave in a restaurant) and 'episodic memory' (mental representations of specific events that one has personally experienced).

Chapter 2

LEARNING TO BELIEVE: A PRELIMINARY APPROACH

Carlo Severi

Is belief an experience?

(L. Wittgenstein, *Notebooks 1914–16*, 1961)

The child learns to believe a host of things, i.e. it learns to act according to these beliefs. Bit by bit there forms a system of what is believed, and in that system some things are unshakeably fast and some are more or less liable to shift. What stands fast does so, not because it is intrinsically obvious or convincing; it is rather held by what lies around it.

(L. Wittgenstein, *On Certainty*, 1969)

Religious rituals are generally associated with the establishment of 'systems of beliefs'. For many anthropologists, belief is necessarily part of a system of related ideas, and this system forms the context where ritual action acquires its meaning. As Wittgenstein remarked, 'When we first begin to believe anything, what we believe is not a single proposition, it is a whole system of propositions'. In such a system (which he calls elsewhere a 'mythology' or 'world-picture'), 'consequences and premises give one another support' (Wittgenstein 1969: 21). According to him, a belief is firmly established in our mind not because it is 'intrinsically convincing', but because it is part of a system, it is 'held by what lies around it' (1969: 22). Actually, it cannot be denied that in many cases to perform a ritual is to affirm a faith, to accept a doctrine. When a Roman Catholic says '*Credo in unum Deo*' he or she is simultaneously praying to his or her God and stating a belief in it. However, is belief always systematic? Is there any difference between belief and

faith? Does ritual action when performed in a religious context necessarily generate a belief? How and when can the performance of a ritual be seen as a particular way to acquire or to 'learn' a belief? What
kind of mental processes are involved in this process? In this brief and
preliminary paper I would like to outline a possible answer to these
questions.

Rodney Needham's analysis of the concept of belief is well known.
In his famous essay on *Belief, Language, and Experience* (Needham
1972), the British anthropologist argued that far from being a universal feature of religion, the concept of belief is only 'the arbitrary product of an intricate and unique historical tradition' (1972: 152). The
content of this notion combines, as he writes elsewhere (1972: 50),
only 'Jewish, Greek and Christian concepts'. To try to understand social
and religious facts belonging to different cultural and linguistic traditions starting from this concept would be, in Needham's perspective,
essentially wrong. For him, there is no such phenomenon as 'believing'
in many non-Western religions. The attribution to human nature of a
'distinct capacity for belief' (Needham 1983: 41) shared by many
anthropologists is the result of an incorrect inference from the Western
use of a verbal concept. 'The crucial mistake', writes Needham, 'has
been the uncritical acceptance of a traditional Western definition of a
mental state called "belief" ' (Needham 1983: 41). His conclusion is
not only that belief is no more than 'an isolated and artificial alternative among the innumerable cultural classifications of human powers',
but also that 'belief does not constitute a natural resemblance among
men' (1972: 151–2). If 'a class must be defined by the invariable presence of certain common properties', writes Needham, then there is no
class of phenomena in human societies defined by the invariable presence of a mental state called 'belief' (Needham 1983: 37).

Since the publication of *Belief, Language, and Experience*, the study of
belief as a religious experience seems to have disappeared from anthropological analysis of ritual action. Many anthropologists have preferred to avoid the topic even when they provided interesting analyses
of ritual symbolism and of its various ways of generating meaning
and effectiveness (see, for instance, Turner 1986, Tambiah 1985,
Humphrey and Laidlaw 1994). Actually, rituals have a paradoxical
relationship to belief. As sequences of symbolic actions, they have
often been defined as attempts to generate a mental state of belief in a
fictive or supernatural dimension of reality. In this perspective, ritual is
seen as a unique way to materialize the existence of a supernatural
world. Pierre Smith, for instance (1979, 1991), has convincingly
argued that this close link to the establishment of a belief should serve
to distinguish 'real' rituals from other contexts of social interaction
(such as feasts, celebrations or dances) that only *resemble* them.

However, the kind of belief Pierre Smith refers to in his studies of African rituals is rather different from the 'Western artificial artefact' analysed by Needham. I cannot reconstruct here the very rich intellectual background of Needham's argument, from Hume's *Inquiries into the Human Nature* to Wittgenstein's various writings about belief (among them the *Notebooks*, *On Certainty* and the *Philosophical Investigations*). Nonetheless, it is clear that the Western idea of belief is, in Needham's eyes, very close to an act of faith. For Needham, as for Hume, what transforms a 'product of our imagination' into a belief is its 'vividness', its 'firmness', its 'solidity'. The effect of belief is, for Needham, 'to make an idea approach an impression in force and vivacity' (Needham 1972: 52). For him, as for Hume, belief is indeed 'nothing *but a more vivid and intense conception of an idea*' (Hume 2000 [1739–40]: 119–20), a certain feeling of the mind which rules out scepticism and doubt. Wittgenstein's position is more problematic. The Austrian philosopher sometimes seems to keep to the same line of thought as Hume (and Needham). For him the 'vividness' of a belief must rule out any form of doubt. At the beginning of *On Certainty* (1969), he remarks, for instance, that belief does not only imply 'certainty' as a state of mind, but it also appears only where 'everything speaks in its favour, nothing against it'. Only where 'grounds for doubt are lacking', writes Wittgenstein elsewhere (1969: 2), something like 'belief' can emerge.

In a long argument developed later in the same book, however, Wittgenstein seems to question this equivalence between belief and certainty. He notes, for instance, that the main difficulty in the analysis of the act of believing is 'to understand its groundlessness' (1969: 24). A few pages afterwards, he adds that 'at the foundation of well-founded belief always lies belief that it is not founded' (1969: 33).

In posing these questions, Wittgenstein comes close to the experience of anthropologists. Actually, the kind of belief generated by ritual ceremonies such as the ones studied by Pierre Smith never really seems to rule out disbelief and doubt. As Højbjerg *et al.* (1999) have rightly remarked, rituals never fail to generate, in daily social life, comments about themselves. This not only means, as every fieldworker knows, that traditional societies, in Europe and elsewhere, are far from being societies of believers. It means, more generally, that a reflexive attitude about religious 'truth' or about the existence of supernatural beings seems very often to be associated to the performance of a ritual action. Ritual action may not only aim to confirm the existence of supernatural beings. It can also challenge them, or be performed in order to test the effectiveness of their powers. If this is true, we should consider religious doubt 'as a condition that sustains the existence of religious ideas and practice ... and as an essential element in the process of acquisition of religious ideas' (Højbjerg *et al.* 1999; cf also Højbjerg 2002: 4).

In an earlier paper (Severi 2002), I have tried to give a first account of the role played by doubt in ritual communication. My starting point was the relational theory of ritual action that Michael Houseman and I formulated some years ago. In a book devoted to the analysis of a ritual of the Iatmül of Papua-New Guinea (Houseman and Severi 1998), we claimed that one of the essential clues for understanding the context of ritual communication is the way in which, through the establishment of a particular form of interaction, a special identity of the participants is constructed.

In the anthropological study of ritual symbolism much attention has been devoted to the various ways in which language as it is used in ritual performances transforms the usual representation of the world and constructs its own universe of truth. A typical way to do so in American Indian shamanism, for instance, is to establish a metaphorical link, a set of analogies or a group of 'mystical' relationships between ritual objects and living beings. From this perspective, a newborn boy or girl can be ritually defined as a 'fruit' (as, for instance, in the Kuna shamanistic chants; see Severi 1993b, 2002). His or her mother will be called in this context 'a tree'. Consequently, the childbirth will be referred to as the 'growing of a bleeding fruit'. Here as elsewhere, the linguistic instrument of these metamorphoses is parallelism, a 'way to thread together verbal images' as Graham Townsley called it, which is virtually omnipresent in American Indian shamanism. In this context, for the shamanistic chant to refer to a 'bleeding fruit' is to refer to the real experience of the woman giving birth to a child and simultaneously to a mythical Tree-Mother bearing fruit.

In the paper I am referring to (Severi 2002), I argued that the same instrument – parallelism – can be used in a reflexive way in order to define not only the world described by the ritual language but also the identity of the person enunciating it. The image of the performing shaman, being made of contradictory yet non-exclusive and simultaneous identities (such as a tree, a deer, a monkey, etc.), entertains a doubt about the always possible assimilation of his ordinary identity into a supernatural one. His image progressively becomes paradoxical and therefore raises unanswerable questions. In Kuna society everybody knows that while chanting a therapeutic chant, a shaman transforms himself into a spirit. However, is the shaman becoming a 'vegetal' or an 'animal' spirit? Is he transformed into a boar, a deer, a monkey or a jaguar? Will he be able, as he claims, to perform that transformation again and again? I have argued that ritual action builds a particular kind of fiction, a special context of communication in which any positive answer will imply doubt and uncertainty, and vice versa. This complex definition of the enunciator has an immediate perlocutionary effect: a certain kind of uncertainty is always generated. If we follow Pierre Smith's suggestion that we should consider 'real' rituals to be only those ceremonies that lead to the establishment of a belief, we should conclude that linguistic communication becomes ritualized only when a particular way of elaborating a complex image of the enunciator unleashes that particular tension between belief and doubt that defines a ritual-reflexive stance. In this sense, ritual is deeply different from ordinary social life. If in social daily life, as Wittgenstein has remarked, 'the child learns by believing the adult' and, as a consequence, 'doubt comes always after belief' (1969: 23), in a ritual context belief always *implies* a relationship with doubt.

However, the kind of analysis of religious rituals as patterns of complex relationships that I have tried to develop until now envisages the question of the acquisition of belief only implicitly.[1] In this chapter, I would like to approach this question more directly, taking the point of view of the anthropology of memory. Of the minimal requirements for defining social memory, I will consider here only the distinction between encoding and recollecting. Usually, we tend to think that the relationship between the encoding and the recollection of a representation is rather simple. Recollection appears to us as an almost automatic way to reproduce an originally fixed mnestic trace, be it the name of a person, his or her date of birth, his or her telephone number, etc. Actually, the work of many psychologists has shown that, encoding and recollection, as mental processes, are not symmetrical. They are fundamentally different processes. Encoding implies the fixation of some traces in one's mind, essentially through the use of categorization. Recollection is far more complex, since it involves a process of reconstruction implying both inference and imagination. We will see that it is useful to keep this distinction in mind when studying the way a belief is established and propagated in a religious tradition.

The *Pater Noster* Perspective

Our Father, who art in Heaven ... How is a religious belief like this one culturally transmitted? Many religions have found their own solution to this problem. The Catholic Church has for centuries asked children to memorize brief texts containing a certain number of 'articles of faith' in order to transmit a set of fundamental beliefs. *Pater Noster* and *Credo in Unum Deum* are perfect examples of this kind of learning.

Obviously, this process of memorizing a prayer 'by heart' also has a social aspect: while expressing a particular semantic content, the recitation of a memorized prayer has the social function of establishing strong links among believers. To pray together is a way to establish a common memory, as well as a way to become part of a group of people declaring themselves 'united' by a common faith. In this perspective, the process of learning a religion appears to be *semantic-based* (related to the understanding of a specific text), *explicit* (publicly declared) and *depending on a relatively straightforward process of memorization*. This process, which often implies the use of mnemonic devices, appears to consist in a sort of passive encoding of data in one's memory. Once the text is memorized, the belief is acquired.

This approach to belief is not very popular among anthropologists for various reasons, both good and bad. However, it should not be underestimated. This kind of brutal enforcement of the rules of a pre-established mnemonic technique in order to ensure belief is actually very common, and far from being limited to the Catholic Church. This kind of use of a 'mechanic memory' can become equally important in very different cultural traditions. Let me refer to an example drawn from the Kuna shamanistic tradition (Severi 1993b). During his period of instruction, the Kuna shaman's pupil spends long days in his master's hut where he must show unfailing respect and obedience. Nearly every day he brings him presents and often goes on working for him for years. In return, his master, whom he calls *saila* ('chief'), welcomes him to his home and passes on to him his knowledge of the chants. This teaching is based on two different forms of learning. One, which is purely verbal, involves the young disciple's memory (his 'good mind': *nononuetti*). The master recites a verse of the chant and gets the disciple to repeat it until he has learned it by heart. The sole object of this exercise is to have him memorize the text. Complying with the traditional rules, the pupil often learns whole sentences whose meaning escapes him.

The other method of learning employed by the Kuna shamans involves the deciphering of a series of images: the pictograms. For instance, the master will show his disciple drawings representing a sick person stretched out on a hammock, the ritual brazier where cocoa burns, spirits who effect the cure, mythical 'villages' inhabited by the spirits who caused the sickness, etc. These images, which he must first engrave on his memory and then learn to copy, are supposed to help him to recall with absolute accuracy a text where these persons and objects are mentioned. This twofold organization of mnemonic teaching corresponds to the particular structure of the Kuna chants, which generally consist of verbal formulae that are constantly repeated with variations (Severi 1997, 2004a and b). Using an image as a mnemonic support, the Kuna young specialist is supposed to succeed in acquiring a very specific text. We can draw the conclusion that the use of 'mechanic memory', which in the Kuna case is applied both to the memorization of words and images, is widely spread in human cultures and therefore deserves careful attention. This perspective (we could call it the *Pater Noster* perspective) has the advantage of underlining, even if in a superficial way, the role of memory in the acquisition of a belief. The role played by memory in this process, although operating in very different ways is crucial, and should not be neglected.

However, this approach also has many disadvantages, both theoretical and empirical. Let us consider it from a purely theoretical point of view. First of all, this perspective makes us think that the content of a religious belief has to be stated explicitly to become firmly established. Quite deceptively, belief appears here in a logical form of this kind: 'a proposition P is a shared belief for a group G if and only if every member of the group G believes that P is true'. Secondly, this approach makes us think that the content of a belief is more important than its pragmatic aspect. Admittedly, for a Roman Catholic, to pray in a church is a public, conventional or even optional activity. However, from the point of view of the Church, to pray can also be a private act. One can always pray for oneself in one's own room: what counts is how deep and sincere the 'faith' of the believer is. Finally, and more importantly, this approach tends to oversimplify the mental processes involved in belief and it says nothing of its relational context. As a consequence, many aspects of the process of the establishment of religious belief in a ritual context are left aside by this 'proposition-based' perspective on belief. The role of doubt is neglected, and it seems crucial in the establishment of belief through ritual action, for instance, in the case of shamanistic traditions (Severi 2002). From this perspective, as Wittgenstein wrote (1969), belief does not only imply 'certainty' as a state of mind, but it appears only where 'everything speaks in its favour, nothing against it '.

Let us consider now two objections resulting from ethnographical facts. The first concerns the relationship between belief and the content of a mental representation. The work of many anthropologists (my favourite examples are Barth 1975, 1987) has repeatedly shown that a belief can be established without referring to an explicit and clear definition of its content: in these situations the context of the belief is far more important than its content. A typical example of the establishment of a belief with no clear content is the case of the so-called mana-terms. The study of a Kuna mana-term, the shamanistic notion of *purpa* (usually translated as 'soul', 'vital principle', etc.) has for instance shown that the particular complexity of a mana-notion is the result of the complexity of its ritual use. In order to define this category, we do not merely have to reconstruct a network of related ideas

(such as 'force', 'character' or 'personality'), we also need to reconstruct the pragmatic conditions that ritually define the action of
shamanistic chanting. In other words, explicit knowledge is shared
among the Kuna about the technique of ritual recitation that enables
a shaman to cure an ill person and not about the semantic content of
this category. Rather than elaborating a clear-cut definition of the
invisible properties of the world, the shamanistic tradition conveys a
complex representation of the action of *chanting about* the world
characterized by the presence and the force of a 'soul'. In this case, the
transmission of a belief is based on the pragmatics of the notion and
not on the clear understanding of its semantic content (Severi 1993a).

A second empirical objection concerns the relationship between
belief and scepticism. The approach founded on the propositional form
of belief tends to imply that the 'natural' contrary of belief is perplexity, or unbelief. Ethnography shows that this is not always the case: a
failed ritual, while threatening the 'faith' of the believers, can also
cause a scandal and generate violent reactions (Severi 1993a, 2004c).
This fact very likely implies that the psychological background of belief
may be more complex than we expect. In order to understand these
unexpected aspects or consequences of the establishment of a belief,
let us examine another case where belief is firmly established even if it
is weakly defined from a propositional point of view. As we shall see, in
this example (drawn from Houseman and Severi 1988, where we discussed it for other reasons) the context – the set of rules governing the
game 'to believe', so to speak – plays a more important role than the
content of the representation remembered.

The Monstrous Wolf Perspective

A young English writer, Richard Holmes, made the same journey on
foot in Lozère, in Southern France, as Stevenson had a hundred years
before. Holmes (1983) remarks that the people that he met seemed to
believe in the same legends as Stevenson wrote about in his account of
the journey (Stevenson 1986 [1879]). The local people still speak of
'the Beast', a monstrous wolf that is said to feed on human flesh and
attack at any moment anywhere, that cannot be caught by any
means, that is perhaps immortal and so forth. Among the common
explanations, then as now, for the Beast's fearful behaviour, Holmes
notes one. It consists of the assumption that a group of a particular
species of wolf, a group consisting of only three specimens, once tasted
human flesh and can no longer do without it. This explanation, which
may seem commonplace, is in fact quite brilliant and highly instructive for the analysis of the various ways a representation can be cul-

turally transmitted. Let us consider it closely. The fact that only one specific species is involved provides an explanation for the Beast's particularly savage behaviour. Secondly, the Beast does unheard-of things precisely because it is a special kind of being. The fact that several animals are involved accounts for the Beast's frightening ability to be in several places at the same time. And finally, Holmes notes, this explanation, which mentions three wolves (not two), always includes at least one specimen of this pseudo-species about which nothing is known. This third unknown figure ('the animal still unaccounted for', as Holmes brilliantly writes) will then serve to interpret any not easily explicable future misadventure on the part of the Beast. This, it may be assumed, is why this explanation has enjoyed so much success and why the story of the Monstrous Wolf has persisted through time. There is no doubt that a situation of this kind entails a process of endless improvisation (it will always be necessary to invent a little, if only to 'fill the gap' left by the third wolf) and a particularly complex type of establishing a context, involving both fiction and belief. In fact, it is precisely through this process that the people of Lozère can today, and could in the past, believe in the existence of the Beast without their rationality being able in any way to be called into question.

The role played by fiction and imagination in this situation could lead to the conclusion that no memory is operating here. However, this would be the consequence of the wrong idea about memory. The Monstrous Wolf's strong persistence in time shows that recollection is not an automatic way to reproduce an originally fixed mnestic trace. It consists rather in an active intervention on it, which implies both inference and imagination. Despite appearances, memory is in the case of the Lozère legend as important as the acquisition of a prayer learnt 'by heart'. Actually, this case shows that to look at the establishment of belief from the point of view of memory can enable us to make an important distinction between semantic-based and pragmatic-based phenomena of cultural transmission. The Monstrous Wolf, due to the contradictory features involved in its definition, implies a memory process (a process of constant re-learning of religious belief) based on the re-elaboration of hints, through inference and imagination. As opposed to the *Pater Noster* perspective, its representation illustrates a process of reinvention based on the pragmatic context of belief acquisition, not on the understanding of a specific semantic content. Through this process of recollection, *a context orienting imagination is acquired.* Once this context is established, to believe in supernatural beings ('spirits' or 'monstrous wolves'), far from implying a faith, coincides with the exercise of one's own thought and imagination. As in the case of the 'third wolf' that accounts for inexplicable episodes with regard to the Monstrous Wolf's behaviour, the representation of belief becomes a space where imagination is inscribed.

The distinction between the two perspectives that I have outlined here (the '*Pater Noster*' and 'The Monstrous Wolf') could provide for a preliminary definition of the process of 'learning to believe' that I have tried to formulate in this paper. Following this perspective, the process of 'learning to believe' should be seen as involving a two-level structure. One level concerns the memorization of the semantic content of the religious message. A second, more important level concerns the unconscious acquisition of the context where apparently 'new and free' inferences, emerging as part of a social process of recollection, will enrich and confirm the establishment of the belief.

A study of this process may shed new light on the establishment of the curious kind of 'belief without certainty' that we find in ritual contexts. It may also lead to a better understanding of the fact, noted by Wittgenstein (1969), that in a system of beliefs, 'what stands fast does so not because it is intrinsically obvious or convincing, but because it is held by what lies around it'.

Note

1. The book I have written with Michael Houseman on the Naven ritual contains an attempt to account for the learning of some crucial aspects of ritual action in relational terms (Houseman and Severi 1998: 236–51).

Chapter 3

MENSTRUAL SLAPS AND FIRST BLOOD CELEBRATIONS
INFERENCE, SIMULATION AND THE LEARNING OF RITUAL

Michael Houseman

Much of what follows is a first attempt to conceptualize Neopagan and New Age ceremonial in relation to ritual activity of a more classical variety. Present-day ritual crafting is approached as a means to test and reconsider certain ideas regarding the nature of ritual action in general. Relying on data drawn largely from the Internet, I base my analysis on a contrast between episodes that mark a young woman's first menstruation in two different modern Western traditions: ritualized face-slapping and contemporary menarche rites. In both cases, participants rely on inferential interpretation and on empathic simulation in order to make sense of these exceptional events. They do so, however, in quite different ways. Taking this divergence into account prompts speculation regarding the principles governing the organization and transmission of ritual behaviour.

Inference and Simulation

The arguments presented here proceed from the idea that it is useful to envisage ritual behaviour as enacting special patterns of relationship, at once between participants and, in an embedded fashion, with other human and non-human entities: spirits, ancestors, objects, liturgical pronouncements, places and so forth (Houseman and Severi 1998;

Houseman 2000, 2006). These enactments are efficacious in that
they provide the participants with indisputable grounds for subsequent discourse and action, both within and beyond the ritual frame,
that presuppose the relational configurations acted out in the course of
the performance itself. How are such ritual relationships acquired and
passed on?

There is a commonplace notion that learning consists in a transmission of knowledge where the relationship between the communicating parties provides the context for a transfer of information
between them. This paradigm, however, is not very helpful insofar as
the acquisition of relational patterns is concerned, for it is precisely the
connection between the communicating parties – the 'context' –
which is the object of transmission. Indeed, the transmission of relationships relies less upon conveying specific information than upon
partaking in particular interpersonal situations. Circumstances in
which relational patterns are communicated thus tend to instantiate
the patterns themselves: 'What is a secrecy?' 'I can't tell you', 'What is
competition?' 'I can define it better that you can', and so forth. What
one may be said to learn through such interactions is not so much a
role or a way of behaving associated with one or the other of the positions occupied by those involved, but both positions at once as they
relate to each other. In short, one acquires a pattern of relationship.
Recognizing that what holds true for relationships in general applies to
ritual relationships as well, avoids splitting into two separate issues
what are in fact interdependent aspects of peoples' continued commitment to ceremonial events: developing the capacity to perform
them and acquiring the personal inclination to do so.

Coordinate involvement in ritual, or in any activity for that matter,
implies the participants' ability to make sense of their own and others'
behaviour. This is what allows them to react appropriately to each
other's reactions and underlies their commitment to the reality they
jointly enact. However, in order to make sense of what they are doing,
the interacting parties must be able to appreciate their and others'
actions as linked to their and others' intentional and emotional dispositions. A growing body of research suggests that this involves at least
two, quite different communicative operations, neither of which is
entirely conscious or infallible (for an overview, see Davies and Stone
1995; Carruthers and Smith 1996). The one, usually referred to as
'theory of mind', consists in drawing inferences about others' mental
states from their observable behaviour. Such inferential interpretations rely on the (adult) human capacity to mentally entertain representations of (others') representations, that is, meta-representations.
Consider George and myself. He and I evaluate each other's dispositions, and react, as a result of inferences founded upon the perception

of each other's actions. Because I know something about George, and because my encyclopaedic knowledge tells me that crying often connotes sadness, and because I have some general notions about what emotions, intentions, beliefs, actions and so forth might be, I am able to infer from George's tears that he is feeling sad and react accordingly. Authors differ as to what extent this implies the possession of a high-level, overall folk-psychological theory (school of thought called 'theory theory'), or of low-level modular mechanisms for the processing of various types of meta-representation (e.g., Sperber 2000). They all agree, however, that some sort of inferential interpretation of others' behaviour is involved.

Another type of operation, recently corroborated by the discovery of mirror-neurons (see, e.g., Blakemore and Decety 2001), consists in a process of empathic simulation. According to this view, persons do not so much represent others' mental states, as they are led by others' behaviour to approximate these states themselves, thereby putting themselves as it were in the other's place. Here, it is the subject's own experience that provides the basis for understanding others' dispositions and reacting appropriately: not 'what do I think she thinks' but 'what do I (as her) think'. Consider once again George and myself. Each of us is involved in an internal simulation of the other's perceived actions; we evaluate each other's dispositions, and react, as a function of our own emotional and intentional experiences arising from this simulation. My own experience of sadness as occasioned by my simulation of George's crying, allows me to recognize his sadness in his tears. Here again, authors differ considerably as to the nature of the mental processes involved. For some, it entails the elaboration of complex simulative models implying differing degrees of conscious introspection, off-line cognitive functioning and/or agency-ascription devices (for a recent example, see, e.g., Jeannerod and Pacherie 2004). For others it is a passive empathic experience amounting to the direct perception of others' intentional and emotional dispositions (e.g., Gallagher 2001).

Inferential interpretation and empathic simulation are often presented as rival explanations, implying very different conceptions of how the mind works (e.g. Berthoz and Jorland 2004). However, it is generally assumed that in the course of ordinary, everyday (adult) interaction, both these ways of communicating are continually in play, each providing a measure of correction for the other. But is this also true in the case of ritual? There are good reasons for thinking that things may be somewhat different, if only because the pragmatic premises that implicitly underlie peoples' participation in ritual and non-ritual events are not the same. Everyday interaction proceeds in large part from the tacit assumption that, in principle, the participants'

outward behaviour expresses or notifies their emotional and intentional states. However, because this equation is often uncertain (dis-
simulation is always possible), everyday interaction inevitably entails a
process of negotiation in which the participants' positions with respect
to each other are being continually worked out. In a ritual situation,
however, in which the patterning of behaviour is sharply constrained,
the presumed connection between private dispositions and outward
behaviour is oriented in the opposite direction. It is indeed one of the
hallmarks of ritual that the participants' emotional and intentional
dispositions to not so much inform their actions (other than the intention to carry out the actions in question, Humphrey and Laidlaw
1994), as they are informed by them. Whereas the underlying question
in ordinary interaction is 'given what I feel (and what I evaluate others
as feeling), what should I be doing?', in the case of ritual it is 'given
what I am doing (and what I perceive others doing), what should I be
feeling?' While ritual participants are expected to experience emotional
and intentional states in the course of their performance, the exact
nature of these states is largely irrelevant to the organization of the ritual performance itself. In short, under the special conditions of ritual
interaction, emotional and intentional dispositions are presumed to
proceed from actions rather than the other way around.

    With this issue in mind, let us consider two very different types of
ritual events, both occasioned by a young woman's first menstruation
in modern Western societies.

Menstrual Slapping

The first ritual event is the still fairly common though increasingly
abandoned custom one researcher (Thompson n.d.) has called the
'menstrual slap': a mother (or in some cases a grandmother), upon
being informed by her daughter that she has her first period, slaps her
daughter's face. This practice has been portrayed in several commercial films (e.g., Kurys' (1977) *Diabolo Menthe*, and Goldwyn's (1999) *A
Walk on the Moon*) and I have found close to a dozen references to it on
the Internet. It is alternatively held to be of Greek, Turkish, Jewish,
Lithuanian, Slavic or Eastern European origin.

    Even when the unexpected slap is not very hard – one witness
described it as 'firm tap' (Appel-Slingbaum 2000) – it still comes as
quite a shock. The women subjected to this practice retain a vivid
memory of the smack they received in large part because of its
apparently unwarranted, incongruous character. The slap's
anomalous nature is indeed heightened by the positive attitude shown
by the slapping party. Witnesses mention that the slap was preceded by

congratulations and/or followed by a show of affection; one third-party account recalls that 'As Helen reeled from shocked disbelief, shame, anxiety and confusion, Grandma [who had slapped her] smiled and invited her for tea' (Rayni n.d.). When the slapping party is prompted to explain her behaviour, the results leave much to be desired: 'It's for good luck', 'It's an old Jewish custom', 'I don't know but my mother did it to me', 'Don't ask me why you get slapped! YOU JUST DO!' (Pogrebin 1994; Appel-Slingbaum 2000; Howell 2001; Rayni n.d.; Satterwaite n.d.). Some women, reflecting back on the experience, often later in life, try to figure it out: might it have been a punishment for pride at menstruation? An indicator of 'Eve's legacy of childbirth and pain' (Hoffmann 1996)? A warning not to disgrace the family by becoming pregnant out of wedlock (Taylor 1988)? 'Something to do with introducing a girl to the pain of womanhood' (Rayni n.d.)? One mother told her daughter it was 'to open [your] eyes' (Costos *et al.* 2002), while another woman wonders if it were not 'to "slap sense" into a newly fertile girl [...], to "awaken" her out of her childhood slumber' (Appel-Slingbaum 2000). Several accounts maintain that this practice aims to bring blood and colour back to the cheeks of the menstruating girl, '[to] keep her looking healthy despite the fact that she is bleeding' (Rosenblatt and Frame 1996; also see anonymous testimony at www.mum.org/slap.htm). The *Anthology of Lithuanian Ethnoculture* also suggests something along these lines:

> [...] the mother having learned about her daughter's first menstruation would slap the girl's face and utter a ritual formula: 'bloom like a rose, be beautiful' or similar words. The ritual practice was intended to predestine the girl's physiological development. It was believed that even the manner in which the act of slapping was performed could determine the duration of menstruation (Jurkus n.d.).

The logic suggested by these latter explanations recalls F. Héritier's (1989) ideas of the upper and lower halves of the body being virtual mirror images of each other. The reddened cheek belies the loss of vaginal blood, an externally applied pain standing in the stead of an internally occasioned suffering. The slap acts as a suction pump, as it were, drawing to the face blood that would otherwise flow from the womb: the harder the slap (i.e., the redder the cheek), the shorter the young woman's menstrual period and, one might add, the longer the time during which she is held to be fertile. Thus, even such fragmentary material suggests that quite a lot is going on here on the level of possible symbolic interpretation: not only the face/womb analogy, but also the evocation of awakening and opening one's eyes and the mention of blooming roses (both classical metaphors for the onset of menses in Western European cultures).

However, the complexity of the menstrual slap is above all relational. As Costos *et al.* (2002) put it, 'The tradition of a mother slapping her daughter's face upon learning of her menarche is among
the most contradictory messages that can be transmitted'. Indeed, at
least three different relationships seems to be acted out simultaneously in the course of this short episode. On the one hand, the
slap is an explicit acknowledgement of the fact that in one essential
respect, as a biologically mature woman capable of bearing children,
the daughter is henceforth the mother's equal. It is their shared identity that prompts the daughter to confide in her mother in the first
place, and it is a recognition of this that accounts for the mother's
congratulatory attitude. On the other hand, this symmetrical relationship is associated with at least two other, clearly asymmetrical
ones. To begin with, the purposeful infliction of violence by the
mother upon the daughter bears witness to a radical, hierarchical
difference between these two parties: one is the offspring of the other.
At the same time, the slap also attests to (may indeed be seen as a
tacit reaction to) a reverse asymmetry: whereas the mother's
aptitude for procreation is in decline, the daughter's is in ascendancy,
such that the daughter is destined to replace her mother in the
latter's child-bearing role.

By combining these different, contradictory relationships in a single
sequence of action, the menstrual slap gives rise to an exceptional
relational configuration in which womanhood and motherhood are
inextricably connected. Mother and daughter jointly act out this complex relationship in the course of the ritual, and this affords them with
a novel experience that stands as a legitimizing touchstone for behaviour and discourse – the menstrual slap included – to the effect that
adult female status and an aptitude for child-bearing go hand in hand.
In this way, menstrual slapping does not so much create certain ideas
and values pertaining to female procreative function as it contributes
to their perpetuation by packaging them, along with the ambiguities
they imply, in a partially inscrutable yet highly memorable and emi-
nently transmittable form.[1]

So how do mother and daughter (and other witnesses) make sense
of this event? The degree of emotional arousal and bodily commitment
it entails surely prompts them to attribute some measure of meaning
to it. At the same time, menstrual slapping is typical of many rituals in
that it makes systematic use of what Carlo Severi and I (Houseman
and Severi 1998) have called 'ritual condensation', in which nominally contrary patterns of relationship are acted out simultaneously.
This feature, whereby ritual acts may be readily recognized as distinct
from mundane activities, has important consequences for the
functioning of empathic simulation and inferential interpretation.

Menstrual slapping is plainly a source of intense emotional and intentional bewilderment. As one woman put it: 'a lot of mixed feelings here!' (Costos *et al.* 2002). As a result, empathic simulation plays but a limited role in the participants' appreciation of this episode. It is indeed difficult to see how the mental replication of such an attention-grabbing yet paradoxical performance might allow the participants to evaluate each others' dispositions in such a way as to provide them with a clear understanding of the situation. This is especially the case for the newly menstruating daughter who is stunned into hurt perplexity. However, as the mothers' lame and often despairing justifications suggest, they also share in the emotional and intentional confusion that menstrual slapping entails. There is really only one, over-arching simulative operation that all the participants (and observers) may be presumed to be engaged in, and that is the diffuse but shared feeling that those who undertake this ritual are personally implicated in doing so: the identities of those who give and receive the slap are not fortuitous.

The situation is more complicated for inferential interpretation. As demonstrated by the women's and others' conjectures regarding the meaning of the menstrual slap, the latter is highly evocative. Violent punishment, procreative power, the loss and circulation of blood, personal accomplishment, feminine rivalry, uterine continuity and more provide the grounds for a variety of (often after the fact) inferences regarding the possible significance of this exceptional event. Ritual condensation, however, not only endows menstrual slapping with a rich, polysemous symbolism. It also combines its disparate and partially contradictory aspects into a performative totality whose enigmatic nature remains unexplainable by the participants themselves, and difficult to account for in terms of ordinary intentionalities and patterns of interaction. As a result, interpretative speculation, however elaborate, is revealed as incomplete and conceptually unsatisfactory; the explanatory urgency elicited by the face-slapping experience remains unfulfilled. The participants are thus led to infer that these anomalous actions, irreducible to the interpretations they may occasion, are in some difficult-to-define fashion meaningful in and of themselves. The menstrual slap takes on a markedly self-referential character: its presumed significance, which resists being put into words, is held to be totally accessible solely by its performance, whose enactment may thus be said to provide the conditions of its own reiteration.

As already suggested, ritual performances are typically organized along lines similar to those sketched out for the menstrual slap. Making sense of such ceremonial events relies largely upon interpretative inference, whose necessarily unfinished character prompts the participants to invest their actions with special, albeit difficult-to-grasp meaning. In such cases, the transmission of ritual relationships consists essentially in the replication of these partially inscrutable actions themselves. A very different situation obtains in the case of Neopagan and New Age menarche ceremonies.

Menarche Celebrations

Neopagan or New Age first menstruation rituals are called 'first blood celebrations', 'menarche rites', 'red parties', 'womanings', 'coming of age rituals', 'first moon celebrations' and so forth. Scripts for such undertakings can be found on the Internet as well. Often they are associated with advertisements for specialized books, magazines or 'passage to womanhood ceremonial kits'. The latter come complete with candles, pendants, easy-to-follow ritual scrolls, moon calendars, herbal teas and other paraphernalia. My favourite is a two-inch tall 'Menstrual Goddess' produced by the Bell Pine art farm of Oregon ('she is absolutely adorable, and even better in person' gushes the birthwithsol.com Internet site) in which, once again, face and lower body are combined in a single image.

Some of these scripts are so liturgically elaborate as to cast doubt upon the likelihood of their ever having been performed, whereas others, on the contrary, are too vague or whimsical to merit much attention. Still others amount to somewhat atypical but otherwise perfectly ordinary events, such as the baking of a red cake or the granting of three wishes (e.g., Davis and Leonard 2003); menarche parties also deserve mention (e.g., Crossman 2003). There remain, however, a fair number of outlines and descriptions that deserve serious consideration.

One Internet site describes menarche ceremonies in the following general terms:

> Different rituals can take place during the ceremony, reenacting the transition from childhood into womanhood. Often a special alter is built with little goddess statues, seashells, red roses and other symbols of menstruation and womanhood. Sometimes the girl will choose a favorite childhood toy to throw into the fire, symbolizing the release of her child-like ways, and receives a special piece of jewelry as a token of her new role as a menstruating woman. The girl can also be tied together to her mother with rope or ribbon, representing the bond of mother and child. The maiden then wiggles free or is released by the grandmother and runs to a special place away from the party to sit in seclusion and reflect on her new role as a young woman. When she returns, the older women take time to recall their own first periods, share stories about the joys and pains of menstruation, offer advice regarding sex and sensuality and have many laughs and

tears about being a woman. Gifts are given to the young maiden such as chocolate, jewelry, fancy clothes and menstrual products. Parents sometimes offer the girl special privileges, such as a later curfew or permission to wear makeup or get a body piercing. After the ceremony is over, a great feast takes place with song and dance late into the night, followed by a slumber party with her closest friends (Mystical Mountains n.d.).

Men are occasionally involved in these ceremonies in a peripheral fashion, by giving a red flower to the girl (Norhala 1995) or by preparing a meal beforehand (cf. Bhran n.d.). In some cases, the girl's father has a role to play as well: after having spent some time with the adolescent going over childhood pictures and choosing a stuffed toy, he formally hands the girl over to her mother, acting as the guardian of her childhood state, keeping the toy 'as I will keep the memories of your childhood' (Beyond the Realms n.d.). However, for the menarche rite itself, whether a community-wide festivity, a family celebration or limited to the girl and her mother alone, the participants are women. Here, for example, is the coming of age ritual for girls as performed by the Binghamton Pagan community of upstate New York:

> The coming of age ritual for girls we do here in our community is very beautiful. All the women of the community are part of the circle. The young woman (girl) is given a ritual bath of herbs (by her mother) and then dressed in white. She is told to bring a reminder of her childhood with her to the circle. She is then blindfolded and lead to the circle by her mother. The women in the circle stand one behind the other with their hands on the hips of the woman in front of her and spread their legs to form a 'birth canal'. The young woman crawls through the birth canal symbolizing her rebirth into womanhood. She is then un-blindfolded and her mother says whatever words she would like to share with her and then asks her if she is ready to leave her childhood behind (but also reminding her to always remember the child that lives in all of us). All the women in the circle wear red and bring a gift for the young woman (the gift is traditionally something red – candles, flowers, etc). Then we share red grape juice and jelly filled donuts (symbolic). Each woman in the circle then shares the story of her first menstruation. Some stories are sad, funny, but each is our own experience. Then we all gather around her and chant 'She changes everything She touches and everything She touches changes'. Then the circle is opened (Binghamton Pagan Community n.d.).

Finally, M. Fellous provides a short description (Fellous 2001: 119–23) and film (Fellous and Renard 1993) of a family-scale menarche rite she observed in Portland, Oregon (USA) in 1993:

> At the foot of the couch, Tess, 14 years old, a stuffed animal [...] held tightly in her hands, is curled up against Hannah, her godmother, two years her

elder, who underwent a similar rite two years earlier. Seated on the floor, surrounding Suma, Tess's mother, are a group of her friends. On the rug next to them are various objects symbolizing femininity and fertility.

The ritual begins after sundown and is orchestrated by a local ritual leader: 'So this evening we honour Tess' first step in becoming a woman'. Following her directions, the seven participating women sit in a circle, introduce themselves and purify themselves by smudging with lavender and mountain sage. Then to the accompaniment of drumming and singing ('Earth my body, water my blood, air my breath and fire my spirit'), they 'open a sacred space', convoking absent family members as well as Gods and Goddesses 'who are the archetypes of those psychic elements we will be referring to tonight'. After a time of meditation (the 'molten core of the earth' is mentioned), Tess's mother tells an African folktale. After a moment of silence, each woman begins to make a personal 'power object' held to 'symbolize' her relationship with her menstrual cycle.

> Tess and Hannah, go out into the night to find an object that is supposed to symbolize this moment in her adolescent life. The women remain inside, weaving a crown of flowers. When Tess and Hannah return, Tess is made to symbolically cross the threshold by passing under the raised arms of the women who, playing the tambourine, accompany her to the bathroom where Hannah will bath her, make her up and dress her in a new dress.

During this time, Suma, Tess's mother, eyes closed, seated in a circle with the other women, is invited by the leader to 'call out a quality that you want to let go of [...] and then we'll speak it back'. 'Possessiveness' says Suma and the gathered woman respond in chorus 'Suma is letting go of possessiveness'; other qualities follow: 'the past relationship with her', 'the control over Tessa', 'envy and jealousy of my own children'. 'And what are you opening to?' the leader asks. Suma answers 'My own aging process' and once again this is taken up by all the women together: 'Suma is opening up to her own aging process'.

When Tess emerges from the bathroom, washed, dressed and made up, she is greeted by cries of joy and the sound of drums, rattles and tambourine. The women stand in a circle around her and the crown of flowers is placed upon her head. 'Welcome back as a woman' says her mother, 'Welcome to the circle of women'. The women circle around her, chanting her name while clapping hands and playing the tambourine. Each women then presents Tess with a gift 'that symbolizes her new-born femininity'. Finally, the circle opened at the beginning of the rite is closed and everyone shares a meal composed of red foods and drinks.

While both practices share a number of themes, Neopagan and New Age menarche rites contrast sharply with menstrual slapping. There is no unexpected bodily violence, little uncertainty and a tearfully joyous time to be had for all concerned. This is due in part to differences in the conceptions of womanhood these performances mediate. However, in order to identity the distinctive properties of contemporary menarche celebrations as instances of ritual activity, I would like to pursue the comparison on a more formal level. In what ways do the principles that underlie the organization and transmission of these ceremonies – specifically with regard to the roles played by inference and simulation – diverge from those at work in menstrual slapping?

Menarche Celebrations as Ritual

Perhaps the most obvious difference (beyond considerations of length of performance and number of participants) relates to the texture of ritual action. The ceremonial behaviour of menarche rites, while at times unusual and fairly elaborate, is, in itself, remarkably unproblematic and transparent. There is none of the ambivalence and opacity to be found, for example, in the unexpected, unexplainable menstrual slap. In other words, the meanings of the participants' actions are, in principle, readily accessible to them and fully intelligible in terms of their everyday feelings, intentions and representations. Grape juice, jelly-filled donuts and other red items are held to 'symbolize' menstruation, the women who spread their legs apart are deemed to 'form a birth canal', relating personal anecdotes is taken to educate the young girl about womanhood, sharing food is held to enact feminine solidarity, etc. This straightforward nature of ritual behaviour is further accentuated by the practitioners themselves who, in the course of the performance, often take pains to explicate the significance of their actions. One woman, for example, describes how, for her daughter's menarche ritual, she prepared a box wrapped in red paper:

> Inside, under many layers of tissue paper, lay a smaller box, crisscrossed by a red velvet ribbon. That box held a small clay statue of the Goddess of Menstruation. 'Just as Tisa [her daughter] had to go through all those layers to get to the little statue,' I said, 'I would like us [the participating women] to go through all our layers and reach deep inside and share our thoughts with her.' As we passed the statue around, we talked about some of the women we admired, our role models (Soster-Olmer 2001).

In short, there is not much to be found here in the way of ritual condensation understood as a simultaneous enactment of opposites.

The abundantly commented upon actions that make up menarche ceremonies are markedly unambiguous. They lay no paradoxical 'thought traps' (Smith 1979) and are held to harbour little mystery in and of themselves.

In menstrual slapping, the performance of richly evocative yet obscure behaviour at once encourages inferential interpretation and thwarts its satisfactory resolution. The behaviour in question thus acquires a self-referential quality and a measure of indisputable legit-imacy. This is not what happens in Neopagan and New Age menarche rites where, on the contrary, inferential interpretation is systematically trivialized and therefore sharply curtailed. What further understand-ings are there to be drawn from enactments that are made to be as self-evident and unequivocal as possible? As a source of meaning 'beyond the information given' (Brunner 1973) whereby participants make sense of these events as special, out of the ordinary yet efficacious per-formances, inferential interpretation plays but a limited role. The only inferences with sufficient relevance (Sperber and Wilson 1995 [1986]) to be readily entertained, concern the connection between the ritual performance and analogous activities presumed to have been undertaken by others elsewhere or in the past.

The liturgical formulae, songs, gestures and objects employed, the exegetical commentary they elicit as well as the oral and written sources consulted, all bear witness to the idea that present-day menar-che rites derive from the ceremonial behaviour of indigenous (and non-Western) peoples and/or ancient (pre-Christian) civilizations (for an extreme example, see Stein 1990). Implicit and explicit reference to such precursors, presumed to be uncorrupted by oppressive (e.g., patriarchal) ideologies and the shortcomings of modern Western soci-ety, is indeed a constitutive feature of these ceremonies and a source of the authority the participants attribute to their performance. How-ever, speculations as to the nature of these connections remain strik-ingly open-ended. To begin with, contemporary ritual crafters typically incorporate elements drawn from a variety of traditions. More importantly, however, and contrary to what one might expect, those who perform these rites are pointedly not trying to reproduce ancient or tribal ceremonies as faithfully as possible.

Neopagan and New Age menarche rites have some recurrent fea-tures: the relinquishing of a childhood toy, the prevalence of the colour red, bathing, seclusion, a moment of privileged communica-tion between mother and daughter, episodes connoting transition such as crossing a line, entering a circle or passing under spread legs or raised arms, adult women telling stories about menstruation and womanhood, gift-giving, etc. They are nonetheless strikingly variable from one community or family group to the next, and even within communities and families their performance is highly labile. One rea-son for this is that these celebrations are often cobbled together by con-cerned mothers and friends from diverse sources: books, Internet sites, commercial kits, amateur or professional ritualizers and so forth (see, e.g., Koon 2004; Rudolph 1998). More significantly, however, and in keeping with the decentralized, personalized bent of Neopagan and New Age practice in general (Pike 2004), menarche rites are deemed to be most effective when consciously adapted to the peculiarities of the situation at hand and the individual participants concerned. Thus, for example, the advice repeatedly given to those who would organize such rites is that the girl herself be consulted regarding who to invite, how they should dress, what food will be served, etc. (e.g., Davis and Leonard 2002; Thistle 2005; Soster-Olmer 2001). According to its practitioners, a menarche rite, often undertaken in explicit opposition to certain aspects of mainstream popular culture (menstruation as 'the curse', etc.), should be a harmonious and festive occasion, in which the gathered woman endeavour to provide the newly menstru-ating girl (and her mother) with the means of assuming her nascent womanhood in the least traumatic and most creative way possible. From this point of view, what precise items of behaviour make up a given menarche rite is of secondary importance. What counts above all is the spirit in which they are carried out: the supportive intentions these items of behaviour are held to express, and the personal, 'empowering' effect their performance has, not only on the girl herself, but on all the women present (e.g., Roberts 1994; Hobbs 2005; Zenack 2006; Reid n.d.).

Unlike menstrual slapping, Neopagan and New Age menarche rites are not partially unintelligible yet stipulated enactments held to har-bour essential yet difficult-to-define realities, and alleged to be passed on more or less unchanged from one generation to the next. Rather, they are eclectically recomposed, largely self-evident performances, consciously tailored to particular circumstances and analogously linked to 'traditional' or 'archaic' practices that serve less as models than as resources. In view of these differences, many anthropologists would question their very status as rituals.

Might it be, however, that the complexity of Neopagan and New Age ceremonial, absent on the level of action itself, is to be found else-where? I suggest that this is indeed the case, that the complexity of these rituals resides not in the paradoxical properties of the items of behaviour undertaken, but in the ambivalent identities of those who undertake them. They are to be judged not by the condensed quality of their actions but by the enhanced quality of their agents. This is related to the fact that in rituals such as these, coordinate participation and understanding depend essentially upon empathic simulation.

For Neopagan and New Age practitioners, their ceremonies are directly linked to ancient and/or tribal societies. The ritual performed here and now is taken to echo others performed previously and/or elsewhere. However, as mentioned above, the overriding concern of Neopagan and New Age ritualists is not to replicate these antecedent rituals, but rather to recapture the spirit in which they were performed. The idea is not to do now what a Celtic priestess, say, did in her day, but to do what such a priestess might do if she were practising today as a middle-class European-American. In short, creative adaptation is preferred over direct reiteration.[2] In acting out in this way the imagined behaviour of postulated prior performers, Neopagan and New Age ritualists are engaged in simulating these prior performers' intentional and emotional states. The items of behaviour they undertake are presumed to proceed less from their own personal dispositions than from those they attribute to such pre-eminent if largely hypothetical others. However, when these items of behaviour are enacted, it is of course the participants' own intentional and emotional dispositions (and not those of the simulated parties) that are affected by their performance. At her daughter's menarche rite, a woman and her close friends each contribute a flower to make a crown that is solemnly placed upon the girl's head. For them, these particular actions do not so much reflect their own feelings and beliefs as they express the sentiments and convictions of wiser ilk than they – Arthurian magicians? Dionysian priests? Native-American shamans? – whose attitudes they seek to emulate and in whose ceremonial footsteps they try to follow. However, as they add their flowers and as the crown is placed upon the young woman's head, all of them, each in her own way, is personally affected and transformed.

This more or less explicit simulation of postulated forerunners entails a 'vertical' refraction of the participants' agency: paradoxically, the participants' private emotional and intentional states are informed by ritual actions which are held to express the dispositions of antecedent others as these are conjured up by the participants themselves. A similar, largely implicit and more markedly empathic 'horizontal' refraction also takes place between participating persons. In order to make sense of their collective undertaking and to interact accordingly, the participants rely to a large extent upon an ongoing replication of each others' dispositions. Their actions are dictated above all by what they feel the other participants might be feeling. In this way, the participants are led to assume, and react as a function of, multiple, potentially contrary, points of view. The mother is prompted to identify not only with her daughter, but also with her own mother and with the other women present. These other women identify both with the mother, with her daughter, with each other, and perhaps, with their own mothers and daughters. Fellous' observations regarding Tess's mother's introspective ruminations echoed by the friends around her are directly relevant here:

> Later, [she] developed her thoughts further, saying how this separation was like a cycle in her own life, re-enacting her own adolescence and her separation from her own mother. It was as though time had contracted: [she] was, in turn, herself, her mother leaving her, her daughter leaving her, and her daughter emerging from her womb (Fellous 2001: 121).

The daughter is led to identify with her mother (in one case she wore her mother's wedding dress), with the other women present, with the female role models they represent and tell stories about, with 'the child inside' she is enjoined to never forget (e.g., Soster-Olmer 2001), and with the Goddess herself (she is often told that she is the Goddess, e.g., Hawthorne 1993).

The salience of Neopagan and New Age menarche rites derives, then, less from the singular character of the actions performed than from the exceptional intentional and emotional sharing their performance entails. What counts above all is not the execution of certain odd sequences of behaviour, but the institution of certain unusual intentional and emotional configurations. In short, the ritual efficacy of enactments such as these relies more upon the patterning of agency than upon the organization of action. In menstrual slapping, the participants' private dispositions are presumed to proceed from the behaviour they carry out and not the reverse. As I have mentioned, this is one of the distinctive hallmarks of ritual. It is also the case in Neopagan and New Age ceremonies, but with a simulative twist that implicitly discriminates between the participants' personal intentions and emotions (occasioned by the actions they undertake) and their simulations of the intentional and emotional states of others (that provide the basis for these actions). The vertical and horizontal refractions that arise from this discrimination set up an ongoing reverberation between the participants' replication of others' dispositions, the collective representations of emotions and intentions realized in their joint enactments, and the private feelings and understandings these enactments bring about. In doing so, these refractions define a novel interactive context in which ordinarily contradictory patterns of agency come into play at the same time: intentional and emotional experiences are made to circulate among participants increasingly endowed with multiple subjecthood. Within the relationships acted out in this context, the participants become very much more than what they may appear to be: mothers, daughters, fellow women, moon children, goddesses, priestesses, worshippers, lovers and friends. What their individual feelings and convictions lose in precision they gain in multi-faceted convergence; they are instilled with additional if partially unintelligible significance as the interdependent aspects of an exceptional totality instantiated in the ritual performance itself.

Condensation and Enhancement

Menstrual slapping and first blood celebrations both enact special relational patterns in which nominally contrary modes of relationship are simultaneously enjoined. This is what makes these performances so difficult to account for in terms of everyday interaction and intentionality. Moreover, both these enactments are held to be efficacious in their own right: by informing the participants' emotional and intentional states, they provide them with unarguable, experiential grounds for subsequent discourse and behaviour that presuppose the exceptional relational patterns acted out in the course of their performance. For these reasons, both types of events deserve to be recognized as rituals.

They are structured, however, according to different principles. Menstrual slapping is founded upon 'ritual condensation' in which a concurrence of opposites pertains chiefly to the organization of the actions undertaken. Menarche celebrations, on the other hand, are founded upon what we might call 'ritual enhancement' in which this concurrence pertains above all to the constitution of the agents involved. In the first case, singular agents undertake composite, pluralistic actions, whereas in the second, singular actions are undertaken by composite, pluralistic agents. Thus, while the complexity of the menstrual slap, and correlatively, the symbolism its performance gives rise to, relates to the participants' outward behaviour, that of menarche rites relates to the participants' emotional and intentional dispositions.

I have argued that the participants' capacity to make sense of the relationships they act out in the course of action-centred rituals such as menstrual slapping, relies heavily on inference. While their respective identities are not in themselves problematical, the behaviour they pursue (a celebratory infliction of unexpected pain by a trusted family member) is designed to be at once unquestionably attention-grabbing and intrinsically ambiguous. Inferential interpretation of this condensed behaviour is thus strongly stimulated, but prevented from reaching a satisfactory conclusion. This gives rise to the supposition that the anomalous behaviour in question is imbued with some special, difficult-to-define meaning accessible only by means of its performance. In ritual enactments such as these, the participants' intentional and emotional dispositions are held to be largely contingent. As a result, empathic simulation is of subsidiary importance in their understanding of these episodes. Mainly, it induces among participating parties the shared feeling that the anomalous behaviour they undertake is directly relevant to them, that those who are engaged in these performances are personally implicated in the relationships they enact.

In agent-centred rituals like Neopagan and New Age menarche celebrations, empathic simulation intervenes in a more obvious fashion (this had led several authors to liken their performance to [pretend] play, theatre or art, e.g., Luhrmann 1989, Pike 2001, Magliocco 2004). The items of behaviour that compose these events are made to be as straightforward and accessible as possible. However, because these items of behaviour are animated by the explicit and tacit simulation of intentionalities and affective states attributable to postulated forerunners and co-participants (entailing vertical and horizontal refractions of agency), the identities of those who undertake them are rendered inherently equivocal. It is the performers themselves rather than the actions they pursue that become imbued with special significance that is hard to define in ways that do not refer to the performance itself. In situations such as these, inferential interpretation intervenes in a subordinate fashion, principally as a means of legitimately accounting for the enhanced quality of the ritual performers: drawing on disparate ceremonial and exegetical features, it prompts the participants to entertaining hazy speculations regarding the supposed link between the special relationships they enact and those realized in the course of ceremonial activities previously undertaken by others.

It should be emphasized that while inferential interpretation plays a leading role in events founded upon ritual condensation, and empathic simulation plays a dominant role in events founded upon ritual enhancement, in either case, both communicative processes are required. Whereas inferential procedures allow participants to invest their performances with additional meaning and authority, simulative operations commit them to the personal relevance of the relationships they enact.

While the two ritual styles outlined here are not strictly incompatible, they do imply divergent orientations in the organization of ceremonial activities.[3] Correlatively, they also suggest two quite different ways of thinking about learning ritual, that is, about how ceremonial enactments capture the minds of those who participate in them in such a way that these persons acquire not only the ability to undertake them but also the incentive to do so. On the one hand, within the context of action-condensing performances, learning ritual consists in acquiring the capacity to carry out certain highly evocative, partially incomprehensible actions, all the while sharing with other participants the feeling that those who accomplish these actions are personally concerned by them. On the other hand, within the context of agent-enhancing enactments, learning ritual consists in acquiring the capacity to pursue multiple empathic simulations while sharing with other participants the conviction that the activities undertaken are equivalent to those previously performed by others. These two modes of transmission, in turn, imply divergent conceptions of tradition or 'deference' (Bloch 2005) whereby ritual performances may be appreciated as necessary recurrences rather than as arbitrary inventions. In cases such as menstrual slapping, where ritual relationships are transmitted through the reiteration of ritual actions, tradition is construed as a set of practices whose perpetuation relies on unaffected repetition. In cases such as Neopagan and New Age menarche celebrations, where ritual relationships are transmitted by means of the reproduction of ritual agents, tradition is taken to refer to a set of intentional and emotional dispositions whose perpetuation derives from acts of conventional imagination.

Acknowledgements

I would like to thank G. Lindquist, M. Moisseeff, V. Servais and E. Viveiros de Castro who kindly read and commented upon a previous version of this text, as well as the members of the 'Texts in progress' workshop of the African Worlds Study Centre (CEMAf, Ivry). Finally, I thank my students at the Ecole Pratique des Hautes Etudes (Paris) for having willingly put up with the numerous exploratory sessions that allowed me to work out many of the ideas presented here.

Notes

1. The issues addressed in this episode can be found in any number of cultures, particularly those in which adult female status is closely associated with the ability to bear children, and becoming a woman is deemed to be predicated upon the relationship between a young woman and her own mother. In such conditions, the attainment of womanhood may become problematic, for the acquisition of procreative capacity whereby womanhood is defined is often held to follow a zero-sum rule according to which every winner implies a corresponding loser.

2. See Fedele (2006a, 2006b) for an example pertaining to menstruation. For political issues raised by 'cultural borrowing', see Pike 2001: 123–54; Magliocco 2004: 205–37.

3. It might be thought that a newly invented rite necessarily starts out as agent-centred and acquires action-centred qualities over time. While the emergence of new action-centred rituals in many parts of the world belies this idea, it is obviously necessary to document agent-centred rituals elsewhere than in contemporary European-American culture.

Chapter 4

THE ACCIDENTAL IN RELIGIOUS INSTRUCTION
IDEAS AND CONVICTIONS

David Parkin

Two Approaches

Deeley (2004) has provided a reassessment of Geertz's early five-point definition of religion. He uses it as a framework in tracing the affective-cognitive process by which ideas become religious convictions. The mesolimbic dopamine system of the brain and its moods and motivations are constantly re-activated through the repetition of particular rituals which, reciprocally, are increasingly associated with such moods and motivations. This constantly re-activated syndrome of mood, motivation and ritual practice forms the basis of socially acknowledged, enduring religious beliefs. Deeley draws parallels from work by familiar names in cognitive and evolutionary anthropology which spans what were once distinct sub-fields of the social, cognitive and biological, but which are nowadays linked by research on the 'social brain', some of it aimed at explaining the operation and evolution of religion (e.g. Boyer 2000a, 2001b, 2003; Dunbar 2003; Durham 1991; Sperber 1996; Whitehouse 2000). This is to examine religion from the viewpoint of a 'micro-theory' of concepts (their internal network of associations), to use Boyer's term (1994: 67–68), rather than from that of religion as made up of analogical reasoning resonant of and causally linked to other social forms (e.g. religion is social consciousness).

Although assumptions concerning the 'religious brain' (to use the title of Deeley's paper) have been ingeniously extracted from Geertz's interpretive approach in this way, Geertz's own very recent reappraisal of his ideas on religion stresses something more akin to a Durkheimian and Weberian two-part definition. It is what we might then call an understanding of religion from the 'macro-theory' of concepts.

It is reasonable to concur that belief (in religion) presupposes informal learning processes, insofar as exposure to recurrent opinions and practical demonstration may inculcate unquestioned assertions. To that extent, learning is part of any process of religious commitment, often unconsciously acquired. On the other hand, the world religions, and in some respects the so-called traditional religions, commonly set out in full consciousness to train adepts into embracing such commitment. Thus, the commitment that results from either kind of learning may well be imprinted on the 'religious brain' through ritually reinforced affective-cognitive repetition. But the conditions of collective enterprise that permit such commitment have also to be set up, sometimes prior and sometimes alongside the developing affective-cognitive syndrome, so that people can speak and share gestures that communicate what they perceive as shared belief.

I start, then, from this institutional perspective and, by way of example, from that of a world religion, namely Islam. I conclude by posing questions about the role of unexpected ideas and events in the development of religious conviction and the 'religious brain'.

Analogical Separations

Formal 'learning' from the perspective of a textually based world religion presupposes a distinction which is social before it can be analysed as cognitive: between the hierarchically inscribed, formal literary, exhortatory and rhetorical modes of persuading a listening public to subscribe to an acknowledged belief system or religion, and the informal ways in which individual believers privately, at first, deal with such propagated and textualized beliefs. Yet, it is in this latter area, where ideas, beliefs and putative heresies jostle for acceptance and credibility (see Humphrey and Laidlaw 1994), that accidents of interpretation occur or in which unexpected events are seen by actors as needing to be explained in terms which, even if different in some respects, preserve sufficient familiarity to be regarded as continuous with earlier explanations. If we gloss this as only a process by which ideas become convictions, we miss the essential component of accident or even serendipity by which the 'new' or uncomfortable ideas come to actors in the first place (cf. Pieke 2000). It might be suggested that research on the social or religious brain should now also throw light on the mental incorporation of cognitive accident (perhaps through the better known notion of cognitive dissonance). For this, we need first to identify the social conditions under which persons respond to epistemological accident, for which I use Geertz's review of his definition of religion as a starting-point.

He reminds us that, for him, 'Religion ... tunes human actions to an envisaged cosmic order and projects images of cosmic order onto the plane of human experience ... [that a believer constructs or discovers] another world to live in – whether we expect ever to pass wholly over into it or not – is what we mean by having a religion' (Geertz 1973: 90 and 2005: 7, and bracketed inclusion taken from Geertz 2005 ibid.). He then goes on to re-examine his definition as it had been applied to the two societies he studied, Muslim Morocco and religiously diverse but heavily Muslim Java. He further notes that his views at the time did not accord with the 'secularization thesis' of the 1960s and early 1970s, namely that 'the rationalization of modern life was pushing religion out of the public square, shrinking it to the dimensions of the private, the inward, the personal, and the hidden ...' (Geertz 2005: 10). We can, moreover, agree that the thesis nowadays also seems untenable in the face of an apparently rising radical or fundamentalist religious consciousness, accompanied by activism, among all the so-called textualist or world religions, of which Islam receives most prominence in this regard, but is not in fact alone. So-called 'traditional' religions such as animism, with or without pantheism, are by definition locally bound and are not normally associated with global spread and influence. That said, it can be argued that their local provenances overlap interminably, as if by way of a tangled skein, so that, in many parts of the world, they continue to inhabit or work their way into the practices and assertions of world religions, showing sometimes remarkable similarities across time and space, with shamanism, divination, spirit possession and ancestral veneration being examples.

Geertz's definition, like all such, can be challenged in the truncated form in which it is presented. But, in fairness, it is meant to be understood in association with ritual, myth, spirit beliefs, spiritual discipline, creed and piety and other practices which, when described in relation to each other make it clear that we are talking about what we conventionally understand as religion, even if, through metaphor, these attributes may be applied to any kind of secular ideology.

The largely Durkheimian premise of the first part of the definition, that the cosmic and experiential should mirror each other, and the other-worldly Weberian background to the second idea, that we make up another possible world to the one we live in, fit the Abrahamic religions, including Islam, better than others. We have, of course, nowa-

days largely moved on from definitions to questions of process (though
the two are often mutually involved): how did religion evolve, what
are its cognitive dimensions, and how is religion always either pene-
trating or withdrawing from what is otherwise known as the non-
religious – principally politics, law, morality and the claims of natural
scientists?

Learning religion is part of the process, partly riding on memorization of liturgy and partly on exposure to like-thinkers. From the viewpoint of its clerics, learning a religion is for any one individual clearly
a standardized and yet personal process of absorption of precepts and
convictions such that they are not just appealed to in particular situations, as one might pull down an instruction manual on how to
behave at a party, but become unquestionably a constituent part of
that person. The idea that we can separate the cosmos (a transcendental world) from the world we otherwise inhabit (our earthly world)
is fundamental to the Weberian, Geertzian and Abrahamic view. But I
would argue that there is a meta-separation of crucial emotional and
cognitive significance to believers. It is contained in, for example, the
common idea that God and other-worldliness is within each human
who, at the same time, is driven also by this-worldly concerns. This
internal separation, which reflects that of the cosmic and earthly, is
the basis of Abrahamic ideas of original sin, sinning during life, temp-
tation, piety, resurrection and entry into paradise or heaven, or, conversely, descent into hell. It is a separation of affective-cognitive
pathways which threaten to become entangled.

The personal conflicts and crises arising from this felt danger of
merging the separable are indeed addressed through formal liturgy as
part of the initial learning process, as when an initiate, convert or catechist memorizes commandments and didactic parables and is taught
that disobedience resulting in transgression may incur punishment
and divine wrath. But the turmoil of inner states that may arise from
such teaching also informs that person emotionally in ways that may
vary by individual, resulting in different and sometimes extreme
strategies of coping. Such strategies include praying as many times
and devotedly as possible, carrying out good deeds and acts of piety
and charity, reading texts either to further understand their deeper
significance or as an act of hallowed repetition, sacrificing oneself or
loved ones to advance, defend or simply acknowledge deity and the
creed.

Such acts of worship may be ordained in moderation by the texts or
those who provide religious instruction, but can sometimes be taken to
extremes by the believers themselves, a matter of subjective and relative definition. We might speculate, for instance, that suicide bombing
in the cause of Islam is regarded by most ordinary Muslims as an

extreme act of self-sacrifice, who might also regard a man spending most of nearly every day praying in the mosque and neglecting family and other duties as an act of extreme piety. As actions judged to be either moderate or extreme, they are the opposite poles of a socio-emotional spectrum. At one end clerics normally try to standardize 'moderate' belief and practice (cases of clerics blatantly inciting followers to so-called extremism are surely rare). At the other end, pupils may seek to mark out their individuality in what they and some others deem to be special efforts, including martyrdom. Shifts along the spectrum, in either direction, accompany changes in individual life-cycles as well as being responses to challenges to the religion.

Dichotomies are at best heuristic and at worst essentialist. The separation of formal standardization as an aim in religious teaching from its unintended emotional and cognitive consequences seems justifiably heuristic. It points up the fact that, in invoking a precept or holy text (usually claimed as written), an Abrahamic religious believer may do so either dispassionately as might someone citing a standard legal code, or through passionate appeal to its absolute authority, power and effects. But, in delineating this contrast, the dichotomy opens up a third possibility. The believer may waver between passion and calculation and at some point doubt the relevance, significance and veracity of the invoked religious clause, and regard it as inappropriate to the situation at hand. It is this latter, third possibility entailing emotional and cognitive ambivalence that I regard as in fact a major factor driving religious continuity. It is, in other words, the paradox that through the pain suffered by many believers who undergo religious doubt and ambivalence, religious propositions may sometimes emerge as means of resolving such uncertainty and clearing away the pain. The assertion resolves the ambiguity and dissolves the internal suffering. From the viewpoint of orthodoxy, such ambivalence is the 'shadow', so to speak, that inevitably accompanies the formal learning processes of religion, which, after all, seeks 'enlightenment' (e.g. the much cited *nur* or equivalent in the Abrahamic creeds).

Cognitive and emotional ambivalence is not absent from the learning processes of, say, natural science or other so-called rational positivistic modes of reasoning and teaching, whose course is also driven ultimately by scepticism. If we were to retain some distinction between science and religion, it would be that, in principle, the latter asks its tutees to make faith the basis of their convictions while science advocates empirical demonstration. In practice, of course, religious clerics commonly point to the evidence of 'miracles' or the 'wonders of life' as 'scientifically' illustrating the truth of the creed, while scientists often ask the rest of us to accept their claims as a matter of faith, given our alleged incompetence as non-scientists to test them. Perhaps the dif-

ference is that, ideally in science, students are taught to doubt and
question, while in religion they are not. The difference between science
and religion may, then, come down to a question not of their respective
ritual practices but of the ways they are each learned, or claimed to be
learned.

Now, the three types of religious reflection and response given
above, clinical and calculating, passionate and absolute, and ambivalent bordering on sceptical, most obviously rest on religious learning
as a formal process of due instruction, with designated teacher, pupil
and written or oral texts. Compared with Judaism and Islam, perhaps
relatively few modern Euro-American Christians have that kind of
intense formal exposure to teachers and texts, instead learning their
religion more informally (see Jenkins 1999), (though the growing
strength of religious creationism may well return Christian learning to
a level of textual or Biblical intensity on a par with that in Judaism and
Islam). For the moment, the three kinds of response are much more a
part of religious learning for young people in Judaism and Islam, who
are more likely to attend schools or institutions of instruction, of
which the Muslim madarasa are a rapidly and globally increasing
example (Loimeier 2002). In drawing a great deal from his own field
experiences of Islam in particular, Geertz's definition of religion echoes
the pairing of the textual basis of instruction and the various local
countervailing practices and beliefs against which the Islamic texts
and clerics constantly push. This contrast between textual formalism
and, sometimes unwritten, local vernacular practices and ideas, is
indeed consistently characteristic of Islam's often long-rooted presence in sub-Saharan Africa and Malayo-Indonesia. Unlike most of the
Arabic-speaking Middle East and North African Maghreb, where Islam
has on the whole long since vanquished competing gods, the battle is
always on in parts of Africa and Malayo-Indonesia either to suppress
the local and traditional in favour of the pan-Islamic or at least to
accommodate it in ways acceptable to Muslim clerics in the region,
even if such ways are pronounced as unacceptable practices and inno-
vations (*bida'a*) by Saudi-derived Wahabi and Salafi reformers and
missionaries.

A Religion's Inner Epistemological Struggle

There are then the personal dilemmas of any individual believer-sceptic who wrestles with the task of reconciling the formal demands of
religious text to actual practice and logic in particular situations.
Caulked on this task is that of how to bring together wider Islamic
issues raised by the Wahabi with the persistence of local people's

indigenous views of Islam. Lambek has discussed the tensions inherent in this kind of situation in the western Indian Ocean (beginning with a paper on contested knowledge and authority (Lambek 1990), as have I over the years along and about the East African coast (focusing on such contentious activities as the *maulidi* celebration of the Prophet's birthday, veneration of saints, prolonged and lavish mortuary rituals, medical use and invocation of the *jinn* and other spirits).

The East African coast is populated by non-Muslims as well as Muslims, who nearly all speak Swahili as a first or second language. As I have suggested (2000: 98–99), 'wisdom' is regarded as acquired through contrasting means among the two peoples. Muslim men and women of learning are expected to have gained their understanding from prolonged attendance at *madarasa* and, later, possibly at an Islamic college, either in Lamu, Kenya, or, increasingly, in Saudi Arabia. There is a long-standing East African coastal tradition of intellectual debate and philosophical exchange reminiscent of Socratian dialogue (Kresse 2006). Local Swahili intellectuals generally blend indigenous and Islamic ideas and formal instruction, but sometimes separate them. Kresse describes the concept of *utu* (the Bantu concept of humanity) as developed by one of a number of such local scholars, some of whom use Islamic notions rather than Bantu concepts as their philosophical starting-point, while yet others mix them. However mixed, such Bantu-Islamic epistemology is seen to rest on some degree of textual learning, some of it explicitly religious.

By contrast, such non-Muslim neighbours of the Swahili as the Giriama and related Mijikenda peoples commonly claim that, despite the knowledge nowadays acquired through formal secular schooling, traditional wisdom is still the preserve of elders who have lived long enough to bring together their acquired experiences of life into reasonably coherent statements about the world and cosmos. It is a knowledge or wisdom that is not drawn from texts but premised on many facets of the indigenous religious categories of animism. While overlapping at various points nowadays with both Christianity and Islam, such animistic wisdom throws up issues that are addressed in terms which predate and are independent of the two world religions. Novice healers undergo apprenticeships of seven years in the practice of a single senior healer before they can practise on their own, during which time they learn by example and word of mouth the properties of herbal and other medicines and how to collect, apply and talk to them, a task which is heavily embedded in moral as well as therapeutic considerations (Parkin 1991: 174–80).

In short, among Muslims instruction through designated religious teachers and texts is the primary basis of a reputation for knowledge. It is not by itself a function of ageing, and indeed a number of prominent sheikhs celebrated for their Islamic knowledge are only in their 40s. The idiom of Islamic knowledge is that it should be propagated to as many believers as possible, ideally across all social and ethnic boundaries and incorporating outsiders. Among the non-Muslims, indigenous, primarily animistic wisdom is acquired in many cases through the exposure to experience that social ageing brings, and, in healing, through practical apprenticeship. The use of texts is expected to be absent, for to write down such traditional wisdom is tantamount to betraying its secret nature to outsiders, a common enough feature of many societies. This is despite the presence of and enthusiasm for 'western-style' school education which exists alongside but does not penetrate animistic epistemology, and despite the fact that, sometimes nowadays, people do write down for private (but not public) consumption traditional religious ideas passed on to them by their elders.

The contrast is well illustrated by personal fieldwork experience. Becoming a recognized non-Muslim Giriama sage was a possibility for me only after some twenty or so years of acquaintanceship with elders and their successors, this being part of my own ageing process. For instance I was sought out as someone who knew the system of clanship and naming, both indicators of marriage possibilities and prohibitions, but which younger Giriama claimed to be forgetting. In my case, I could 'remember' these facts by referring to my notebooks compiled over the years, while Giriama elders rarely had anything but their own memory to rely on. By contrast, becoming a Muslim sheikh is through a publicly acknowledged if difficult route laid out by the religion: first, convert to Islam and be very pious; second, become an *ustadh*, or junior religious teacher, after oneself receiving formal Islamic instruction, preferably at an Islamic college; and, third, through copious, imaginative writings, mosque sermons and lectures, earn in due course the title of sheikh. Oral and literary transmission thus each broadly characterize the two modes of getting wisdom. Moreover, the oral transmission of animistic knowledge is by and for fellow Giriama and no-one else, while the texts on Islam are open to all who read Swahili and, ideally, Arabic, and, globally all those beyond who want to know more about the religion of the Prophet and wish to convert.

Given the secretive feature of animistic religious knowledge, often glossed by Muslim clerics as 'witchcraft' and 'superstition', it is perhaps not surprising that Muslim clerics denounce it as threatening to Islam itself, which, after all, celebrates the accessibility of the Qur'an and Hadith and other holy books to all peoples. The main reason given for denouncing animism is that it entails the worship, veneration or active appeal to many gods or spirits (*shirk* or *ushirikina*) rather than the one and only God. The animism becomes in effect pantheism. The alleged threat posed by secrecy and the pantheon is, from the Muslim clerics' viewpoint, that rank and file Muslims will continue to fear, venerate and make use of non-human spirits and to believe in human witch power over and against their belief in God and His Word as laid out in the holy texts. And it is indeed true, from our understanding of the logic of witchcraft, that animistic categories often provide a more complete explanation of misfortunes, including death and disease, and the remedies to deal with them, especially among those coastal Swahili Muslims whose forebears converted from animism to Islam only within the last few generations and for whom 'customary' animistic treatments and beliefs are drawn from earlier ideas of well-being.

Again, from the Muslim clerics' viewpoint, this is sometimes regarded as the shadow that accompanies the formal features of Islam. But it is also a kind of buffer zone. On one side are local Swahili Muslim scholars who wish to preserve their version of a local form of Islam which incorporates *maulidi* ceremonies, mortuary rituals, and ancestral and saintly veneration, without actually straying over into worship of many gods. On the other side are Muslim outsiders such as the Wahabi who wish to purify Islam of these *bida'a* practices, seen as the thin edge of the wedge encouraging pantheism. Between them are the traditional, pre-Islamic beliefs and practices concerning spirits, the ancestors, and the reciprocal relationship between humans and animals and plants, which constitute a buffer zone in the sense that local people may see some explanatory and therapeutic benefit in these entities, while non-locals see them as irrelevant and ungodly, and forbid them.

The Giriama and other coastal non-Muslims are, then, part of the Swahili Muslim constitution historically and in terms of their respective evolution as religiously defined entities. That is to say, in these intense mutually involving situations, non-Muslims are constitutive of Muslims. The latter define themselves, not only by reference to abstract textual codes and parables, but also by pointing out the on-going struggle for Islamic purity undergone by any coastal Muslim surrounded by non-Islamic spirit and animistic beliefs.

Far from Islam being learned simply through an unambiguous route of text and teacher, as might be assumed by the intensive and prolonged learned recitation of the Qur'an by children in *madarasa*, it is also learned through the threats posed to it. It is at the moments of epistemological and theological crisis that a contest ensues as to which Islamic values should be pronounced as the most appropriate. No homogeneous Muslim response to crisis can be assumed, for rival clerics, schools, sects and orders may each argue from a particular corner. What is indeed striking about theological discussion in, say, Lamu, Mombasa, or Zanzibar, is the diversity of views proposed on an issue,

for instance on birth control, stem cell research, bridewealth and age
at marriage, on whether Ramadhan everywhere in the world should
begin by sighting the moon from Mount Arafat in Saudi Arabia or
from the various local sightings, and the extent to which so-called 'traditional' customs and beliefs (including what Wahabi call *bi'ida*)
should be included within a local definition of Islam. Diversity of views
is helped by the relative hermeneutic ease by which any text, including
the Qur'an, can be regarded as amenable to endless interpretation, a
task readily undertaken by rival students of the holy books, but one
which, paradoxically, runs up against the equally insistent claim by
any one rival that a proposition emanating from the Qur'an is the true
word of God, and that His truth is absolute and certain and for which,
therefore, there is only one interpretation.

Madarasa and Competition in Zanzibar

Islamic learning is, then, characterized by flux as well as programme,
by the passion of contest as well as through textual inculcation. In
this flux, the unexpected is as much a feature as the diversity of rival
views, and indeed feeds into the latter. I have elsewhere written of a
sermon by a maalim which was interrupted by a bustle and noise
caused by a group of youths fighting with each other at the far end of
the area where the congregation were gathered (Parkin 1985a,
1985b). The maalim, a skilful preacher and player of words, captured
the incident to his own advantage, pointing to it as illustrating how
wayward young men could become if they lacked attention to religion
and allowed themselves to be influenced by non-Islamic practices. The
air of drama was serendipitously brought effectively into the service of
the maalim's sermon, for which he was commended.

By contrast, the cholera epidemics in Zanzibar Stone Town were
tragic, occurring suddenly and killing many hundreds of people, after
flash floods had caused sewerage to contaminate drinking water
through leaks in pipes and drainage. This was one explanation among
a number which oscillated between blaming government's negligence
or peoples' own carelessness in their use of water and 'dirty' food. But
the accident of cholera deaths was also clear evidence from the pulpits'
viewpoint of Muslims' own lack of piety, which needed to be remedied
by increased prayer and attendance at mosque and better Islamic
behaviour, a plea to which many people responded. The problem of
contaminated drinking water was linked to that of stagnant pools
attracting mosquitoes and hence malaria, and the two were further
expanded into a new western-influenced discourse on 'environmental
pollution' alongside the existing Muslim concern with moral pollution.

Let me here show how even the curriculum of a school may be shaped by unplanned events. There is in Zanzibar, as throughout the Swahili coastland, a wish to include secular subjects within traditional ones, provided they are underwritten by Islamic principles. Islam, it is said, is after all a way of life, both more than a religion and more than a prescription for behaviour, being rather a comprehensive act and vision of the beginning and end of humanity, a sentiment that echoes those who pronounce themselves Muslims first and last and therefore unable to put the state before their religion.

But the secular educational drive has introduced variation and competition between the *madarasa*, with some parents wishing their children to be versed mainly in Islamic precepts and secondarily in other subjects, and others preferring a concentration on these other subjects and content to have them embedded in a pervasive Islamic ethos rather than as emanating from a focus on holy texts. The difference may be slight or considerable, depending on the choices made by the school's management, which themselves may change.

The effects of the Zanzibar revolution of 1964 on the provision of Islamic education were considerable (see Loimeier forthcoming). Before the revolution, a Hadhrami-derived network of scholars called Alawi (see Bang 2003) controlled Qur'anic schools, while key scholars, often drawn from the Omani-derived Al-Farsy lineage, worked closely with the colonial government in setting up such schools with curricula that combined secular with Islamic subjects. For a period, dating from 1964 to about 1972, the hard-line anti-religious and anti-Arab revolutionary leader, Abeid Karume much reduced or eliminated Qur'anic schools. His assassination in 1972 ushered in a more tolerant religious attitude. Radical Islamic reform groups of the Salafi and Wahabi kind, made up of individuals often educated in universities in Saudi Arabia, Sudan and Egypt, came to dominate the provision of Islamic education.

However, as the years have passed, Sufi ideas, particularly those of the dominant Qaddiriyya and the much smaller Shadililyya and other brotherhoods linked to them, have become stronger in Zanzibar, by insisting on carrying out the *bida'a* of *maulidi, dhikr* processions, elaborate funerals, saint veneration, and lavish celebrations of the ending of Ramadhan and return of pilgrims, and by including the teaching of these practices in schools they have set up. There is indeed a struggle currently waged between the reformist groups' schools and those linked to Sufi groups. While the former receive at least informal support from members of the ruling government political party, the CCM, the Sufi groups are seen as part of the mainly Omani-derived or Omani-linked opposition, which includes some Muslims of South Asian origin, and which is affiliated to the new political party, CUF.

This describes the opposition in terms which are more clear-cut than is the case in reality, for many Wahabi and Salafi also support the CUF, but gives the general picture.

Out of this struggle the Sufi-based schools have had to devise new ways of meeting the unexpected challenges posed by the other schools and groups opposed to them, whose clout has been reinforced by the recent increase in the number of immigrants from the mainland to Zanzibar, who are not normally Sufi, nor even Muslim.

Founding a School and Working a Creed

I studied one such Sufi-based school intermittently over a few years in Zanzibar Stone Town and present it as an illustration, both of the way the curriculum is affected and of the fluctuating emphasis on Islam as a taught element within a wider curriculum. What I want to show in due course is how, despite the attempt to formalize the teaching of Islam, this and other schools are faced with having to respond to and accommodate unexpected events of the kind described above. I argue moreover that, far from crippling the pedagogic process, such accidental occurrences provoke new ideas at least among the adult teachers, some of which become religious convictions. This process is of the same kind as faced by the individual adult Muslim believer-sceptic who, in his or her dilemmas, learns both to accommodate new facts and ideas to their understanding of Islam and also, in some cases (though by no means all), makes these the basis of new assertions about the world. Learning religion is thus two-dimensional in that it is premised on staged targets to be completed one after the other and yet has to reach religious understanding in ways not covered by such formal stages.

The school has in fact been set up by a member of the Omani Al-Farsy lineage, who is a young cousin of the famous, now deceased, Sheikh Abdallah Saleh Al-Farsy, himself once Chief Kadi of Zanzibar and later of Kenya, colonial education officer and inspector of religious instruction for Zanzibar government schools, translator of the Qur'an into Swahili, and a scholar renowned for his extensive writings, lectures and sermons. The school's founder is in his mid-thirties and known locally as an *ustadh*, a scholar and teacher at an early stage and sometimes spoken of as someone who may in due course earn the title of sheikh. He set the school up in the tradition of the Shadiliyya order, as he put it, a matter of some significance as we shall see when we come to discuss other aspects of his own career development. All his pupils are from Shadiliyya families. The school takes in a dozen or so nursery and primary children on a part-time basis, some of whose

work is to learn to recite the Qur'an, and some 15 secondary level children who study full time at Form I and II levels. The children have
already, in the preliminary school known as *chuo*, undergone some or
all of the training required for a recitational knowledge in Arabic of
the Qur'an.

Teaching is from Monday to Thursday and Saturday, Friday being
omitted as the holy day of prayer. The nursery children study from
8.30am to 11am, and the primary from 2.30pm to 4.30pm. The full-
time Form I and II teenagers study morning and afternoon. When the
school was first set up in 2000, most of the teaching was built around
18 central, religious, topics, ranging from the Qur'an itself to the
hadithi, many forms of prayer and meditative exercises, law and the
rules of Qur'anic interpretation. In setting up his school, the *ustadh*
attracted parents who wished their children to have a mainly Islamic
Shadiliyya education, with secular instruction built around this. In
fact, the founder had previously had a school with more pupils which,
though regarded as successful, had in effect been taken over by a rival
group, headed by a mainland immigrant, which had access to the
building which the school had leased and so disbanded it in the form
created by the *ustadh*. The rival group significantly reduced the role of
Islam in its education provision. Some Shadiliyya parents withdrew
their children but others continued to send them, given the absence of
an acceptable alternative and out of a wish to have their children educated in a Shadiliyya institution.

In January and February 2003, however, the *ustadh* also reduced
the more explicit religious themes and increased the teaching of English, French, Maths, Accounts, Civics, General Science, Commerce,
History, Geography and Swahili, all subjects that are taken in public
exams, alongside Religion, which is other than just Islam. Some 40
minutes continued to be given over first thing in the morning to three
sessions of Sufiist prayer, devotional chanting and meditation, known
as *wadhifa, salatu, saaltuka*, and *faatha*. The founder insisted that he
had in this way retained a judicious mix of religious and secular teaching (*masomo ya dini na masomo ya dunia*). At the same time as altering
the curriculum in favour of secular subjects, the founder became affiliated to the Naqshabandiya Sufi order, claiming it to be a 'branch' of
Shadiliyya and therefore not inconsistent with his original inspiration
nor something which should deter Shadiliyya parents from sending
their children to his school. He had made contact with Naqshabandiya
proselytizers and was in due course sent a robe (*juba*) from a highly
placed sheikh in Turkey, which denoted membership of this order. The
order in fact probably came into being in the fourteen and fifteen centuries, and its links with Shadiliyya are essentially historical rather
than current. It was claimed, moreover, that the order (perhaps

numbering 50 million worldwide) is mildly more sympathetic to some
of the Wahabi objections to 'ecstatic' conduct than either Shadiliyya
and Qadiriyya. But, despite this public face of Naqshabandiya, the
school retained many features of Sufism, including the singing and
chanting of prayers (in the style of *maulidi*) much enjoyed in the morning by the pupils but much criticized by Wahabi. Of course, even
within a single order, there will be variations of belief and practice
and, as with other aspects of religion, we are dealing here with a question of claims being made locally by small groups of people in Zanzibar
against a knowledge that, however diverse each may be, such orders
are globally widespread, influential and powerful. The school founder,
in receiving his Naqshabandiya robe and a turban and fairly regular
but small financial donations to help his school, was hardly tapping
into this global power in any major way. The significance of his action
has to be seen in the local Zanzibari context of a competition to set up
schools combining Islamic with secular education. The *ustadh* had
refurbished part of a family building in setting up the smaller school in
2000 to replace the larger one he had lost. While continuing to attract
some of the disaffected Shadiliyya parents, he expressed the fear that
they would gradually compromise their Sufi beliefs and come to regard
the heavily secular school as more beneficial to their children. Numbers in the new, smaller school did indeed fluctuate and withdrawals
became common, usually to be replaced as parents became disaffected
with government schools which often lacked teachers. In reducing the
element of religious instruction in his school, in legitimating this by
arguing that Naqshabandiya encourages a greater proportion of
secular teaching, and in claiming the latter as a branch of Shadiliyya,
the *ustadh* redefined his school and made it more able to compete with
the other larger schools of the kind that had displaced him.

The changes do not end here. He then developed an interest in the
plurality of Sufi orders and in social pluralism generally, making these
the theme of many of his talks, lectures and teachings, focusing on
issues that emphasized ecumenical solutions. An example was his very
strong support for the traditional and most practised view that Ramadhan and other religious events should begin by local sightings of the
moon and not that from Mount Arafat, this being in effect part of the
argument that the many different local traditions of Muslim holy
events should prevail over the Wahabi insistence on standardization.
He justified his view by reference to what he called one of the many
'scientific miracles' of the Qur'an, many of whose verses predict
knowledge yet to be realized among humans and explain scientific
principles which have been discovered. He went on to give explicit support for the idea of diversity within Islam, and within its persuasions,
according to the wishes and circumstances of the peoples in their

lands throughout the world. The ideas of pluralism and diversity which he came to enunciate became a conviction, as he put it, that Islam was God's gift to help peoples address problems and dilemmas which were bound to be different throughout the world, given the varied conditions of their social, political and economic lives, and that it was the nature of this gift that should constitute the basis of religious learning and not just debate on abstract universal principles. I do not think it unrelated that he also married a woman who was not only of non-Omani background but was Ismaili of South Asian origin, saying that this was consistent with modern developments. It is true that there has been a general departure from the strict insistence of a generation or two before that Al-Farsy members marry endogamously or, if necessary, at least other high-placed Omani lineages, although this case seems extreme. What is significant is the acknowledgement by Omani generally in Zanzibar that such mixed relations and expectations nowadays exist.

Conclusion

It is too early to say how much a doctrine in favour of the teaching of diversity within Islam will be accepted more widely in the *ustadh*'s locality, if at all. It is, however, one which could indeed be taken up. As a radical view, Islamic diversity could well become propagated as an innovative creed by, say, a charismatic figure, not necessarily the *ustadh* himself, who turns the idea into a conviction. The accident of competing claims over educational provision and local-level political invention produced the conditions under which alternative solutions and views could be born. The shift from idea to conviction then becomes a matter of persuasion, and therefore of religious learning. The skill of charismatic teachers and preachers is to repeat a key message forcefully (e.g. that Islam thrives on its diversity), but in ways that seem varied and so engage attention, via sermon, poetry, exhortation, prayer and conversation, all in different registers. In this way an unusual or uncomfortable underlying idea becomes generally acceptable. The next stage is for the clerics to work it back into an explicit, unambiguous message of single register, divested of its varied presentational forms, but of unquestionable doctrinal significance for speakers and audience alike. This is the religious conviction, the repetitive message par excellence. Here, we are back to questions of dopamine release in the brain arising from ritualized verbal and conceptual repetition and its link to mental representations. Can the idea of accident in mental representation also be mapped neurologically? After all, the very idea of accident presupposes shock or surprise, unanticipated excitement, and *post facto* reaffirms the fear but also fascination of uncertainty. Is there then a cognitive parallel of such development? Whitehouse has offered an explanation of how mainstream religion can spawn, so to speak, minor and sometimes temporary cults, perhaps prompted by a myth-dream in the manner associated with Melanesia (Whitehouse 1995: 193–99 and *passim*). He sees the mainstream as 'doctrinal' religiosity and the splinter cult as 'imagistic'. Is the transformation of an accidentally acquired idea into a religious conviction something of the reverse process: of a semi-articulated image catching religious leaders off-guard becoming in due course an enunciated religious principle?

As I have noted, Islam is in many parts of the world externally defined by the presence of persisting indigenous pre- and anti-Islamic elements, which constitute the boundaries beyond which Islam should not go. It is also internally contested through the divergent views of reformists and local 'traditionalists', the former accusing the latter of *bida'a* practices. In both cases, there is clearly here a believed tension between local, indigenous or vernacular understandings of religious practice and transmission and allegedly global learning (in fact Wahabi and therefore Saudi but presented as of world-wide application). The tension does roughly map onto a distinction between doctrinal Wahabi and Sufi and animistic imagistic practices. I would argue that the diversity of the latter is the fount of creative challenges to the proponents of doctrine, even causing constantly re-discovered interpretations of the Holy Book, as in the examples given above. It is a process by which, paradoxically, the indigenous challenge, far from being suppressed by doctrine, can work its way through repetition and routinization into doctrine. It might even be doctrinally counter-intuitive to begin with (e.g. spirits cannot exist for there is only one God), but, through localized repetition, become an unquestioned religious assumption (e.g. there is only one God but *jinn* and angels also have a place).

Chapter 5

ON CATCHING UP WITH ONESELF
LEARNING TO KNOW THAT ONE MEANS
WHAT ONE DOES

Michael Lambek

What is education? I should suppose that education was the curriculum one had to run through in order to catch up with oneself, and he who will not pass through this curriculum is helped very little by the fact that he was born in the most enlightened age.

Kierkegaard (1968: 57)

Whatever the one generation may learn from the other, that which is genuinely human no generation learns from the foregoing. In this respect every generation begins primitively, has no different task from that of every previous generation, nor does it get further, except in so far as the previous generation shirked its task and deluded itself. The authentically human factor is passion ...

Kierkegaard (1968: 130)

Shamanism is like acting or playing music – received knowledge and training combined with originality, skill, and performance. To know what you are saying and doing, you must learn from others, but to be any good, you must add something of yourself.

Stephen Hugh-Jones (1994: 35)

Nothing is simple in the kingdom of analysis. The first thing the topic of 'learning religion' demands of us is consideration of what we mean by 'learning' and what we mean by 'religion' and how the answer we give to each will shape the answer we give to the other. There are, of course, no absolute or definitive answers to these questions and in this paper I formulate them pragmatically, with respect to the body of ethnographic material I wish to address. This is not to say that I stick to local formulations of 'learning' and 'religion' or that I am advocating an extreme nominalism, but rather that I develop a mode of analysis or interpretation that seems pertinent for grasping a particular set of practices and elaborate a more general point that they seem to illuminate. I argue that to learn religion entails learning to take one's acts seriously and thus to acknowledge one's share of responsibility for their felicitous outcome.

Knowledge, Practice and Wisdom

In an earlier work (Lambek 1993) I observed side by side and in some detail three traditions – Islam, astrology and spirit possession – as they were engaged in by Malagasy-speaking villagers on Mayotte, a French controlled island in the Comoro Archipelago of the Western Indian Ocean. I argued that the respective means by which learning took place in each was related to the ideas within each tradition regarding what constituted knowledge and how widely it should circulate. Drawing upon Schutz's (1964) distinction among experts, well-informed citizens, and 'the man on the street', I showed how in practice people alternated among these different orientations towards knowledge and also how they respectively articulated the three traditions in their own practice. This includes comparing how well or deeply invested in particular bodies of deliberative or procedural knowledge members of a community are; how deeply committed to them; and how adept at drawing upon them. With respect to inquiring how people acquire depth one might shift from the Schutzian categories to the five levels of practical knowledge described by Flyvbjerg (2001: 9ff., borrowed from Dreyfus and Dreyfus) ranging from novice through competent performer to expert.

In studying more specifically the lives of spirit mediums on the island of Mayotte (and subsequently in northwest Madagascar (Lambek 2002a) I have also found it useful to disentangle three levels of engagement, from learning to host a spirit or perform in character as that spirit, to working actively as a spirit medium, and then to becoming a strong or mature member of society in a manner that incorporates having spirits and working as a medium (Lambek 1988). In the abstract, these are successive levels of appropriation, maturity and judgement, but in practice advancing at each level contributes to the next, cultivating an art of living (Nehamas 1998; Lambek 2003). In the end, learning religion could mean becoming wiser, exercising ethical judgement more soundly, balancing deep passion with equanimity, and living a better life.

Performance

In this paper I strive toward the same goals but from a somewhat different angle of analysis, akin to practice but not identical with it, namely performance. Learning to perform means learning to imitate or iterate.[1] I approach this through a discussion in the philosophy of speech acts. Speech acts, and more specifically the category that Austin (1965) termed 'illocutionary', can be taken as a kind of kernel or elementary structure of what I mean by performance, or ritual performance, more generally. They are formally iterated acts that produce a marked difference in a state of affairs or bring a new state of affairs into existence. Performing an introduction or making a promise has this in common with uttering a prayer or carrying out a sacrifice, an act of purification, blessing or worship, with establishing the social identity of an infant or disposing of a corpse, and with committing an act of sorcery or an act of sorcery removal.

However we wish to locate religion, it is possibly useful to consider it as composed of something different from ordinary utterances and everyday acts, whether for practitioners or from the perspective of arm's-length observers like ourselves. But these acts and utterances do not need to be extraordinary either; they may entail nothing more than slight shifts and reframing of ordinary speech and ordinary acts, no more than the difference between not eating a certain food because you don't like it or because it is declared taboo (Lambek 1992). A question then is whether such non-ordinary acts and utterances are parasitic on ordinary ones, 'etiolations of language' in Austin's terms.

Of course, to take such an approach requires us also to look at the mystery and marvellousness of the ordinary and it might even be to conclude with Wittgenstein that what is authentically religious *is* part of the ordinary and that all the *talk* of religion, the metaphysics, as opposed to the *acts* of religion, is rationalization and misleading. But that is an issue I cannot address here.

The iterative performance of the priest, shaman or spirit medium can be usefully compared to that of the stage actor or the musician but it is not the same as either of these (just as performing a character on stage or film is not the same as performing a piece of music). Most obviously, performance on stage is less illocutionary than perlocutionary (rhetorical, persuasive), but religious performances include a perlocutionary dimension as well. Secondly, stage and film acting maintain certain boundaries – victims of gunfire do not really get shot and lovers (with the exception of porn) are not supposed to get sexually aroused, and even then, not emotionally aroused. In certain forms of mysticism quite the opposite is true. In general, one can argue that what we call religious performance is comprised of a variety of genres or kinds of acts that can be distinguished precisely according to whether and how the performance is understood in relation to the performed (the signifier to the signified) and – precisely because this is not simply a matter of an abstracted text, but of an embodied performance – the relationship of the performer to the performance, the actors to their acts. These approximate more or less to what Rappaport refers to as the canonical and indexical aspects of ritual.

Thus, where Austin can give a precise description of what English speakers intend when they say that they 'pretend' to do something, so too, if I were up to the task, ought I to be able to describe what Malagasy speakers intend when they recite passages from the Qur'an (*midzor*), call spirits to enter them and then speak as spirits, or when they fall ill because they have violated a taboo particular to the spirit said to possess them. Malagasy spirit possession works hard to deny certain boundaries which Western stage actors maintain but it is not without boundaries of its own (which are most evident when people enter or leave active states of possession). Both stage actors and spirit mediums must sustain characterizations, must have the skill to carry off their performances successfully, and must, as Hugh-Jones (*supra*) notes, add something of themselves to the performance. Both must also balance what they reveal and what they conceal and must strive, in particular, for specific, and very delicate, balances between irony and sincerity (Lambek 2003; Taussig 2003). However, as noted, while spirit possession is like performing on the stage in many respects, they are not the same kinds of acts.

From this perspective, learning religion includes learning to perform specific genres and acts of iteration (and possibly of unlearning the ordinary or everyday) to which are intrinsic certain kinds of intention. It is a question of framing, of adding sanctifying brackets to certain acts and utterances, of speaking and acting under quotation, in italics, or *sous rature*. Competence in the performance of iteration includes learning how and when to move among these stances, to remove the brackets around iteration or raise them to a higher rather than a lower power from ordinary life. By higher power, I intend underlining the seriousness with which an act is performed, by lower power I think of such forms of iteration as 'pretending.' The deployment of iteration thereby has an ethical dimension and competence in such deployment could be part of what is meant by ethics. This can include learning when and how to perform with irony, to suppress it, or even, as Kierkegaard propounds, to transcend it.

While for Kierkegaard religion is defined by absurdity and faith and is the product of passion, in the philosophical tradition I am describing it is a matter, in the first instance, of the structure, cultivation and performance of possibly non-ordinary, but generally not extraordinary, iterative acts and utterances. Habitual usage may make them come to seem very ordinary indeed.

Seriousness

At the heart of any theory or practice of iteration there is the question of what I obliquely referred to above as the iteration taken to a certain power: of the relation of the performance to the intention of the performer. As Laurence Herault (this volume) notes for contemporary catechists in Switzerland, 'the faithful do not mimic what Jesus did, they re-enact it'. But how does one make, recognize, or learn the difference? In Christian thought and in Western philosophy this is often phrased as the question of sincerity. As Stanley Cavell, on whose discussion of iteration I have been drawing, puts it, that human utterances and acts can be imitated 'betokens, roughly that [they] are essentially vulnerable to insincerity (you may say false consciousness)' (1995: 58). Augustine's anxiety as to the difference between a sincere and a theatrical confession haunts this tradition, yet I think this is but one cultural refraction – others might be stage fright (Geertz 1973) or grace (Bateson 1972) – of a widespread feature of the human condition, a vulnerability to the ruptures inherent in (self-)consciousness, not an exclusively Christian problem. Indeed, what is phrased as the problem of insincerity with respect to action is analogous to the problem of scepticism with respect to knowledge. In the absence of a better term I will refer to the general quality of action and the relationship of performers to their acts that is at issue here as one of seriousness.

How do we know when we are being serious? How do we come to acquire the conviction that an act of iteration is not simply one of mimicry but real and consequential on its own terms and how are we able to recognize seriousness in others and in ourselves? One could add: is it possible to be serious (or sincere, or have conviction) without knowing that one is (or does)? Is it necessary to intend or profess seriousness in order to *be* serious or to act seriously?[2] There is also the matter of whether sincerity or conviction are important in local ideology and whether they are made evident through introspection or by means of the outward success of the performance itself. Finally, how can or does religion, when fully 'learned', overcome or quash the anxiety of knowing whether we are serious? How can learning religion address learning to know that we do indeed mean what we say and intend what we do?

I will follow certain of Cavell's reflections on what he rightly calls these 'immeasurably complex' issues (1995: 55) concerning the seriousness and sincerity of acts and utterances. Austin asks whether a performative utterance like a promise must be spoken 'seriously' in order to be taken 'seriously' and whether

> their being serious consists in their being uttered as (merely) the outward and visible sign, for convenience or other record or for information, of an inward and spiritual act; from which it is but a short step to go on to believe or to assume [without realizing] that for many purposes the outward utterance is a description, *true or false*, of the occurrence of the inward performance. The classic expression of this idea is to be found in the *Hippolytus* ([Euripides] 612), where Hippolytus says ... 'My tongue swore to, but my heart (or mind or other back-stage artiste) did not.' Thus 'I promise to ...' obliges me – puts on my record my spiritual assumption of a spiritual shackle (Cavell ibid., quoting Austin 1965: 9–10).[3]

Austin suggests that distinguishing an inner from an outer voice provides people with illegitimate excuses and he continues to argue himself that, 'Accuracy and morality alike are on the side of the plain saying that *our word is our bond*' (Cavell 1995: 56, quoting Austin 1965: 10). For Austin, the performative utterance is what counts; inner doubt is a mere infelicity in an otherwise successful performance.

In other words, I would say, (outer) seriousness is not to be confused with, seen as a mere expression of, reduced to, dependent on, or viewed as lesser than (inner) sincerity.

A question is whether such a promise is an 'ordinary' use of language or some kind of iteration, a non-ordinary usage, in non-ordinary circumstances. Cavell writes (in parenthesis):[4]

> (When Hippolytus says, 'My tongue swore to, but my heart did not' is he an actor on a stage? Does he think he is, that is, take himself to be on some inner stage? Does Austin imagine one or other of these possibilities to be in effect? Does Austin think we, or anyone at any time, may not be able to tell these differences? Or not tell them in the case of Hippolytus because we cannot tell them in ourselves? Is there something in the figure of Hippolytus that would confuse Austin about all this? (His slam at the 'back-stage artiste' suggests that there is.) I am trying not to let such questions take over.) (ibid. 56–7)

Rappaport – who cites the same passage from Austin (Rappaport 1999: 121), but does not cite Cavell – is beset by a somewhat analogous problem, namely the possibility that human language offers us for deceit and alternative, and he accepts Austin's analysis as a means toward a solution for unambiguous communication. Rappaport (1999) demonstrates (by means of a lengthy argument that unfortunately I reduce here to mere assertion) how ritual addresses the problem by affirming the social relevance and priority of the exteriority of the tongue's 'doing' over the interiority of the heart's 'saying.' Ritual makes certain acts and utterances definitive and renders internal feeling irrelevant to their effects. In other words, ritual effects the production of a specific class or genre of performative acts in which seriousness is established from the outset. It doesn't matter what performers think to themselves, the act of participating in a ritual commits them to accepting both the public message and the meta-performative means by which such communicative acts are enabled and specific messages are established. (An easy illustration is the person who gets married while being uncertain of the wisdom of the act or cynical about the authority of the ceremony.)

Rappaport, like Geertz before him (1973), thus draws upon the philosophical critique of private language. It is as though the public advocation of seriousness, established through ritual, trumps any private concerns with sincerity. For Geertz this enables the anthropologist to interpret culture without recourse either to inaccessible layers of subjectivity or dubious theories of mind. For Rappaport it is important because ritual insulates social order from the vagaries of human ambivalence and passion.

Rappaport's argument builds upon Austin's and also strengthens it by emphasizing the way ritual reinforces the performative effects of otherwise ordinary utterances. But Cavell would not be entirely convinced. He continues to 'wriggle' over the issue, in large measure because he worries that dismissing ostensibly non-serious forms of language as merely parasitic on ordinary language is politically dangerous (insofar as it targets the arts, parody, etc., and 'takes non-seriousness to be a declaration of self-exclusion') (58) and because (if I have understood him correctly) taking the transparency of ordinary language at face value obviates a position of personal responsibility and philosophical scepticism. Cavell continues to ask, '*Must* we mean what we say?' (1976, my emphasis).[5]

Conviction

I accept Austin's point that seriousness is not a matter of an outer performance corresponding to a prior inner intention and that the outer performance is therefore not to be judged as true or false with respect to some hypothetical inner one. Arguments concerning public versus private language are enormously helpful. Austin (and other philosophers of language) demonstrate the consequences of public utterances and Rappaport adds the way that ritual both reinforces or enhances illocutionary force and commits performers to accept the liturgical orders in which they are participating. But they omit a good deal when it comes to learning religion; that is to say, they omit a good deal if learning religion is to mean more than acquiring deliberative and procedural knowledge and if we recognize that participation in ritual acts can have a significance for participants or raise concerns that exceed (or otherwise depart from) their public acceptance of the liturgical order of which their own acts are a part. One does not need to posit an independent 'inner artiste' in order to ask what the acquisition of religious knowledge or competence comes to mean for those acquiring it; what the performing of specific acts comes to mean to the specific individuals who carry them out; and what kinds of performance anxieties attend to specific liturgical regimes. It remains valid to consider the passion with which certain religious adepts pursue their goals or accede eagerly, happily or with equanimity, to the challenges religion places before them, or conversely, when they worry whether they have things right, are as virtuous, powerful, or effective as they are supposed to be, and so forth. In sum, a central problem in learning religion – and not just Protestantism, though it may be found most acutely there, in the form of sincerity – is acquiring conviction. Kierkegaard summarizes the problem succinctly when he writes of learning 'to catch up with oneself'.

Even when one has learned to smoothly inhabit a way of life and a set of practices that comprise it, these practices and this way of life will continue to throw up challenges — and indeed must do so (within reason) if they are to retain our interest. Intrinsic to the idea of a challenge is discovering whether we have been up to it. Learning then entails both meeting specific challenges and recognizing that they are meetable, that in general we are up to meeting the challenges that this way of life, this set of practices, throws our way. In the case of ritual this includes learning that the certainty of acceptance entailed in performance does trump the vagaries of belief and scepticism.

Seriousness entails a commitment to ensuring that the performative acts in which one participates are carried out felicitously; conviction (here) can be understood as the knowledge that they can be. These can only be realized after the fact.

What can go wrong in the performance of ritual? Austin elaborates a typology of infelicities. In his inimitable language, or rather, in his inimitable capacity to draw upon and to finely discriminate among the resources of ordinary language, Austin distinguishes two broad kinds of infelicities. There are *misfires*, which are acts purported but void, and *abuses*, acts professed but hollow. *Insincerities* are a category of abuses in which the thoughts, feelings, and intentions for subsequent conduct are inappropriate. They are what exercised Austin about Hippolytus and have exercised many since. Austin points out that it won't do to call upon insincerity to rescue oneself from a poorly judged act, as though to say 'but I didn't mean it' could serve as a valid excuse; nevertheless, the recognition of one's own insincerity can cause considerable anguish.

In the arguments propounded by Austin and Rappaport insincerities are not sufficient to produce misfires, that is, to void the act itself. But in the case of spirit possession I am about to discuss, the problem of knowing or trusting one's own intentions – of knowing whether one is serious, or how serious one is – is relevant precisely because of such a threat to the outcome. That is to say, the uncertainty of knowing what one wants or what one is capable of is salient not as a form of insincerity but because it risks the disallowance or vitiation of the act itself. The performance anxiety here is that if one doesn't 'really' have a spirit or the right spirit, the possession ritual will be a misfire, either a *misapplication*, in which (following Austin's definitions) the persons and circumstances are inappropriate for the act, or worse, a *misexecution*, characterized by the flaw that the procedures cannot be executed by the participants correctly.

While this is not a matter of insincerity, it shares with insincerity a tension between knowing the correct convention and doubting one's ability to carry it through. That is to say, it suggests a want of conviction and a threat to the seriousness of the act and occasion.

Acquiring Conviction

The problem of sincerity faced by speech act theorists is somewhat artificial so long as it is phrased in terms of the analysis of single utterances. This has been a weakness of the philosophy of language. Indeed, there is a certain irony in that while speech act theory turns the study of language from semantics to pragmatics, it has tended to do so abstractly, by means of artificial examples analogous to the way Chomsky illustrates transformations in sentence structure or, in Cavell's case, by means of quotations from written texts. Even when speech act theory draws upon conversational analysis (or rather, when conversational analysts draw upon speech acts), the study is likely to remain closely bound to specific instances and narrow, immediate contexts, as manifest in the transcriptions. Yet seriousness (conviction, confidence, sincerity) is not something that one 'has' or starts with, or that is self-evident in any individual segment of discourse (that is, not a property of any backstage artiste) but something that one learns – or grows into. Anthropologists know this: Rappaport sees it as a consequence of participation in ritual; Geertz (1973) writes of the acquisition of specific moods and motivations; and Asad (1993) emphasizes the role of disciplinary power in inculcating specific dispositions. Further, if learning is something that, as Kierkegaard argues, one must do for oneself, it occurs in the context of supportive (and coercive) relations with others and it may in fact entail internalizing or introjecting others. Conviction, is not unconnected to what one could call a growth in confidence or self-confidence in the language of western psychology (or ethnopsychology); faith in the language of Christian theology; or disposition in the language of Aristotle or Bourdieu.

Conviction, then, does not take place instantaneously, nor is it evident in (or 'behind') a given utterance; it is not the matter of a single speech act. Nor is conviction a direct object or objective of learning (but rather an indirect object of deutero-learning, Rappaport 1999: 304-5). It is less an active endeavour than a kind of passion; one becomes surprised or overtaken by one's own conviction. It is thus analogous to what Aristotelians describe as the cultivation of character; indeed, in proper measure, perhaps it can be seen as a virtue. If conviction is not necessary to produce a given speech act, it may be necessary for the happy (I do not say 'felicitous') living of an ethical or religious life. It can inform speech acts but it is also informed by them. It builds gradually. Nor is it a prior or private matter, the fancy of some 'inner artiste', but the product of public ritual and of interpersonal relations, albeit relationships that take place both in the outer, social world, and inwardly by means of identification, introjection and individuation and introjection, (cf. Harding 1987 for a striking illustration). In a slogan, conviction is confiction, the product or meta-product of a project of world-making engaged in with others.

Of course, conviction is rarely unassailable. What we are after might be qualified as 'working conviction'. Learning religion entails acquiring conviction in the course of acknowledging scepticism.

These points are well argued and illustrated in Lévi-Strauss's famous essay on the Kwakiutl shaman (1963) who first practises what he considers to be pretence and in the course of doing so and observing the effects of his actions and the response of others comes to understand them as truthful and his work as serious. We could go on to say that thenceforward his acts are performed with conviction, that the irony entailed in understanding his deception gets reframed or transcended. In learning the techniques of the shaman and in performing *as if* one were a shaman – thus insincerely or without conviction, one eventually surprises oneself by *becoming* a shaman, by realizing oneself as one, by discovering that one *is* a shaman.[6] Shamanistic performance becomes serious. Taussig's acute recent reinterpretation (2003; cf. Whitehead 2000) makes the point that the dialectic between conviction and scepticism, between the word or symbol and the body, or between revealing hidden mysteries and exposing the trick, remains open rather than closed. The mystification of performativeness remains vulnerable.

Alongside public certainty is performance anxiety. This is a world 'backstage', as it were. But it is not the 'backstage artiste' of Austin's scorn or the ghost in the machine but merely backstage to public ritual – the practical, informal, and sometimes unconscious, sometimes public ways by which religious adepts convince themselves of what they know, of the seriousness of their enterprise and the sincerity and strength of their own engagement. The point here is not to establish or rely upon a distinction between inner and outer, evident though that may be in tragedy, but to describe a space that is neither specifically inner nor outer. Scepticism is no more – or less – private or internal than is conviction.

Spirit Possession

Spirit possession raises squarely the question of the parasitic nature of certain kinds of iterations and the problem of seriousness and conviction. If it provides a good entrée into questions of learning religion, conversely learning offers a productive way to think about possession. When I began studying possession the reigning paradigm was epidemiological and the arguments concerned who got possessed and why. It was a matter either of risk or instrumentality and very mechanical. Changing the register to 'learning' from 'infection' or 'strategy' enables one to think more broadly about the circumstances of possession, the complexities of taking on a character, the growth of insight, the intrinsic irony of possession as a cultural form, and about the value adepts find in engaging in such practices.

Possession has no explicit pedagogy. The ideology in Mayotte states that possession is not deliberate; it cannot be learned and should not be sought out. It is spirits who decide to possess humans, not the reverse, and spirits who then must be educated, and so its eventuality and course are unpredictable. Thus, how people learn possession and their reflections on that process are best grasped retroactively. In fact, its development is intimately tied to biographical features.

The following material is based on discussions I have had with the main protagonist, Mohedja Salim (all names are pseudonyms), during 1975–76 and again in 1980, 1985, and subsequently as she reminisced about her first experiences with spirits. Had space permitted I would not only have presented a much more extended account but also have included the perspective of her husband Tumbu, whose own acquisition of knowledge, spirits and conviction was closely tied to that of Mohedja. Indeed, the two play off and reinforce each other so deeply that presenting only a portion of Mohedja's side offers a partial and overly simplified picture. Sometimes Mohedja and Tumbu gave me identical accounts of events and sometimes they differed; they differed too over time, but each conversation supplemented the others and was consistent with them in its general thrust. While the discussions purport to report on events they also help realize or consolidate what they describe, like memory work more generally, both forming a narrative and assimilating its content to the self of the narrator.

When I first met Tumbu and Mohedja in 1975 they had been married some 25 or more years, a mutually satisfactory union of unusual durability for Mayotte. They lived in the village of Lombeni Kely where they cultivated dry rice and cash crops and where they were each consulted as healers. They were each possessed by several spirits of different types and age. Here I discuss only the onset of Mohedja's senior (elder) *patros* spirit. Patros is a category of spirit said to be indigenous to Mayotte but the names of individual patros are recorded in Arabic books consulted by astrologers. In some mediums the patros spirits become healers. They make use of a variety of medicines and techniques, including local medicinal plants and astrology, and in some mediums they also extract sorcery from the bodies of clients. Patros display themselves publicly at ceremonies known as 'drums' (*azulahy*) at which they congregate, dance and eat strange foods. A feast is held when a patros announces its name and thus legitimates its presence in a new medium (Lambek 1981; cf. Janzen 1992).

Tumbu and Mohedja drew on their patros spirits not only to heal and advise others but also to address their own concerns and those of their immediate family. The spirits spoke with a degree of confidence or certainty not readily or directly available to Mohedja and Tumbu themselves and helped them to make decisions and to act with determination.

Mohedja was raised in the village of Chirongue. Her father died when she was quite young and she had two older male siblings. When she was in her teens she moved with her mother to Lombeni Kely. Tumbu had just returned there after several years working on the island of Anjouan. Although their backgrounds were quite different, a marriage between them was quickly arranged. They married around 1948–49. Within two years, Mohedja gave birth to their first child, Nuriaty.

The Arrival of Mze Bunu

Mohedja said she was only the second person in Lombeni Kely to get a patros. There were already plenty of patros in Chirongue and Mohedja used to go to the ceremonies and watch the dancing. But she was afraid to eat the cakes served there because she had been told that if she did so, she too would get a patros.

Mze Bunu rose shortly after Nuriaty was born. Mohedja recalled that she was very sick for six months after giving birth and that no one could cure her. She was bedridden and so ill that often she did not know the time of day or who was talking to her. They tried all sorts of cures, blessing rituals (*shijabu*) and sacrifices (*swadaka*) but to no avail. People feared for her life, as did Mohedja herself.[7]

Finally, her older (half-)brother Samba arrived from Chirongue. His patros spirit rose and said the stars were against him being the curer, that he was not compatible (*mwafaka*) with her case. At this Mohedja became even more despondent and was sure she was going to die since Samba was already a very successful and well-known healer. But Samba said that he would try anyway lest it be said that he had refused to help his little sister. He made her an amulet and fed her medicine composed of a handwritten Koranic verse dissolved in water (*singa*). Mohedja – actually the spirit that was now manifest – tore off the amulet. But for the first time in six months she was able to get up. However, two days later she was as sick as before.

Samba's spirit then advised them to seek Samba's (classificatory) elder brother, Kasimu Juma (no direct kin relation to Mohedja herself) as the healer (*fundi*). Kasimu's spirit, Mze Bunu, rose and announced that a spirit was bothering Mohedja. Mohedja laughed over this as she told me, since it turned out that it was Mze Bunu himself who was troubling her, though he did not say so at the time.

On his first visit Kasimu extracted a *sairy* and gave her medicine to drink. The *sairy* is the material manifestation of sorcery and its removal (Lambek 1993) but Mohedja is certain there was no sorcery in this case.[8] The *sairy* was simply a product of the arrival of the spirit. 'Big' spirits, especially those intending to manifest themselves as *fundis* (knowledgeable healers) in their hosts, often enter people of their own accord (rather than being sent by sorcerers), making them sick. Patros require the removal of a *sairy* before they will stop making the host sick and rise to her head.

In the distinction between spirits sent by sorcerers and those coming of their own accord, Mohedja is suggesting that the spirit is ego-syntonic, that its arrival is acceptable and even desirable, that the spirit is there for her. It is not clear whether she knew at the time that it would become a *fundi*, but it appears that she and her *fundis* were attempting to transform her illness into something positive. It is interesting that right from the start of her marriage she is tacitly setting the course for a possession career.

Kasimu said he would return and that in the meantime they were to cook a red chicken, setting aside the blood, and also provide a red cloth. Gradually during that week she improved until she was able to get out of bed and even walk about a little – after six months! At the end of the week Kasimu returned with the other leading patros *fundi* from neighbouring Lombeni Be. Together they asked her spirit to rise. A patros rose in her right away and even drank blood that first night. This event was sufficient to constitute the '*ishima*' (courtesy), the first ceremony of a possession cure (normally it is a large public event but this was not generally a part of Kasimu's practice). Kasimu asked the spirit what it wanted for the *azulahy be*, the big ceremony (that would serve to fully and publicly establish the spirit's relationship to Mohedja and to cure her) and the spirit requested a red goat. Kasimu gave Mohedja more medicine and she became well and was soon going out to the fields again.

The spirit said that Mohedja should hold the big ceremony. But Tumbu, who did not yet have a spirit himself and was not interested in them, refused. And so, after a year, Mohedja became sick again, though not as gravely as before. Tumbu continued to refuse to sponsor the ceremony. Finally, Mohedja lit some incense and spoke directly to the spirit, saying that if he wanted his ceremony, he was bothering the wrong person since she did not have the means. He had better do something about Tumbu since it was he rather than she herself who was the obstacle. Two days later (in another version, 'That very night ...') Tumbu himself fell very ill. Without informing Mohedja he sought a diviner. The diviner told him that his wife's spirit lay behind his illness; he had broken his promise to the spirit and should hold its ceremony. Immediately he rushed off to seek a large red goat. When Mohedja saw it she asked what it was for; she was truly astonished. Tumbu replied it was for her ceremony, and she knew that her trick had worked. But to this day [Jan. 5, 1976, some 23 years after the event] she has never told him what she did, for fear of having him accuse her of trying to commit sorcery against him.

The two of them went to Kasimu Juma's to schedule the ceremony. By this time Kasimu had married some distance away. When Kasimu's spirit rose Tumbu also asked what medicine he needed to cure himself. The spirit replied that holding the ceremony for Mohedja would be sufficient, nothing else was necessary. Tumbu asked a second time to be very sure he didn't need any medicine of his own. [This remark is characteristic of Mohedja's precision in reporting such matters.] Then they amassed the goods they needed for her ceremony and set aside rice to make cakes.

Before her ceremony, Mohedja went to Lombeni Be to invite people there who had patros spirits. But they laughed at her and said they wouldn't come since she didn't really have a patros. The reason they thought this was that throughout the past year, whenever they had held patros ceremonies in Lombeni Be, Mohedja had never participated as people with spirits are wont to do. She heard the drums from afar but never felt moved to follow them, nor did her patros rise at the sound. Both she and they didn't know that on his first appearance Kasimu Juma had specifically told the spirit that he didn't want him going and dancing at other people's ceremonies.

Mohedja grew discouraged and she thought to herself that maybe people were right and she didn't really have a patros after all. On the day of her ceremony very few people attended. The people in Lombeni Kely came to watch but none of them had patros yet. They urged and urged her patros to rise, singing and clapping, but nothing happened and Mohedja kept thinking that maybe the Lombeni Be people were right. Finally, she heard a guest from another village say the whole thing was a waste of time and there was no patros. They had never heard of a patros that asked for a ceremony and then refused to rise to celebrate it! Mohedja felt very upset and embarrassed. People were getting tired and wanted to go off to sleep.

All this time Kasimu Juma had been in trance and his spirit had been chatting with Tumbu and others. Now the spirit announced that he was leaving and the people said that if the spirit did so, that would be the end of the matter. But the moment Kasimu Juma left trance Mohedja entered it! People danced until, at the appointed hour, the spirit was bathed and re-emerged to announce his name. He was Mze Bunu, the same spirit as that of her *fundi* Kasimu.

Then the others understood why her patros had not risen earlier. He was already up in Kasimu and a spirit cannot be in two places at once. The reason they had not thought of this before was that they were all still quite inexperienced at dealing with patros. Nowadays people can often tell the identity of a spirit from the first time it rises in a new host, although it has often puzzled Mohedja how they do this, since, she says, she herself generally cannot.

Learning to Mean It

I have used this story elsewhere, under other names, in order to illustrate the suspense of an emerging identity and the rule-bound nature of the dramatic process. What is striking for the present discussion is the way in which Mohedja is determining who her spirit will be even while this knowledge is denied to her conscious mind. It is she, with the assistance of Kasimu, who has given direction to her emerging identity, who has, in a sense taken control even while in apparent subjection. Not only has she demonstrated autonomy in selecting the identity of her spirit, but (as I cannot go on to demonstrate here) the particular identity she has selected is also salient her own self-construction. Nevertheless, she has not yet realized her own conviction and is uncertain whether she has a spirit or who it is (i.e., whether she can carry through). The felicitous public performance, including the tense moments of ostensible misfire, confirms her judgement and manifests her competence. What she describes is the course and means of her own conviction, learning to 'mean it', and coming to recognize where she stands.[9]

In recounting these events Mohedja also demonstrates another side of what we might mean by 'learning religion'. That is, not the learning equivalent to enculturation but that comparable to acculturation. Mohedja portrays the entire community as ignorant of the way patros work. She is learning what it means that she is not in trance while her *fundi* is, even if we surmise that subconsciously she already knew this. At the same time, she is taking something of a risk; the ceremony could have failed. But the risk and its upshot only add to her own growing confidence as a medium and *fundi* herself. The events are not only illocutionary in their effects, but perlocutionary. They establish with certainty the identity of the spirit, the intimate connection (tacit collusion) with Kasimu, and Mohedja's competence as a medium. They indicate also (to us) that possession is not a mechanical process nor is it a matter of simply responding to social expectation.

This account of Mohedja's development of conviction is incomplete. For example, in 1985 Mohedja told me that Mze Bunu had started healing people through her before she held his *azulahy* or he had given his name. I have not addressed the profound importance of this spirit for the remainder of her life, the ways in which conviction and seriousness continued to build. What the account begins to illustrate is the fact that to 'learn spirit possession' is not only to learn how to enter and exit trance or to perform competently as specific spirits or with their help, but to take their presence seriously and to practice with conviction. Someone like Mohedja learns to fully accept the reality of spirits, to live with them and, more fully, as herself. Moreover, this reality happens through public performance and is collectively realized. Speaking through Mohedja (18 Oct. 1975), Mze Bunu told me that he does not like to rise in many people and would possess no one else in Lombeni. For the next thirty years this proved to be the case.

Conclusion

In the field we distinguish as 'religion', conviction derives not only from facility *with* iterative performances or the objective vehicles or instruments of larger powers but from agility *as* their vehicle, instrument or subject. Subjects are not prior to or independent of the iterative performances on which they draw and from which they learn to trust their knowledge, inspiration and judgement (while balancing this with reasonable scepticism).

The problem named 'insincerity' with respect to Protestantism, is a locally (ideologically) informed refraction of a property intrinsic to, but also potentially resolved by, iteration. We only 'catch up with ourselves', come to realize that we do indeed mean what we say (or intend what we do) after the fact, in light of felicitous performances. This is surely part of what it means to 'learn religion'.

Acknowledgments

I hereby acknowledge the part of others. A first version of this paper received stringent and appropriate criticism at the international symposium 'Learning Religion: Anthropological Approaches' held at the Institute of Social Sciences, University of Lisbon, 8–10 September 2005. Research has been generously supported by the Social Sciences and Humanities Research Council of Canada.

Notes

1. See also Taussig (1993). I have preferred to avoid the word 'mimesis' because of its Platonic connotations (Lambek 2000b).
2. On self-deception see Lambek (2003). On the multivalence of the verb 'to act,' see Turner (1982).
3. Cavell goes on to show that Austin himself has been unfair to Hippolytus who did not utter this phrase as an excuse and who did not break his word.
4. Cavell is extremely fond of both parenthesis and quotation; of course, the problem of how to interpret their contents is formally similar to the problems of seriousness and iteration that he is addressing.
5. 'Cavell is seeking to draw us into a position where we are denied both the possibility of an epistemological guarantee for our beliefs and the possibility of a sceptical escape from those beliefs. Of course, this is hard for us to bear, but it is here that we must learn to, as Putnam [1992: 177] puts it, "wriggle"' (Critchley 2005: 48).
6. See also my discussion of the way in which the healer of sorcery works his technique upon himself (Lambek 1993: Chapter 9).
7. Post-partum delerium was a part of many women's experience. In one case I observed in 1976 a woman became psychotic shortly after giving birth and died soon after. Mohedja has often been ill upon giving birth, but this is the only birth accompanied by spirits.
8. Mze Bunu was accompanied by another spirit on whom the sorcery was displaced (Lambek 2002b).
9. Mohedja's ostensible ignorance of her spirit's identity, all the while acting in such a manner as to make it a certainty, is only one way a possession cure can play out. Often the host and her healers already know the name, but to mention it before the spirit introduces itself at the correct moment during the ceremony would produce a misexecution.

Chapter 6

HOW DO YOU LEARN TO KNOW
THAT IT IS GOD WHO SPEAKS?

T.M. Luhrmann

For now we see though a place darkly, but then face to face; now I know in part, but then I shall know just as I also am known.

(1 Cor. 13:12)

Nearly a hundred years ago, when Europeans were intoxicated by reports of newly colonized natives who worshipped strange gods with ancient rites, when the new school of English anthropology laid out a ladder of intellectual evolution as orderly as a London timetable, the Parisian philosopher Lucien Lévy-Bruhl spun a philosophical psychology that was so radical, so preposterous in its claims, that few English thinkers took it seriously and the one who did – E.E. Evans-Pritchard – rejected the ideas so thoroughly that he never even mentioned the Parisian's name in the famous book he wrote to refute him. For many scholars, even now, Lévy-Bruhl's name carries the whiff of something unseemly. This is a shame, because our newly sophisticated cultural psychologies are beginning to show us just how much he has to offer.

In his early work, Lévy-Bruhl argued that the distinctive feature of the 'primitive' mind was that such primitives experienced themselves as participating in the external world, and the external world as participating in their minds and bodies. A man might believe that his enemies would have power over him if they simply knew his name; he might believe that his dream was a visitation by a real and external spirit. By the end of his life, Lévy-Bruhl had decided that participation was a religious mode of thought experienced by primitive and modern alike. Those who have grappled with his work, however, have tended to

focus on the question of whether other, not fully developed people –
tribal Africans (in Evans-Pritchard's case) or children (in Piaget's case)
– do indeed think differently from the way that we do. Because of this,
Lévy-Bruhl is rarely read today.

Yet Lévy-Bruhl's work raises extremely interesting questions when
read from the perspective of learning, not of innate or essential difference. His description of participation captures the central experience
of divinity for many American evangelical Christians: that humans
can experience divinity intimately, and that in such intimacy that the
internal mind and an external reality in some way participate in each
other. The paradox is that these evangelical Christians create the experience of participation not because they still linger in the child-like or
pre-modern state Lévy-Bruhl's critics assumed he was describing, but
through deliberately engaging the sophisticated intellectual apparatus
of the highly schooled mind. They *learn* to feel God in their bodies and
in their minds.

The emphasis in anthropological and psychological studies of cultural transmission (as in the work of Pascal Boyer, Harvey Whitehouse
and Justin Barrett) has been upon cognition – on what kinds of cognitive features survive as a concept passes from one generation to
another. These are deep and important questions, but they are not the
whole of religion. The experiential dimension of religion rests upon
the way people learn to use cognitive concepts to interpret their minds
and bodies, and the practices people learn which change bodily experiences in relation to those concepts, to make those concepts real. That
is what they are learning to do when they learn to experience participation. This essay lays out that process and its significance for cultural
psychology.

The Vineyard Christian Fellowship

I joined a Chicago Vineyard church, as an ethnographer, in April
2004, as a continuation of work begun in California on the growing
points of American religion (see Luhrmann 2004). I attend most of
the Sunday morning gatherings, joined a weekly housegroup for a
year, and have participated in many of the courses run by this Vineyard (for example, the Alpha course, designed to convert the curious
and bring the new believer to greater commitment) and by other Vine-
yards (for example, a local Vineyard's course on The Art of Hearing
God). I have formally interviewed over thirty members of the congregation and talked informally with dozens more.

This church is one of what are now called the 'new paradigm' Christian churches (Miller 1997). Such churches pair conservative Chris-

tianity with a casual, youthful social style tolerant of the rock music, dancing and movies labelled as vices by their conservative Christian forebears. (Admittedly, they reshape those activities into Christian forms.) They typically meet in gyms, not churches; they use a rock band, not a choir; their membership is young, and their music, contemporary. They describe themselves as 'Bible based' and 'Jesus centered'. By this they mean that the Bible is the only authority and that the point of one's life on earth is to develop a personal relationship with Jesus. The route to this relationship is thought to run through prayer.

One cannot overestimate the importance of prayer in this kind of church. It is the means to Jesus and to God, the tool with which you build the relationship that will literally (as it is understood) save your life. Prayer is modelled as the central act of your life. The Bible (as people told me repeatedly) says that you should be in prayer constantly, and while no-one at the church feels that they are, they easily say that near continuous prayer is an attainable goal for which one should strive. And the goal of prayer is to develop a direct, personal, and vividly felt relationship with their creator experienced through *dialogue*, through an interaction between two intentional consciousnesses.

The experience of participation arises through prayer, and in particular, through two features of the way prayer is taught and learned. First, people are encouraged to *interpret* God's presence in the everyday flow of their own awareness and to seek in it evidence that they might be hearing a voice spoken by another being. Under the influence of this cultural encouragement, people look for movement in their peripheral vision, and interpret it as the flash of an imp. They shift their attention from the fan to the computer, and wonder whether perhaps they hear a distant angelic choir.

An evangelical book, *Dialogue with God* (Virkler and Virkler 1986), introduced to me as a central text for a Vineyard course on 'the Art of Hearing God', provides a clear illustration of this encouragement (and see also other popular books on the subject: Willard's *Hearing God*, Bickel and Jantz's *Talking with God*, Foster's *Prayer*). The author begins by saying that he used to live in a rationalist box. He yearned to hear God speak to him the way God spoke to people in the Hebrew Bible – and he believed that God still spoke to others the way He did in ancient Canaan. (This is a common belief in evangelical Christianity, albeit a controversial one; more conservative evangelical Christians believe that revelation was complete in the Bible. The sales figures of such manuals as *Experiencing God* – over four million since 1990 – suggest that many, however, are with the Vineyard on this point.) Alas, he was unable to hear God speak to him until he realized that God's voice often sounds like his own stream of consciousness, and that the Christian just needs to know how to pay attention to his own awareness in order to hear God speaking directly and clearly. 'God's voice normally sounds like a flow of spontaneous thoughts, rather than an audible voice. I have since discovered certain characteristics of God's interjected thoughts which help me to recognize them' (1986: 29). That is the point of the book: to help you to identify what, in your experience of your own mind, are God's thoughts. 'You need to learn to distinguish God's interjected thoughts from the cognitive thoughts that are coming from your own mind' (1986: 31). God's voice, the book explains, has an unusual content. You will recognize it as different from your ordinary thoughts. You feel differently when you hear God. 'There is often a sense of excitement, conviction, faith, vibrant life, awe or peace that accompanies receiving God's word' (1986: 30). What the author tells you, in effect, is to learn to experience moments in your own subjectivity as the presence of an external being.

Second, congregants are encouraged to engage in specific practices that lead them *to become absorbed* in their own thoughts. This is a different kind of psychological phenomenon than interpretation, which is the application of cognitive concepts to memory and experience. Practices which create greater absorption lead the subject to attend to internal phenomena and to disattend to external sensory stimulus. All of us go into light absorption states when we settle into a book and let the story carry us away. There are no known physiological markers of an absorption state, but as the absorption grows deeper, the person becomes more difficult to distract, and his sense of time and agency begins to shift. He lives within his imagination more, whether that be simple mindfulness or elaborate fantasy, and he feels that the experience happens to him, that he is a bystander to his own awareness, more himself than ever before, or perhaps absent, but in any case different (Tellegen and Atkinson 1974; Davidson and Davidson 1980; Luhrmann 2005). It seems to be the case that the ability (or interest) in absorption varies between individuals, but for those who are able to experience absorption to some extent, the psychological, anthropological and historical record is clear that a capacity for absorption can be trained (Spiegel and Spiegel 2004 [1978]; Bourguignon 1970; Lambek 1981; Carruthers 1998; Luhrmann 1989). And as the absorption grows deeper, people often experience more imagery and more sensory phenomena, sometimes with near-hallucinatory vividness (Fromm and Katz 1990). The techniques which encourage absorption are the techniques of intense focused prayer that we think of as part of older eras and more exotic spiritualities – Christian mysticism, Zen Buddhism, Siberian shamanism. But they are front and centre in today's American evangelical Christianity.

Dialogue with God makes it clear that quiet concentration – an absorption practice – enhances the likelihood of hearing God. The book's central example of a man who knew what to do to hear God's voice begins by saying that he 'knew how to go to a quiet place and quiet his own thoughts and emotions so that he could sense the spontaneous flow of God within' (1986: 6). The author provides explicit exercises to help his readers do likewise. He sells a 'centering cassette' for that purpose on their website. In fact, he recommends a 'prayer closet', a place where you can go, unplug the phone, and be fully quiet in prayer. He recommends writing in a journal to contain and discard distracting thoughts; he recommends simple song to focus the mind in worship; he recommends breathing techniques to breathe out your sin and breathe in the healing Holy Spirit; he recommends the complete focus of the mind and heart on Jesus. He acknowledges that many of these techniques seem very eastern, but distinguishes them from Zen and other forms of meditation on the grounds that eastern meditation contacts 'the evil one', while he uses the techniques to contact God. The four keys of dialogue with God, he says, are: learning how to recognize God's voice in your everyday thought; learning to go to a quiet place and be still; attending to dreams and visions; and writing down the dialogue so that you remember it and it becomes real for you.

We should pause at this fourth key. Why write it down? Yet Vineyard congregants do. They used written language to capture their prayers, and they did so, I thought, as a means to make their inner prayer process more tangible and not of the self. Most people that I met at the Vineyard seemed to have a 'prayer journal'. They'd write down their prayers, either before or after they prayed them, sometimes praying through the act of writing. They would check back from time to time to see what prayers God had answered. 'I like looking back in my prayer journal and seeing what God has done for me after I've prayed', said one congregant. 'It makes me feel so good'.

Many of the contemporary manuals encourage this kind of written engagement. They think of it as hands-on involvement. It does involve the reader; it also externalizes and concretizes an inner, subjective experience, and blurs the boundary between what is within and without. 'Don't just *read* this book', insists a current best-selling manual, *The Purpose Driven Life* (over twenty three million copies sold). '*Interact with it*. Underline it. Write your own thoughts in the margins. Make it *your* book. Personalize it! The books that have helped me the most are the ones I have reacted to, not just read' (Warren 2002: 10). It is advice many evangelical Christians take about their Bible. In other religious traditions, sacred texts are treated reverentially. The Torah is written on a sacred scroll, kept in a special cabinet, and its removal and reading are the central acts of the Sabbath service. Once, while attending an orthodox service, I dropped the Artscroll printed copy of the Tanakh (the Hebrew name for the Torah, the prophets and the writings, what Christians call – when slightly reorganized – the Old Testament). The woman next to me stooped down to pick it up before I did, and kissed it before she handed it back. But evangelical Bibles are scrawled on, highlighted, underlined, starred, stuffed with notes and post-its, personalized with the possessive aggression of an urban boy spraying graffiti on a wall. *Mine.*

When people pray, when they write down what they experienced in prayer, they are looking for words and images they feel that God might have spoken to them. The Sunday morning gathering begins with what is called 'worship', which lasts for some thirty minutes. The techies dim the lights, the band plays and lyrics are projected on the screen. Unlike older church hymns, you do not sing *about* God but *to* God, simple songs of love and yearning. Many congregants know most of them by heart. They not only sing them on Sunday morning, but they buy CDs and they play them recreationally. On Sunday mornings, as the band plays, people stand at their seats, eyes shut, swaying back and forth, hands clasped or raised in praise, deeply content. (Meanwhile, latecomers are wandering in for coffee and donuts at the back. It is intense and casual, both at the same time.) After a few songs, the band will pause and the leader will pray softly into the silence. 'God, we love you so much. Help us to hear you clearly today, come into our midst ... Holy Spirit, come ... Come ...' And people wait (even the coffee drinkers). They 'wait on God' to see if they experience something (that they can identify as God) in their thoughts, their minds, their bodies.

After the worship, there is a break for coffee, followed by somewhat under an hour of 'teaching', reflections on a biblical passage by the pastor or another congregant. At the end of the service, someone says, 'if you need prayer, please do not leave until you get prayer'. This is the part of the service for which some people have come. Six or so members of the prayer team will be lined up on one side of the gym. While other congregants shrug on their coats and chat, these prayer team members lay hands on those who come over to them, and pray out loud to God on their behalf. During the process they look for what the Vineyard pamphlet, *How to pray for an hour ... and enjoy it* calls 'promptings of the Holy Spirit': crying, peace, warmth, tingling. They also look for specific images that they feel are God's intervention. Mundane psychological experiences – thoughts, images and feelings – are taken to be God's participation in a dialogue with the praying person.

The explicit emphasis on experiencing God in your mind and body – on participation – creates the problem of discernment, a problem with a long tradition within Christianity but with a real theological role only in a Christianity in which God's signs and communications are vivid, real and concrete. The word 'discernment' has a series of specific theological connotations (Lienhard 1980) – in the beginning, the gift of the ability to identify the difference between good and bad spirits. Here I use it simply to describe the congregant's attempt to distinguish between God's communications, and the congregant's own ideas. For the contemporary evangelical, the problem of discrimination is a direct consequence of the intimacy of God's presence, for while God reveals himself in your body and mind, you can be mistaken in the signs of his presence.

When congregants spoke about the problem of determining whether they had accurately discerned God's voice, they often spoke of testing or examining their sense that God had spoken to them. The first 'test' was whether what you had heard or imagined was the kind of thing you would say or imagine anyway: if it was, you had no need to wonder about an external being's presence in your mind. Elaine explained to me how she heard God speak to her in her mind. 'It is kind of like someone was talking to me. That's how real it is. I get responses'. How do you know? I asked. 'God speaks to me', she replied. What do you mean by that? I ask. You can hear him with your ears, outside your head? No, she responded. 'For some people God speaks with a distinct voice, so you'd turn around because you think the person's right there. For me it hasn't happened like that. Well, I mean kinda, there has been kind of that sense, but not like you'd turn your head because someone was there'. Can you say more about those God experiences? I prompted. She explained that she did not hear the voice like it really was another voice, but it was more than a passing thought. It was clearly, she felt, not her thought. She went on to give an example. 'When people were praying over me and I'm just receiving it [meaning the prayer] and all of a sudden I hear, 'go to Kansas'. Because I was debating whether to go to Kansas, but I hadn't been thinking about it within a 24 hour period'. That's what made it distinctive to her: she wasn't thinking about it, it wasn't something she would have thought about right then. 'It makes you want to say', she continued, 'where did that come from?'

The second test was whether it was the kind of thing that God would say or imply. This was often articulated as making sure that what you thought God had said did not contradict God's word in the Bible. This caution was explicitly expressed in all the written material and nearly every casual conversation on the topic. *Dialogue with God*, for instance, states clearly (and repeatedly) that 'if the revelation violates either the letter of the Word or the spirit of the Word, it is to be rejected immediately' (1986: 8). God is a loving God; a revelation that tells you to hurt yourself or someone else, people said, came from the Enemy, not from God. 'You need discernment', the pastor said. 'There's a letter written from Paul when he says, don't put out the fires of the spirit but test everything and hold on to what is good. We don't expect that God would want someone to cut themselves, or tell them to jump off a bridge. That is not God'.

The third test was whether the revelation could be confirmed through circumstances or through other people's prayers. With this test, prayer moved into the social realm. People would check with each other to see whether they have 'gotten' similar images. They asked people to pray for them, and sometimes followed up to see what those prayers had revealed. It was a common conference exercise to pray for someone and then go around the group to see what common images had emerged and what meaning they had for the subject of the prayers. At one conference, the leader instructed us to write down the images we felt we had received in silent prayer over someone so that other people's remarks would not 'contaminate' what we said. As we went around the room after the prayer, many of us mentioned yellow or orange items: foxgloves, a cartoon character, a yellow canoe, a Chevy Convertible. The subject beamed, and said that it was so cool to know that God knew her favourite color.

The final test was the feeling of peace. Prayer, and God's voice, are thought to give you peace and comfort. If what you heard (or saw) did not, it did not come from God. Stanley and Trish struggled when Trish, a medical student, was assigned for residency to a city that had not been her first choice. (There were many medical students in the church and, as was often the case, the residency match took many of them to their third, fourth and even fifth choices.) For Stanley and Trish, this meant separation for at least a year, and while their daughter was still a toddler. They were not sure what to do, and whether God intended Trish to abandon medicine altogether. They prayed and prayed. The pastor held a prayer meeting at their house so that people could pray over them. Their housegroup prayed over them. People prayed with them in church. Eventually, in part because of what they thought, felt and experienced in prayer, they decided to accept Trish's assignment. And as they did so, they began to feel 'peace': a sense of settled acceptance which they took as a sign that they had correctly interpreted God's words to them.

Discernment thus is clearly a *social* process, in that there are socially taught rules through which God is identified. Those social rules interact with the psychological consequences of practising absorption states. Those who experience heightened absorption and its associated consequences – greater imagery, greater imaginative engagement and increased internal or external sensory phenomena (Luhrmann 2005) – learn to interpret those phenomena as signs of God's intentional presence in their lives.

Nora's story represents well the way one learns how to pray, and how one's everyday experience changes with the psychological development of absorption practice and the social acquisition of the rules of engagement. Now in her early 50s, Nora became one of the most active and most powerful prayer warriors in the Vineyard church. People say that she has a 'gift' for prayer. Yet all this is relatively new to her. She spent her youth in a nondescript Protestant church and converted to Catholicism when she met her husband in her 20s. Then she believed in God in an abstract, distant way. It wasn't until she was in her mid- 40s that she began to want something more. She began getting up very early in the morning to read the Bible, trying to understand the text, and to feel it come alive to her. She spent hours in attentive, meditative reading.

Nora found the Vineyard through an ad in the paper. She'd wanted a diverse church, with contemporary music. When she showed up that first Sunday, and found herself standing along with the others for worship, tears rolled down her cheeks. It was so amazing, she remembers, to sing your love directly to God, not to sing about Him abstractly but to pray in song so concretely to his presence. She said that she didn't even know how to pray at first. She didn't feel connected to God. She began to watch other congregants, to listen as they talked about having a relationship with God and about trusting God, and she felt that they had a kind of peace and joy that seemed palpable, and that she yearned for.

It was the practice of intercessory prayer – learning to pray for other people when they are not present – that gave her the connection to God that she wanted, a sense that she had this real relationship with him. 'It wasn't until I started participating in the intercession ministry that I really felt like it broke through'. What 'broke through' was the experience of having thoughts and images arise in her mind, while she was praying for someone else, and learning to feel confident that these thoughts and images came directly from God.

When I first started having them – this is a story of how I think the Holy Spirit works. It was the first year that I was with the church and the first year I was really interceding for the church. The Vineyard Association was having their national meeting out in California and they asked for intercessors to be praying regularly for that. I took it very seriously, and I prayed [for hours] every morning. And one morning I was just sitting in my prayer chair, I had just finished and I was thinking about a picture. I thought that my mind was wandering. I kept on seeing these boats. And I was thinking about that, and the phone rang, and it was the pastor. He was out in California, and he was calling about something completely different – and it was really odd for him to be calling, it was a small thing. And after we got through with that I just waited, and then I felt moved to say, 'why did you call me?' And he said, 'I don't know. I just felt like I was supposed to call you'. And it clicked then, that the picture I had seen wasn't a distraction from my prayers, but connected to my prayers. I told him about this picture that I'd gotten. And he told me when he came back that several people had gotten the same picture, and that it was about Jesus with his hands on the wheel of a ship! It sounds like lunacy, you know. And yet that's how it works.

She recognized, in other words, that the thoughts she had while praying were really communications from God, and that those thoughts gave her knowledge about the people for whom she prayed.

When I first moved up on the 12th floor, I used to watch out my window. There was this school right there, and there was a really busy intersection. And I used to do what I called 'think' about the people that were driving through the intersection. I would just get like ideas, like they have a medical problem that they're gonna be dealing with today, or there's this on their mind, or I'd watch interactions with kids on the playground under my window and just sort of get ideas about it. I think those were prayers being born, you know, without me really knowing what it was.

She herself implies that this learning process involves both learning to reinterpret her own subjective experience, and learning to alter that subjectivity. On the one hand, she describes her earlier, pre-trained thoughts as containing nascent prayers. On the other hand, she clearly recognizes that her subjective experience has changed. '[Over time, as I have continued to pray,] my images continue to get more complex and more distinct. ... Depending on the prayers and depending on what's going on, the images that I see [in prayer] are very real and lucid. Different than just daydreaming. I mean it's, sometimes it's almost like a PowerPoint presentation'.

Through this process, her relationship with God has become more real. God became a buddy, a confidante, a friend. She had more unusual experiences than she had done before, and she experienced them as concrete evidence of God's interaction with her. For example, she experienced God as speaking to her (occasionally) outside her head, although she had never heard voices before.

It was pretty early on in my relationship with him. I was just all full of myself one morning. I just had wonderful devotions and worships and just felt so close. I went out, and it was the most god-awful day. It was icy rain and gray and cold and it was sleeting. I'm just full of the joy of the Lord, and I say, 'God, I praise you that it isn't snowing, and that nothing's accumulating, and that the streets aren't icy' – and then I went around the corner, and I hit a patch of ice, and just about went down. It was so funny to me. I just burst out laughing out loud. It was just so funny that he would put me in my place in such a slapstick personal kind of way. But then he just graced me the rest of the morning. The bus showed up right away, which it never does. I was reading, and I missed my stop to get off, and *I heard God say*, 'Get off the bus'. I looked up and hollered, and the bus actually stopped, half a block on, to let me get off. I just felt that intimacy all morning. Like when you go from holding a new boyfriend's hand to kissing him goodnight.

What an observer sees clearly in Nora's story is a learning process in which inner psychological phenomena – moments which earlier she would have regarded as her own, wandering mind – are identified as the voice of an external presence. An observer can see that Nora is engaging in intense absorption practices which probably enhance her ability to attend to inner phenomena and probably enhance the likelihood of experiencing unusual psychological phenomena, such as hearing the voice of God. Finally, an observer can see that Nora has learned to experience these moments not as random, curious phenomena, but as the communications of an intentional, person-like entity. That is exactly what Lévy-Bruhl meant by participation: that one experiences one's mind as participated in by another awareness, and as affecting that other awareness, that the outer world is full of intentional, interactive consciousness, a 'mystic influence which is communicated, under conditions themselves of mystic nature, from one being or object to another' (1979 [1926]: 77).

Nora is unusually responsive to absorption practice. That is, compared to most other congregants, she reported more unusual experiences and more intense imagery. She also prayed far more than most: she often prayed more than two hours each day. But while her experience is more dramatic, it is by no means completely atypical. The social rules of learning to experience God are easily elicited from people, as is the report that prayer practice may lead to greater absorption, increased imagery and more unusual experience. Not everyone will have those experiences, but the expectation that practice is important and produces changes is widely shared. As one young woman said:

> Before I came [to church] I never, like I always saw prayer as talking to God, but I didn't realize that he was also gonna talk to me and I needed to just sit there and just listen. So, that's been like the hugest change ... you know, the more you do something the better you get at it, like, if you play a piano piece and you just play it over and over and over again, and then you finally get it ... like that first word [from God], you're like 'whoa, that was awesome', and then you ask and you keep asking for another one, you know, and then, you know, eventually that comes. And then like you ask again and, yeah.

Another part of the social process of learning to experience God's participation in one's life is the process of learning to believe that God is present even when one's discernment seems to have failed. This is commonly cast as the problem of how to handle God's failure to answer your prayers. At the Vineyard, congregants not only prayed often, but they prayed for concrete, specific results. 'God doesn't just want to know that you want to pass the MCAT', a medical school student (not Trish) announced to me in housegroup. 'God wants a number, and he wants to be reminded of it *often*'. That woman did well on her MCATS, and she passed her Boards. 'It's all Him', she said to me. 'I'm not very smart. I couldn't have done it on my own'. But when she entered the residency match, she really wanted to work as an obstetrician, and she really wanted to live in Indianapolis, where her brother was – and she ended up in family practice in St. Louis. She left Chicago because she was so upset, and so mad. 'I'm struggling with God', she said to us. 'I don't know what to say. I'm struggling. Actually, I'm *screaming*'.

So what happens when prayer apparently fails? Disconfirmation – the apparent failure of prayer after you are told repeatedly and specifically that God will give to those who ask – is written into a relationship with God in several ways, all of them associated with increasing intimacy with God, and all of them associated with what is called 'spiritual maturity'.

In the summer of 2004 Elaine's roommate moved out of their studio apartment. Elaine couldn't afford the place on her own, but she inferred from her prayers and from her friend's prayers that God wanted her to stay put.

> It's a lot more money than I was paying before. So my human intellect was saying, live with someone. There's scripture about being in community, having a roommate. But there's a sense [an external sense, a sense that arose from her experience in prayer] that I should really be living by myself. A friend of mine was praying, and she saw me in a studio by myself. I'm like, okay. I respect how she sees. She's been sensing God and the Holy Spirit for longer than I have. So I need to take that into account. It doesn't mean that I'm deliberately going to stay there because of that but I need to test that. You test prophecy. You ask God for more confirmation. That [the confirmation] could be God really saying it to me clearly. It could be someone else having a word or something'.

That confirmation seemed to come. '[Another] person had an image for me about being on the second floor, and studying, and being by the window with light shining in. That was kind of – okay, I remember that. I'm just kind of waiting [for that sign]'.

As the months went by, Elaine kept the apartment, but she also failed to land any job that would help her pay the higher rent. She certainly searched for one. I was her prayer partner in housegroup, and week after week we prayed for specific upcoming job interviews, and in response to specific applications that she had made. Now Elaine began to talk about her sense that God wanted her to depend on him. People often used that kind of phrasing when, after they had prayed for financial help, help had not materialized. They would say that God liked to keep you dependent, to need him badly precisely because you did not have what you needed. Elaine later liked to say that this period had given her more intimacy with Jesus because she realized that he really wanted her to depend just on him.

As God comes to be experienced as an interlocutor, as concrete events in body and psyche come to be recognized as his responses, in the moment, to the worshipper's prayer, God emerges as a real person – what psychoanalysts would call an object – in the worshipper's emotional life. As this happens, the problem of disconfirmation is no longer the challenge to an abstract hypothesis, a theory of reality. The problem of unanswered prayer becomes the problem of why your good buddy appears to be letting you down. This move towards intimacy in the face of the apparent material failure of prayer is an explicit focus of the way congregants talk about spiritual development. As one speaker said in the Sunday morning teaching, after describing the apparent failure of her prayers to get a job, '[He is] my comforter, my all in all, you know, Christ is all I need, I don't need a crutch, here in the love of Christ, not man, I stand. And, so I think the question for us is will we let the overwhelming uncontrollable circumstances of life make our faith go deeper, make us go deeper in God?' Certainly that was the context in which Elaine's travails were understood. I spent a morning with Trish talking about Elaine and her ambitions (because she was ambitious: she wanted intense, powerful, intimate experiences with God, and she wanted to be known for having those experiences.) She's so hungry, Trish said. She wants so badly for God to fill some hole in her life, she wanted so badly to have these intense visions or some kind of amazing relationship with God, and she was going to fail. Trish said this matter-of-factly. She thought that Elaine's prayers were not going to be as effective as she wanted and that her relationship with God would not do for her everything that she wanted. The failure will be good for her, Trish said, wisely. It will be a maturing experience. It will make her relationship with God a better one.

Discussion

Lévy-Bruhl argued, in opposition to the English anthropologists – Tylor and Frazer above all – that reports of the apparently irrational ideas of traditional people could not be understood by extrapolating from the individual psychology of an adult white European. Instead, we must admit that the very psychology of traditional people, the logic which governs what they perceive and how they perceive it, is fundamentally different. In his model of human psychology, perception is a *social* process: one perceives through a dense filter of collective representations which are common to a group and transmitted from one generation to another. 'We might almost say that these perceptions are made up of a nucleus surrounded by a layer of varying densities of representations which are social in their origin' (1979 [1926]: 44). As a result, what is perceived differs radically from group to group. 'Primitives perceive nothing in the same way we do. The social milieu which surrounds them differs from ours, and precisely because it is so different, the external world which they perceive differs from that which we apprehend' (1979 [1926]: 43).

Lévy-Bruhl called the logic that determines this dense filter in primitive societies 'mystical' and he described it as governed by 'the law of participation' in which objects are 'both themselves and other than themselves' (1979 [1926]: 76). Such thought is 'prelogical' in the sense that avoiding contradiction is not its main aim. Here an image, a name, or a shadow may participate in what it represents. That is the primary difference between traditional thought and our own: we aim above all to define reality as independent of subjective representation or response. 'Our perception is directed toward the apprehension of an objective reality, and this reality alone' (1979 [1926]: 59). Lévy-Bruhl grew more subtle in his later work (the *Notebooks*) but in his early work, the contrast is blunt. They experience participation. We (rational Frenchmen) do not.

His ideas were almost immediately rejected, first treated as a bad description (by Evans-Pritchard) and then adopted as an accurate description of childhood thought (by Piaget). In fact he was ahead of his time, although his sharp distinction between primitive and modern was not. He had proposed what we would now call a 'cultural psychology', in which the social world shapes perception itself. It was a deeply Kantian philosophical stance. The noumena – objects in themselves – are never apprehended as they are. They become phenomena, perceived through the categories of understanding held by the observer. What made Lévy-Bruhl's theory visionary is that he argued that the categories varied across groups. Durkheim had argued that the Kantian categories were socially formed, but he derived universal categories from specific social experience (in fact, he derived these universal categories from one Arunta ritual). Lévy-Bruhl pointed out that different social experiences should generate different categories for those different social groups, and he set out to describe that difference.

At the end of his life, in the posthumous *Notebooks*, Lévy-Bruhl abandoned the claim that so-called primitive minds were fundamentally different from those of Europeans. He abandoned the term 'prelogical' (1975 [1949]: 99) and began to write of participation as common to all people, different modes of thought rather than different minds. He described 'a mystical mentality which is more marked and more easily observable among 'primitive peoples' than in our own society, but it is present in every human mind' (1975 [1949]: 101). The mystical mode of thought was both affective and conceptual, and had those features which he had attributed to participation all along: independence from ordinary space and time, logical contradictions (an object is both here and there), identity between objects and their arbitrary features (like hair cuttings and the person from whom they came), 'the feeling of a contact, most often unforeseen, with a reality other than the reality given in the surrounding milieu' (1975 [1949]: 108, 102). He thought that the mystical mode intermixed continually with everyday thought in our minds. For him, the puzzle became, 'How does it happen that these "mental habits" make themselves felt in certain circumstances and not in others?' (1975 [1949]: 100).

The problem of 'different mental habits' is the central problem of today's cultural psychology – but participation has vanished from its intellectual stage. The first serious Anglophone work in cultural psychology focused on classic Piagetian conservation puzzles and Lurian syllogistic challenges. Reporting on such work, Michael Cole (Gay and Cole 1967, Cole and Scribner 1974) pointed out that preliterate people do, indeed, perform less well (as the experiments are carried out) than comparison groups of westerners but that those differences largely disappear when they are schooled. This had also been the conclusion of Patricia Greenfield's (1966) work among the Wolof. Yet the differences did not entirely vanish. Many adults did not conserve, despite western schooling, among Australian aborigines (de Lemos 1969), New Guineans (de Lacey 1970), and Zambians (Heron 1971). Social contact with Europeans also seemed to make a significant difference, for reasons not well understood. More perplexedly, while conservation performance seemed to be related to performance on intelligence tests in a western setting, it was not consistently related in a non-western one. Cole concluded from this that these specific tasks told us little about the actual mechanisms of thought. 'There is no way to test Lévy-Bruhl's assertions about primitive mind by referring to the amount of water in two glasses' (Cole and Scribner 1974: 169).

Over the last two decades, this kind of work has increasingly concluded that cognitive skills are domain-specific. Scribner and Cole (1981) summarized their extensive work on print literacy in Liberia by arguing that almost all effects of literacy were not general, but specific to the use of a particular kind of literacy (the use of the Koran; school-learned English; written Vai in the community). Rogoff and Lave (1984) developed Bartlett's concept of 'everyday cognition' for mathematical skills used in specific, everyday tasks like tailoring. Greenfield (2000), Rogoff (1990) and others began to study local apprenticeship, learning from the subject's perspective. Lave and Wenger (1991) described the local, specific, social nature of many learning tasks as 'situated learning'. The work emphasized that such learning was particular to its setting. As Greenfield put it, learning 'did not necessarily transfer ... learning in concrete situations often remained there' (Greenfield 2005; Guberman and Greenfield 1991). Specific cognitive skills are in some sense bound within a context. Individuals can use those skills within that setting, but they often resist applying those seemingly generalizable skills outside of them.

Meanwhile, in the last few decades many psychologists and anthropologists, mostly calling themselves cognitive scientists, have come up with many ways to demonstrate that most of us do not use formal operations easily, that we operate most easily in familiar settings where we have some practical knowledge of our problems, and that we use a variety of cognitive heuristics to take short cuts in thinking about problems. These short cuts display predictable errors in the way we infer features of people and events (Tversky and Kahneman 1983); they rely on specific cognitive mechanisms like prototypes (Lakoff 1987), scripts (Schank and Abelson 1977), bounded knowledge (Strauss 1992), distributed cognition (Hutchins 1991) and other mechanisms (D'Andrade 1995). These are also evidence for context-specific knowledge, but in this work, context tends to be defined by narrative and representation.

This work on everyday cognition still leaves to one side the problem of participation. To be sure, Pascal Boyer speaks directly to the peculiarity of religious ideas in a significant body of work (1994, 2001b, 2003). But his emphasis is on the shape and content of cognitive ideas. For him (as for Whitehouse 2004), the problem of religion is the problem of transmission. 'People's minds are constantly busy reconstructing, distorting, changing and developing the information communicated by others. ... not all of these variants have the same fate ... an extremely small number remain in memory, are communicated to other people, are recalled by these people and communicated to others in a way that more or less preserves the original concepts. These are the ones we can observe in human cultures' (2001b: 33). Boyer models this process, drawing on cognitive science and evolutionary psychology, as a process of complex inference. People develop rich representations of objects, scenes and individuals on the basis of a comparatively small amount of available information. They do so, he argues, by using cognitive templates. Other of his colleagues have begun to describe sets of these templates as modules which structure the inferences they draw (see Sperber 1994, forthcoming; Atran 2002).

Participation is a different phenomenon, and it is important to this discussion because it is not simply cognitive. To be sure, cognitive models are salient: people use them to interpret their subjective experience. But what participation adds to the discussion is that these experiences of God are sensory. People hear, they see, they feel. They may do so only in their imagination, but these techniques – both the social process of interpretation and the psychological process of absorption, both taught in the deliberate pursuit of cultivating an experience of God – help to make God real for humans. Divinity, by its nature, cannot be sensed. Yet these interpretations help ordinary humans to feel divinity to be real despite divinity's evanescent nature. That is an important contribution to a discussion that tends to approach religious practice from the perspective of different cognitive models. These Christians are not simply modelling the world according to different cognitive constraints. In some fundamental sense, *they live in a different world*, which provides them with different evidence for their cognitive models than the secular observer may have. Moreover, these evangelical Christians create the experience of participation through methods that in fact are profoundly modern. In fact, they do so with the method defined in so much cultural psychology as the definitive difference between the primitive and the modern – through literacy. This is a world dominated by books, by written manuals, in which the use of literacy is embedded in the means to make participation experientially real by writing down prayer experience and identifying God's presence within it. God is made more real through literacy for the very reason Jack Goody (1976) argued that literacy enables the emergence of context-free, scientific thought. Literacy externalizes, distances, concretizes a murky mental process. If you want someone to experience their subjective flow as containing an external presence, literacy is a helpful tool. After all, what these congregants must learn to do is to experience their inner subjectivity differently, as containing not just their own awareness but also the awareness of another. Using literacy to externalize moments of that inner voice helps the subject to experience the inner voice not as a monologue but as a dialogue. So do these books, and the cultural patterns which help them to interpret moments of their own thoughts as containing another presence. So do absorption practices, which ask them to attend more carefully to their inner sensations and may intensify a detachment between inner sensation and an external world.

Yet congregants at the Vineyard have no difficulty functioning effectively with the logical, analytic, communicative skills needed for school and work. They are, in fact, highly competent in work domains and are often widely rewarded for their analytic success. They experience participation, with all its logic-bending features, but rarely in such a way to interfere with the logical skills they might use to navigate the modern world. What they seem to do, in fact, is to use the tools of a sophisticated, literate modernity to create an experience of participation which is bounded in particular ways.

Cole's (1996) most recent theory of culture can help us to understand how they do this. Cole (1996) is committed to three general claims about the nature of this 'context' which bounds everyday thought: that thought is 'mediated' by the use of artifacts, in which he includes not only physical tools like hoes but symbols (conceptual tools) like words and images; that there is something like a modularity, in Fodor's (1983) sense (but in the weak version), to some psychological processes (for example, folk biology, as in the work of Medin and Carey, e.g. Medin and Atran 1999); and that learning takes place through the subject's active construction of knowledge in an environment. These Christians do all that.

First of all, congregants build an experience of participation around a particular 'artifact': the concept of God. In this case, the artifact is a representation, and they limit their expectation of participation to that representation and to other linked representations. (This essay has not discussed the way congregants develop ideas about evil spirits, but at least in the Vineyard context, congregants seem to develop such familiarity with demonic possession later than they develop a familiarity with God, but in a similar manner.) As congregants look for evidence of God's presence, they build a model of who God is, and how he relates to them. At the Vineyard, this God is modelled as a friend in a casual, personal, intimate relationship, and as congregants acquire evidence of divine presence, they chunk information around their model of God and they use that model to interpret the evidence for which they search. They do not use other representations as a possible source to explain their evidence (unless they are also aware of demonic spirits, which has not been discussed here). In other words, if a congregant thinks she has a special message from an intentional being in her mind, she never wonders whether that message is from another human, or from the radio, or from the CIA. Those would be judgements that invited fellow congregants to view her as psychotic, not blessed.

Second, the congregant learns to identify only certain kinds of thoughts as evidence of God's participation in his or her mind. There clearly are social rules which govern the way God's presence in the mind is inferred, and congregants are able to articulate them clearly, as does their didactic literature. They learn to pay attention to their streams of consciousness in a particular way, and (psychologically speaking) they use absorption practices which both draw their attention to inner thoughts, and probably enhance the probability of experiencing what a secular observer would call sensory deception: sensory impressions which do not arise from earthly stimuli. Moreover, this evidence is used to judge existence in a manner different from evidence used to judge the existence of tables and chairs. Congregants treat their interpretation of God's presence in their mind as real evidence – but they simultaneously entertain the possibility that their interpretation might be wrong. From the congregant's perspective, this is the challenge of discernment. Again, these are socially shared understandings that rule out many possible thoughts as evidence for God's participation. Command hallucinations, distressing voices and obviously self-indulgent thoughts are among the thoughts ruled out.

Third, there is a clear understanding that the congregant who experiences God's participation in his or her mind has come to experience that participation through individual active learning. The process of that learning is, again, socially modelled and collectively understood. Spiritual maturity is understood to be the endpoint of that journey, and the model of spiritual maturity presents the believer as someone who begins with a representation of God-as-explanation (and giver of rewards) and moves to a model of God-as-relationship, God as the reality within which to carry out logical analyses.

Through this learning process, centered on a particular representation, bounded in socially defined ways, experienced through intense personal engagement, God becomes real for people. That the learning process incorporates the senses probably makes God feel more real. Many years ago Daryl Bem wrote of 'zero-order beliefs'. 'Our most fundamental beliefs are so taken for granted that we are apt not to notice them at all' (Bem 1970: 5). In fact, belief in God is not automatic, as the religious community understands: it needs constant reinforcement from repeated Sunday services, housegroup meetings, spiritual manuals, and so forth. But the goal of the practice is to create a sense of God as fundamental, as the frame in which one moves and the ground on which one stands – not a hypothesis to be tested. Bem argued that the belief in the truth of our senses was our most primitive zero-order belief: if we did not believe in our senses, we would go mad. And what Vineyard practice tries to do is to lead its congregants to an experience of God which is validated by the senses through the experience of participation. You learn to experience God speaking in your mind, present in your body, concrete and tangible in the experience of relationship, and thus as fundamental as your sensory awareness of the everyday world in which you live.

Let me close with a final thought. The great debate in the scholarship on medieval Europe has been whether Christianity did, or did not, create the experience of interiority we now call subjectivity. So sophisticated and literate is the participation that these modern Christians experience that an anthropologist may be led to wonder whether not only interiority, but participation is a creation of a complex and self-conscious endeavour – and whether the participation Lévy-Bruhl described so well is in fact a better description of the way modern religion differs from the so-called traditional, rather than the inverse.

Chapter 7

HOW TO LEARN IN AN AFRO-BRAZILIAN SPIRIT POSSESSION RELIGION
ONTOLOGY AND MULTIPLICITY IN CANDOMBLÉ[1]

Marcio Goldman

It is possible for an orisha or an entity to transform itself into a known person and, often, even into an object. It is like when you see an object and identify it as unique while at the same time other people see it in a very distant place. It is something that can happen. Orishas can transform themselves. The orisha is one. The fluids he emanates transform themselves into him. Once he projects fluids then he becomes represented. He can be one and many, a force and the concentration of this force in whatever form he may desire.

(Nivaldo Pereira Bastos, Camuluaji)

Each orisha is multiple.

(Roger Bastide)

Introduction

Candomblé is one of the many Brazilian religions that display elements of African origins. Probably formed from the nineteenth century onwards, Candomblé – at least as we know it today – also embodies, to different degrees, elements of Native American practices and cosmologies, as well as that of popular Catholicism and European Spiritualism. In addition, it is possible to observe more or less marked differences among the various cult groups, depending on the African regions from which came the larger part of its repertoire, and on the modalities and intensities of its 'syncretic' connections with other religious traditions.

Roughly speaking, followers of Candomblé tend to classify their *terreiros* (temples or cult houses) into three great *nations* (besides a larger number of smaller ones, or divisions of the greater), derived in theory from the different African origins of their founders. Thus, the Ketu nation originated from the Yoruba of Nigeria and Benin; the Jeje nation from the Fon of Benin; and the Angola nation from the Bantu of Angola and Congo. There are differences between *terreiros* belonging to distinct nations, but there are also variations between those that classify themselves in an identical nation. In the same way there are many and diverse possible combinations between nations.

Nevertheless, beyond this empirical diversity there are common elements among all of the cult groups. The clearest one is the existence of deities (*orishas*, *voduns* or *inkices*) that possess previously prepared followers during specific ceremonies. This preparation occurs through a complex set of rituals including a relatively long initiation process that generally comprises offerings and animal sacrifices. Although this is not always the case, as a matter of fact a Candomblé group is often recognized among the other Afro-Brazilian religions precisely because it adopts such sacrifices, as well as a more elaborated initiation process, and a more marked distinction between the deities or *orishas* and the spirits of the ancestors and the dead in general.

The main question here is about the nature or texture of the different constitutive elements of all Afro-Brazilian religions, specifically the way they are elaborated in Candomblé. Thus, the investigation of the relationships between the *orishas* (which possess human beings), their followers (who go into trance) and the representations and practices that make these acts possible and understandable must be connected with this sort of ontological problem. To be more precise, I would ask: how does one describe in the best possible manner elements whose nature seems on the one hand extremely familiar and on the other absolutely impenetrable to our most common cognitive and descriptive categories?

As long as each thing or being is said to 'belong' to an *orisha*, the easiest way to describe the system seems to simply involve saying that it is a form of pantheism where a certain number of deities (normally sixteen) share the cosmos between them. In this way, the followers are those human beings who, once initiated, can be possessed by the deities to whom he or she 'belongs'.

However, when one tries to precisely enumerate the *orishas* their number hardly ever coincides with the sixteen normally postulated. Also, each *orisha* presents itself in a variable quantity of *qualities* ('*qualidades*') – types or modalities of each deity. Therefore, the *orisha* considered to be the oldest of all, Oshala,[2] presents himself in a 'young' quality (Oshaguian) and in an 'old' quality (Oshalufan) – the same happens with other *orishas*. Similarly, it is also possible to enumerate an enormous variety of qualities of Oshala distributed along such extremes. It is even said that a certain quality of an *orisha* is 'almost' another *orisha* (a certain quality of the *orisha* Omolu is 'almost' an Oshala). Finally, to complicate matters even further, one can also speak of the 'Oshala of so-and-so', or 'my Omolu', someone's individual *orisha*.

Most if not all of the descriptions of Candomblé are top to bottom oriented, beginning with the enumeration of what followers call 'general *orishas*', going on to their qualities and sometimes ending with a certain number of individual *orishas*' names. This descriptive technique offers but one particular vision of the system. What follows is an outline of a recently begun attempt at elaborating another kind of description, giving greater emphasis to dimensions and elements of Candomblé generally left in the background: the ontological texture of its constitutive elements and relationships, and the question of what an *orisha* is after all.

Afro-Brazilian Studies

Afro-Brazilian religions as a whole are the resultants of multiple and creative processes of reterritorialization (see Deleuze and Guattari 1980), which sprang up in the wake of the brutal deterritorialization of millions of people in one of the movements that gave rise to capitalism: the exploitation of the Americas with the use of slave labour. This harrowing experience engendered the combination of different aspects from a wide range of African thought systems with diverse elements from Christian and Amerindian religious practices. These new combinations simultaneously mixed aspects of social formations rendered impossible by slavery with alternative types of association, giving rise to new cognitive, perceptive, affective and organizational forms. Hence this new situation meant a recomposition of apparently lost existential territories on fresh grounds, along with the development of subjectivities linked to a resistance against dominant forces. The latter, for their part, never ceased trying to eliminate and/or capture this fascinating historical experience. Taken as a whole, this scenario undoubtedly explains much of the fact that even today Afro-Brazilian religions are traversed by a double system of forces: centripetal forces that codify and unify the cults, and centrifugal ones, which tend to pluralize their variants, accentuating differences and spawning divergent lines (see Bastide 1960; Dianteill 2002).

This fundamental coexistence of centripetal and centrifugal forces has never been fully acknowledged within the field of Afro-Brazilian studies. In fact, it is worth noting a tendency to ignore or downplay either one of these two dimensions while treating the effect of this occlusion as a defect of the system itself. Thus, there tends to exist an oscillation between positions that have been classified or accused of being, on the one hand 'culturalist' or 'internalist', and on the other of being 'socio-political' or 'external'. The first one, supposedly facing its object of study from the point of view of its internal structure and from the relations that constituted it from within, would then emphasize the preservation of tradition and/or cultural resistance; the second one (which apparently predominates from the 1970s onwards) would privilege the multiple relations and articulations of Afro-Brazilian religions with other social facts, that is, the place occupied by them within the so-called inclusive social structure.[3]

It is clear that this division is not exclusive to Afro-Brazilian studies and that, as demonstrated by Viveiros de Castro (1999), terms like internal or external are inadequate. Nevertheless, in the beginning of the 1980s, when I wrote my first piece of work as an anthropologist, I believed it necessary to adopt a 'structural' position. This stemmed from the feeling that the more sociological analyses tended to drift into a kind of reductionism, which, by insisting on the idea that religious systems are the reflection or expression of surrounding society, lose the means to comprehend effectively both the different religions in themselves and the actual 'society.' This Durkheimian premise, a legacy from which anthropology has still yet to rid itself fully, prevents us from acknowledging that different spheres of social life are components of a mechanism which is not above them and that these spheres are neither the reflection nor the expression of a transcendent social whole prior to their specific manifestations.

Adopting this line of argument, I then claimed that the structural characteristics of the religious system over-determine its relations to other social subsystems. Hence, it would make perfect sense that a possession-based religion – where the trance is conceived and experienced as a technique for the construction and maintenance of the person – is linked to the experience of illness, thought as the person's disequilibrium. At the same time, the socio-political operations to which Afro-Brazilian religions are sometimes reduced become more intelligible if we take into account the fact that processes such as symbolic status reversal, compensation or social climbing imply establishing continuities between usually discontinuous segments; a procedure that is one of the core characteristics of the ritual system of these religions. Likewise, rather than reducing religious syncretism to a complete incapacity to absorb overly abstract religious precepts, or to the assimilation of unconscious archetypes, or to the acceptance of a class ideology, it would be more useful to consider that a system based on ritual and the exploration of continuities possesses remarkable flexibility and an enormous power to assimilate the new realities with which history confronts it.

In other words, I believed that Candomblé has a kind of structural propensity for connecting itself to certain phenomena, which could not therefore function as the causal explanation for the system as such. Furthermore, I believed it was essential to draw a distinction between the constitutive symbolic devices of the system from their use for diverse and frequently mutually opposed purposes – which, nonetheless, must be compatible with the device's structure.

As is common in anthropology, my conclusions partly reflected the trials and tribulations of my fieldwork experiences. The first of these, which began in 1978 and lasted four years, took place in a small Angola Candomblé *terreiro* located in the periphery of Greater Rio de Janeiro – the *Ilê de Obaluaiê*. This research led me to suppose that the explanatory key of Candomblé lay in the classificatory systems and cosmologies of the cult. Such conclusions were certainly affected by personal characteristics of the *terreiro*'s saint-father ('*pai-de-santo*'), who loved mystical meditations and the construction of intricate cosmological systems – clearly 'bricolaged' from several different sources. Some years later my second piece of fieldwork experience took place in a very different scenario in the *Terreiro de Matamba Tombenci Neto*, which is situated in the Conquista neighbourhood of Ilhéus, a town in the south of the state of Bahia (north-eastern Brazil). This time I stayed there for only three months (against the four years in the *Ilê de Obaluaiê*) but my contact with the group was of a much greater intensity than in the previous fieldwork. Combined with certain characteristics of the *terreiro* and once again with some of the saint-mother's (Mrs Ilza Rodrigues, Mameto Mucale) idiosyncrasies, my experience suggested that, contrary to my beliefs, the fundamental aspects of Candomblé should not be sought only in its cosmology or mythology.[4]

The question today is to seek out a new 'interpretation' of Candomblé. Not, clearly, in the hermeneutic sense of the term – the search for a more suitable or more profound meaning than the previous one – but in its *musical* sense: another mode or style of performing a work that is certainly not mine. For this to occur, it is necessary to begin by repeating that the distinctions between internal and external, inside and outside, cultural and socio-political are both impossible to be clearly drawn and very unsatisfactory.

I would like to briefly consider how a system that stresses continuous flows and cuttings (and not plain discontinuities), multiplicities (and not any dialectic between the one and the multiple), and efficient operations (and not forms of ordering and its practical

implementations) can be transmitted or 'taught'. This is a very important question to the ethnographer who in a certain sense also has to
learn it and to transmit it in the least deforming manner.

How to Learn in Candomblé

In her thesis on Angola (or Bantu) Candomblé in Brazil, Gisele Binon
Cossard observes that a young woman starting in the cult must:

> (...) learn everything relating to ritual and the deities: how to take care of
> their sacred belongings, how to behave during the different ceremonies.
> Little by little, she tries to delve into the secrets of Candomblé, its 'founda-
> tions' [*fundamento*]. She is bound to face many difficulties in the process,
> since nobody, strictly speaking, will teach her a single chant, dance or
> appropriate gesture. As she cannot ask anything she is left to observe, with
> her head and eyes lowered, making sure never to appear too attentive or
> over-interested. Soon she discovers that too much curiosity is actually a
> hindrance: firstly, because elders have no interest in revealing what they
> know, since they run the risk of being surpassed by younger members; sec-
> ondly, because it isn't good to learn too quickly, since anything in Can-
> domblé has the potential to generate extremely tragic consequences for
> oneself and others, if done wrongly. Taking initiatives too early can cause
> discontent among the deities: provoked by the use of knowledge that has
> been poorly assimilated and applied without discernment the deities may
> unleash catastrophes capable of inducing madness and even death. 'Time
> dislikes whatever is done without it', say the elders. Hence much patience
> and perseverance is required, which enables friendships to be cultivated
> and, in trade for endless hours of work, precious knowledge can be gleaned
> by paying attention during conversations. At the same time, the numerous
> chants and dance steps can be learnt by taking part in all the festivals. As
> time goes by, the novice becomes more confident. Knowledge of the ritual
> seeps into her slowly. Gestures and words, dances and melodies eventually
> become indissociable automatisms (Cossard 1970: 226–27).

Aside from being beautifully precise, this ethnographic description is
valuable for another reason. Cossard is French and was initiated into
Candomblé in 1960 by the renowned saint-father Joaozinho da
Gomea, receiving the *dijina* (or saint-name) Omindarewa, meaning
she is a daughter of Iemanja, the sea *orisha*. Fifteen years later, Cossard
founded her own *terreiro* on the outskirts of Rio de Janeiro – where she
is still active today – and became an important Candomblé priestess or
saint-mother. During this process, she completed her doctoral thesis in
Paris in 1970 under the supervision of Roger Bastide.

Having lived through the experience of becoming a saint-daughter,
who must learn without appearing to learn, and an ethnographer

who (in this case at least) can only learn by making it clear that she is *only* learning, Cossard clearly knows what she is saying when she concludes that, in Candomblé, 'teaching is never systematic in form. "This comes with time ..." say the elders. But the fact these habits are acquired slowly means that the initiate's knowledge penetrates the deepest part of her being' (Cossard 1970: 227; see also Cossard 1981; Dion 1998; Fichte 1987).

Imagining a 'systematic form of teaching' necessarily presumes the existence of at least three clearly defined elements: someone active who teaches; someone passive who learns; and a more or less inert set of knowledge to be passed from one to the other. It is the complete absence of these kinds of elements in Candomblé that renders any application of our almost default model of learning unworkable. This conceptual model is essentially hydraulic in kind, implying a ready-made but empty container to be filled by a flow of equally ready-made content derived from another ready-made but full container, which – paradoxically enough – is not emptied in the process. This is the model we need to abandon if we wish to develop a fully relational conception of learning, to be sketched here by aligning this problem with ethnographic data concerning Candomblé.

In this religion – to jump ahead slightly – someone who 'teaches' is primarily a person who is constituted as such over many years through complex processes of initiation involving a dense web of practices, a person whose equilibrium and even existence depend on the rigorous observance of several procedures. On the other hand, someone who 'learns' is a person in the process of being constructed, and his or her success depends on the capacity to endure and develop this process, which involves much more than just 'learning.' Finally, the 'content' to be taught and learnt is far from being a systematic set of basic principles, a 'doctrine' – a term which, as it happens, is a synonym in Portuguese and in English for 'teaching' (and in archaic English, I think, also for 'learning').

What must be learnt is not conceptualized as a perfectly coherent and unified body of rules and knowledge, like a type of overcodified doctrine imposed from above. Novices in Candomblé are fully aware from the outset that there is no point waiting to receive ready-made teachings from a master. Instead, they must patiently put together details gleaned here and there over the years, in the hope that, at some point, this accumulation of knowledge will acquire enough density to be useful. This is called '*catar folhas*' ('gathering leaves'), an expression related to the fact that knowledge and learning are located under the sign of the *orishas* Ossain, the master of herbs, and Oshossi, the hunter. Learning is then conceived above all as a form of search and capture, a pursuit that inevitably involves a certain degree of risk.

The anthropologist should, at least partially, proceed in the same manner. Partially, of course, as an anthropological research cannot fully pursue this kind of procedure since it demands time unavailable to us. On the other hand, attempting to proceed in any other way would at best mean failing to get anywhere and at worst produce a kind of code or doctrine whose existence has little relation to lived experience.

The historical origins of Candomblé and Afro-Brazilian religions in general might explain their apparent lack of doctrine and the decentralized nature of the cult. As Roger Bastide (2000 [1958]: 86) has observed, the fact that 'each house or terreiro is autonomous, dependent on a saint-father or saint-mother who recognises no authority above his or her own. They constitute worlds apart, almost like African islands in the middle of a sea of Western civilisation'. However, aside from observing that these 'islands' possess their own *kula rings*, it is worth recognizing that the decentralization of the cult cannot explain everything as long as it still comes from the point of view of an outsider. A better understanding of what learning means in Candomblé requires the consideration of the many dimensions of an extremely complex and sophisticated system.

Essay of a Candomblé Ontology (Angola)

One of the system's dimensions comprises what would classically be termed as a cosmology and what I would prefer to call an ontology – a very special kind of ontology of course.[5] In terms more immediately comprehensible to ourselves, this ontology can be summarized as a kind of monism that postulates the existence of a single *force*. This force is called *ashe* and is similar to other anthropologically familiar notions such as *mana* and *orenda*. Modulations of *ashe* make up everything in existence and capable of existing in the universe according to a process of concretization, diversification and individualization. Even the *orishas* themselves are no more than a manifestation of a specific modulation of *ashe*. The multifarious beings and things of the world, stones, plants, animals, human beings – but so too colours, flavours, smells, days, years, and so on – everything 'belongs' to the *orishas* insofar as everything shares this force, simultaneously general and individualized. In a sense, each being is no more than a kind of crystallization or molarization resulting from the modulating flow of *ashe*, which starting out as a general and homogeneous force continuously gets more diversified and more concrete.

In a more directly religious language, one can say that *ashe* springs from a common source, which may be identified as Olorum or Zambi, the supreme deity who receives no cult at all; or Iroko (or Tempo), the sacred tree whose sap gave rise to the *orishas*; or other sources, depending on the mythic versions in operation. This flow of *ashe* is, in some way *cut* at different points to constitute at one level what are called 'generic' *orishas* (of which a finite number exist) and at another an unlimited number of individual *orishas*, to which all human beings are ultimately linked (I will return to this key aspect of the system later).

This cosmology or ontology develops into a mythology and a series of complex systems of classification or in other words into a philosophy of nature and society. Above all, the myths present the polyvalence of the deities, conceived at the same time as very heavy essences, natural forces (lightning, thunder, rivers and so on), cultural institutions (war, justice ...), and as individuals who lived in the past (kings, queens, warriors ...). We should also note that rather than just involving simple modes of representations (a flash of lightning representing the *orisha* Iansan), relations of ownership (the sea belonging to the *orisha* Iemanja) or control (sickness being provoked and controlled by Omolu), an extremely complex set of relations is involved here. In a sense, the sea *is* Iemanja, lightning and wind *are* Iansan, and sickness *is* Omolu. Nature, culture, human beings, the cosmos, everything seems to be interconnected in this system. Hence, the components of these different layers can be grouped into classes according to the *orisha* to which they belong – or, in other words, according to the modulation of *ashe* that constitutes them. This makes it quite easy to reduce the system to a classificatory or even totemic logic, insofar as the universe is divided up by discontinuities or differential separations within an initially homogeneous or continuous set. Indeed, many structural analyses of Candomblé have already seen the light of day (see, for example, Lépine 1978, 2000).

However, one of the central aspects of Candomblé lies in the fact that human beings are also divided up between the *orishas*. This notion is related to a distinct body of conceptions concerning the nature of humans, a notion of personhood, or – as I would prefer to call it – an anthropology, in the philosophical sense of the term. As in most other human societies, the person is presumed to be multiple and 'layered', composed of a series of material and immaterial elements. These include the main *orisha* to whom the person belongs (whose 'child' he or she is), a variable number of secondary *orishas*, as well as ancestral spirits, a guardian angel, a soul and so forth. The key point, however, is that the person is not born ready-made but constructed during the long process of initiation by means of a series of rituals or 'obligations.' The person is thus *made* and initiation into Candomblé is called '*fazer a cabeça*' ('making the head'). There is more to this, though.

'Making the head' is actually the counterpart of a process called 'making the saint' (saint being here another name for *orisha*) and initiation may likewise be termed 'making the saint'. This means that not only the person is made during the process of initiation: the *orisha* is also made or constructed.

This constructivism may at first seem at odds with the ontological premises summarized above. But only to an unwary observer, overused perhaps to thinking in the terms established by our religious doctrines and/or philosophical systems. As I have already stated, an *orisha* is not so much an individuality but the result of the cutting of a flow, which can be done at different levels. At one level, the cut actualizes the 'generic *orisha*' Iansan, Iemanja, Omolu, etc., and this process is told in different myths. Initiation, however, never involves the consecration of the initiate to one of these generic *orishas*: 'making the head' or 'making the saint' – the central aspect of Candomblé – actually means the ritual production of *two* individualized entities out of two generic substrates. A more or less undifferentiated individual who becomes a structured person and a generic *orisha* who is actualized as an individual *orisha*: one person's Iansan, my Omolu. These individual *orishas* possess their own names and characteristics, in the same way that people are re-baptized and transformed during their initiation.

The deity is not, therefore, just an element external to the human being, intermittently united with the latter. The *orisha* is *made* within the human being and at the same time its own person is also made. This means that the *orisha* inhabits in a constitutive way what Bastide (2000 [1958]: 242) called the human being's 'inner castle'. Perhaps this explains the crucial importance of possession, the key ritual modality of Candomblé since, as Bastide also suggests, possession involves more than the enactment of a rite: it amounts to a 'lived-experience ritual'. It is in trance that all the dimensions of the system appear to come together to produce a particular synthesis of the experience of the cult: the worlds of the gods and humans converge; the Candomblé adept and his or her *orisha* almost overlap; the various components of the human being tend towards unification and equilibrium, raising humans to almost divine status.

Does this mean that human beings *transform* themselves into *orishas*? Or can we say that between the human series and that of the *orishas* homologous relationships are established? I would rather say that this is not very precise, or at least that this is not all. In the tenth of their *Thousand Plateaux*, Deleuze and Guattari (1980: 286–87) show that the elements of a classificatory system were historically conceived in terms of two models: the 'series' model – where *a* is similar to *b*, *b* is similar to *c*, etc., according to rules of similarity and analogies of proportion – and the 'structure' model – where *a* is to *b* as *b* is to *c*, etc., according to a correspondence between differences and analogies of proportionality or homology. While stating that we 'have not left this problem entirely behind' (Deleuze and Guattari 1980: 287) and that the series-structure pair continues to guide our reflection, the authors introduce the concept of becoming as a means to escape this dilemma. Becoming does not mean either similarity nor imitation or identification; it has nothing to do with formal relations or substantial transformations. Becoming 'is neither an analogy nor an imagining but a composition' (Deleuze and Guattari 1980: 315):

> Becoming is the extraction of particles from the forms one has, from the subject one is, from the organs one possesses or from the functions one fills. Relations of movement and rest, speed and slowness that are closest to that which we are about to become and through which we become are installed between these particles. It is in this way that becoming is the process of desire (Deleuze and Guattari 1980: 334).

In other words, these relations can be thought of as a form of movement through which a subject abandons its own condition (human, for example) by means of a relation of affect established with another condition (animal or divine, for example). We should also note that 'affect' here has nothing to do with emotions or sentiments, naming rather something that affects, alters or modifies – a *becoming* in the sense that a horse-becoming, for example, does not mean that I turn into a horse or psychologically identify with the animal but simply that 'what happens to the horse can happen to me' (Deleuze and Guattari 1980: 193). It is in this sense that we can understand the 'reality of the animal-becoming without us, in reality, turning into an animal' (Deleuze and Guattari 1980: 335). Becoming uproots us not only from ourselves but also from *any* possible substantial identity.

In the same way, it is necessary to observe that the term multiplicity should be understood here through the definition established by Deleuze and Guattari (1980: 15–18, 43–50, 190–92). Thus, not in terms of the adjective 'multiple', which is necessarily opposed to 'one', but as a substantive and an index of a pluralism in opposition to all forms of binarism and its variations. As posited above, in more ethnographic terms we are dealing with the attempt at an ethnographic description of Candomblé that instead of beginning with supposed *units* that compose a whole, assumes from the start the multiplicity of the *orishas*, the rituals, the saint-children and so forth.[6]

Of course, one could very well interpret Candomblé in a serialist key, insisting upon a continuum that would mysteriously link all that exists. One could also interpret Candomblé in a structural way by emphasizing the homologous relationships established between the different series: human, divine, natural, etc. In the first case sacrifice and possession, as operators of the establishment of continuities, would certainly be privileged; in the second they would be replaced by totemism and classification.

Nonetheless, I believe that these keys and the phenomena they privilege do not exhaust our possibilities of exploring the system. If we reinterpret Candomblé through the becoming key, possession, for example, would not mean turning into an *orisha*. In truth, it is clearly said that no-one could stand the infinite power that this would entail and that this would lead to the complete annihilation of the possessed body. For the same reason it is said that general *orishas* never possess their children. If possession is not transformation it also does not consist of simple imitation. Rather it is a type of becoming: an Iansan-becoming that mixes wind-becoming and warrior-becoming; or an Omolu-becoming that combines mineral-becoming with sick-becoming or healer-becoming.

Candomblé should then be seen as more than a purely intellectual or cognitive system – or even as a mystical, emotional and ritual one, at least in the formal sense of these terms. More than a system of beliefs or even a 'religion', Candomblé is above all a set of practices and a way of life. This means taking seriously what every researcher into Candomblé invariably hears, namely that the information passed on to them and the festivals they freely attend are no more than the visible side of something much deeper. More important than the magnificent rites or the beautiful myths is a particular kind of knowledge that is linked to these practices, but which also surpasses them in many directions. This secret knowledge is only accessible to the initiated or more precisely to those among the initiates who are capable of *learning* it. Such knowledge is primarily manifested in those actions that followers call '*fuxicos*' – a term meaning something like the action of tinkering (if we take it in its serious meaning) or, when trying to explain what these involve, 'manipulations'. '*Fuxicos*' are actions meant to produce effects, a search for a pure efficacy, allowing to raise the hypothesis that cosmological, mythological and classificatory systems are all actually in service of this operational process.

Hence, perhaps the core elements of Candomblé are not the great classificatory schemes, the big sacrifices or the visible and spectacular aspect of the stunning public festivals, but precisely that which is undertaken in secret, far removed from the gaze of lay people – the 'manipulations', the *fuxicos*, this know-how that constitutes the distinctive feature of Candomblé, the possibility of a variability and creativity that can only embellish the cult and which distinguishes it from the monotonous codes of the so-called great religions. Were it possible to empty the term 'magic' from the ethnocentric content imputed by those who in the nineteenth century and even today deny Candomblé its religious condition, it would perhaps be the best designation for this aspect of the system – magic *almost* in the sense attributed by classic social anthropology, that of a composition (rather than an imposition) of human will with natural and divine forces.

The prominence of the manipulations explains why the relations between norms and their enactment is extremely complex in Candomblé. As we have seen, the system involves a kind of generalized constructivism, such that believers would probably have little problem in agreeing with the enlightenment proposition that it is men who make the gods – without, nevertheless, circumscribing the cult as an illusion or ideology. If everything is *made* it is always possible to make something happen: negotiate with the gods when their demands are too rigorous; postpone or simplify an initiation required by the *orisha*; eat a prohibited food by bestowing it with another name; eliminate elements that should make up part of a ritual or replace them with other more easily found or cheaper elements ('the important thing is that the bracelets shine', as a saint-daughter said when explaining why her *orisha* Oshum used yellow metal bracelets rather than gold ones). All this and much more is possible, providing the person has the knowledge, strength and audacity to make it happen, since it is obvious that there are risks and the final proof lies in the acceptance or refusal on the part of the deities – and in the latter case, the consequences are usually extreme.

The privilege given to continuous flows (of *ashe*) and the strictly constructive and multiple character of Candomblé ontology and anthropology compromises any attempt to explain the system by means of purely serial or structural models. Thus, learning a religion of this kind cannot mean passive apprehension but rather an experience that modifies all of the elements involved in that process – the matter being 'transmitted' and 'assimilated', but also the agents or subjects who, as we have seen, are engaged in an ongoing transformational process. In Candomblé everything works as in Guimarães Rosa's (1967: 43) formula: 'Living is – isn't it? – very dangerous. Because we still don't know. Because learning-to-live is living itself'.

Multiplicity and Becoming in Candomblé

The idea of a 'Candomblé ontology' comes from the 'Essay of an African (Yoruba) Epistemology', written in 1958 by Roger Bastide as a section of the 'Conclusions' of his *Le Candomblé de Bahia (Rite Nago)*. But it also modifies the terms of the question because Bastide seems to deal more with a very particular ontological modality than with an epistemology – despite the fact that the opposition between such notions is relatively unclear.

In truth the section is part of a long attempt by Bastide at the systematization, conciliation and, perhaps, the surmounting of what he considered to be profound differences between certain anthropological mindsets. Beginning by associating the name of Lévy-Bruhl with an emphasis on participation, that of Durkheim and Mauss to the privilege given to classifications and that of Lévi-Strauss to transformations, Bastide then hesitates in the implementation of his synthesis.

Thus, in 1964, he opposed in almost absolute form Lévy-Bruhl and Maurice Leenhardt, on one side, Durkheim and Lévi-Strauss on the other. He claimed that the latter pair was exclusively interested – in the purest Cartesian tradition – in 'clear and distinct' ideas, while the former pair had opened the way for 'obscure and confused thinking'. The conclusion then is that the two positions are completely irreconcilable: 'there is, I think, no possible complementarity between the two conceptions (...). They follow opposed paths. It is necessary to choose between them' (Bastide 1970: 65).

Eleven years earlier, however, he had attempted to show that Lévy-Bruhl's notion of participation was above all a 'category of action', derived from what Bastide called *dynamism*: 'a vitalist or dynamic philosophy, a theory of Forces' (Bastide 1953: 32). In other words, a kind of primordial philosophy that instead of operating on beings and their relations, as we do, is dedicated above all to the codification and manipulation of 'forces' (Bastide 1953: 38–39). Seen from this viewpoint, participation would be a direct outcome of this philosophy, depending much more on a 'pragmatics' than a 'logic', even when the latter is conceived as affective or simply 'prelogic' (Bastide 1953: 36–37).

In the 1958 text the formulation of the problem is more complex and proceeds by stages. The first step is the argument that Lévy-Bruhl's participation is perfectly compatible with the classifications of Durkheim and Mauss (Bastide 2000 [1958]: 292) – but only insofar as the former may be subordinated to the latter. That is, to the extent that participation depends on a philosophy of the cosmos and above all on classifications, since it only acts within classes (Bastide 2000 [1958]: 293). However, Bastide immediately introduces a complication by arguing that Candomblé's classifications are in reality nothing like our classifications: while the latter comprises classes of beings, the former operates on forces and participations manifesting a much more analogical thinking than our own, which would tend more towards separations (Bastide 2000 [1958]: 293–94). Furthermore, Bastide continues, not only do classifications appear to operate on participations but also any observer of Candomblé will immediately note the operation of what he calls a 'will to connect' (Bastide

2000 [1958]: 298). This is manifested both in the place and the function occupied by the *orisha* Eshu in the cosmological system and, in particular, in the fact that the classifications are constantly 'manipulated'. That is, classifications are enveloped by manipulations that frequently transgress the classes themselves – which from the mythological point of view are actually no more than crystallizations of the manipulations performed by deities (Bastide 2000 [1958]: 294). For Bastide, all of this is particularly visible in the sorcery practices that undoubtedly exist in Candomblé (Bastide 2000 [1958]: 295) and leads to a fundamental conclusion: participation is not a category of thought but a category of action (Bastide 2000 [1958]: 293), a pragmatic category. Attempting to escape sociological reductionism, Lévy-Bruhl's error was less to have denied the universality of logic than his insistence on remaining at the level of thought instead of turning to action: in attempting to overcome sociologism, a pragmatism would have been far better than a psychologism or a (pre)logicism.

The 'Essay of an African (Yoruba) Epistemology' also echoes a beautiful text written in 1953, called 'The African Conception of Personality' (Bastide 1973: 371–73). In this text Bastide writes about an 'African ontology' in which the conception of *Being* would be much closer to medieval western ontology than to post-critical philosophy. After Kant, Bastide argues, the impossibility of intermediary stages between *Being* and *Non-Being* became generally accepted: *being* exists or does not exist, nothing else. Medieval scholars, however, admitted the presence of mediations between these two extremes, 'a scale of existences of degrees of *Being*. Something can exist more or less'. For Bastide, this is actually the central ontological conception of Candomblé: between the uninitiated, closer to *Non-Being*, and the full *Being* of the *orishas*, a continuity could be conceived and constructed in the process of initiation by those who, in order to enter the cult, pass through all the rituals and accept all their duties. A path that is, of course, full of comings and goings, of dangers that become more accentuated as it goes on. If the fulfilment of prescriptions allows passage in one direction, their non-observance, the failures and errors, threaten to reverse the process. It is in this sense that possession appears as a fleeting flash in this realization of *Being*.

To conclude I would note that Bastide's 'will to connect' seems to have been borrowed from a profound observation made by Marcel Mauss in 1923. During the debate organized by the French Philosophical Society to discuss *Primitive Mentality*, Mauss posed five objections to Lévy-Bruhl, and while the first four merely attacked the lack of a sociological basis for the book's conclusions, the fifth one was of a very different kind:

'Participation' is not just a confusion. It supposes an attempt to confuse and an effort to assimilate. It is not a simple similarity but a *homoiosis*. There is a *trieb* from the very outset, a violence of the spirit against itself to surpass itself; from the outset, there is a will to connect (Mauss 1923: 28–29).

Stressing that *homoiosis* means the action of making someone or one-self similar to something else, and that *trieb* means drive – in the sense of impulse or desire – I would add that there seems to be only one problem with Mauss' observation: the suggestion that it is only the 'will to connect' which corresponds to this 'violence of the spirit', when there is no reason not to presume that the operations of separation and classification also demand a comparable will and violence.

To classify or to ritualize are actions that depend on the movements and becomings that constitute not only religions but all human affairs. Put otherwise, we can ask what classifications and participations actually are – or better, what they are for. A rough reply would be that both basically serve to enable action. Not in a transcendental sense, like a logical or emotional plane which would supposedly determine the conditions of all possible experience, but in the sense that classifications and participations operate like maps, diagrams or schemas for actions and manipulations. Hence, the key point is not the fact that manipulations are in accordance with classes or participations, but the fact of manipulations itself. This means that to classify or to participate is more important than classes or participations, and that the latter basically serve to be surpassed, working as supporting bridges or trampolines for action and creation.

Notes

1. This text is a preliminary attempt to re-start research into Candomblé begun in 1978 and interrupted in 1984. In this sense, it consists on the one hand of preliminary notes and on the other maintains relations of continuity and ruptures with Goldman (1984, 1985a, 1985b, 1990). This also means that a more contemporary bibliographic revision was left for later in benefit of an elaboration of some less explored aspects in the more 'classic' texts. Early versions of this paper were presented at different events. I thank Emerson Giumbelli, Leila Ripoll, Eduardo Viveiros de Castro, Ramon Sarró and David Berliner for making my presence in these events possible; David Rodgers and Julia Frajtag Sauma I thank for the translation of the original. I also thank Luisa Elvira Belaunde, Olivia Gomes da Cunha and, especially, Martin Holbraad and Tania Stolze Lima, whose critical observations permitted me to better elaborate an as yet imperfect piece of work.

2. I use the names for the *orishas* as used by the Ketu nation. I justify this option not only because these are the names most commonly used in literature and by the general public, but mainly because the very followers of Angola and Jeje Candomblé tend to do the same in daily, less formal situations.

3. This is how the history of Afro-Brazilian studies is generally told (see, among others, Maggie 1976, 2001; Dantas 1989; Capone 1999). After a long evolutionist

and culturalist phase – during which authors were preoccupied only in finding the African origins in Afro-Brazilian traditions – a more sociological approach, capable of connecting ethnographic observations with the current and more encompassing context, was finally reached. As this is not the place to discuss this version, I limit myself to saying that I do not believe things to have occurred with so much linearity and progressiveness. First, because it is evident that more 'cultural' analyses are still in use, emphasizing tradition as a form of resistance, or trying to establish substantive (and not only formal or ideological) connections between what actually takes place within the cults – in sociological as well as in properly religious terms – and broader social contexts (see, for example, Segato 1995; Serra 1995). Second, a lack of a sociological preoccupation of authors such as Roger Bastide and even Nina Rodrigues – known as the first to have studied Afro-Brazilian religions and who in doing this explicitly wanted to prove the impossibility of integration of Afro-descendants into Brazilian society – is doubtful. Finally, because the obsession with escaping what is considered to be evolutionism and culturalism can end up directing towards anaemic forms of functionalist adaptationalism and manipulative visions of social relations, of academic production and the connections between both. For a critical view of this interpretation of the history of Afro-Brazilian studies, see the important book written by Ordep Serra (1995).

4. Tombenci is a very different *terreiro* to *Ilê de Obaluaiê*. Founded in 1885, by the maternal grandmother of the current saint-mother, its organization is based upon her fourteen children and respective parentage, configuring a real space of sociality where ethnic (a carnival Afro-block is associated to the *terreiro*), kin and neighbourhood relations cross. *Ilê de Obaluaiê*, on the other hand, was a very new *terreiro*, which only really worked as a cult house on feast days. This is probably the best occasion to thank and to honour the memory of Nivaldo Pereira Bastos, Camuluaji, who offered my first access to the universe of Afro-Brazilian religions. And to deeply thank Mrs. Ilza Rodrigues, Mameto Mucale, with whom I continue to learn the little I know about Candomblé.

5. 'Becoming is the being [...], becoming and the being are the same affirmation' (Deleuze 1999 [1967]: 217).

6. In this sense, Bastide's epigraph (taken from Bastide 2000 [1958]: 183) could be rephrased: *each orisha is a multiplicity*.

Chapter 8

LEARNING TO BE A PROPER MEDIUM

MIDDLE-CLASS WOMANHOOD AND SPIRIT MEDIUMSHIP AT CHRISTIAN RATIONALIST SÉANCES IN CAPE VERDE

João Vasconcelos

Introduction

This chapter explores the process of learning mediumship at Christian Rationalist centres on the island of São Vicente, Cape Verde, where I conducted 13 months of fieldwork in 2000 and 2001.[1] Before going into the ethnographic core of the text, I will briefly sketch the history of Christian Rationalism, introduce some basic doctrinal tenets and practices of this spiritualist movement, and outline its social implantation in contemporary Cape Verde. I will then try to understand why exercising mediumship in Christian Rationalist centres is an appealing career to a number of middle-class women in São Vicente, and to describe how they enter it.

I will explore only one of the possible reasons for this appeal: the congruence between Christian Rationalist morality and the ethos of middle-class womanhood. This congruence, I will argue, allows many women to connect their life experiences with a number of images and concepts set in Christian Rationalist iconography and literature, thus infusing them with a vivid existential realness. Knowledge conveyed in doctrinal speeches and printed words and images is brought from a purely referential plane to a self-constitutive one (see Stromberg 1993). Objectified knowledge turns into knowledge made of experience; it acquires an inner realness that is, nonetheless, not a purely individual construct but an intersubjectively fabricated one.

At the end I will elucidate the broad theoretical perspective that runs through my ethnography – even though my hope is that the ethnographic case presented may be thick enough to allow for alternative readings. I will argue that learning religion (or, more accurately, acquiring spiritual knowledge *lato sensu*) is a process through which capturing ideas and being moved by them always walk together. Spiritual knowledge is not a purely referential kind of knowledge, because referents are pointless without a sense of self-connectedness to them. Learning spiritual ideas and to be moved by them may occur either in a progressive or in a more or less sudden way. It may either be a gradual process that subtly develops from childhood throughout socialization, or may take the form of a revelation. In both cases it is a social process, implying the sharing of experiences with others, and not a purely individual one.

This theoretical framework for understanding spiritual knowledge diverges fundamentally from *hard* naturalistic and cognitivist anthropological approaches (e.g. Boyer 1994, 2001b; Boyer and Walker 2000; Lawson and McCauley 1990). The dominant trend in these studies is to focus solely on religious ideas, detaching them from the sociocultural environments in which they are embedded and from the experiences that go along with them, and to try to demonstrate, such as Boyer does, how their respective content and organization 'depend, in important ways, on noncultural properties of the human mind-brain' (1994: 3). According to Boyer, that which characterizes religious representations is their counterintuitive character (the fact that they violate intuitive expectations that inform daily cognition) together with the fact that reality is attributed to them. The combination of counterintuition and realness gives religious representations a cognitive salience that is the key to their success in cultural transmission:

> the idea of spirits being in several places at once would *not* be counterintuitive, if there was not a stable expectation that agents are solid objects and that solid objects occupy a unique point in space. In the same way, the notion of statues that listen to one's prayers is attention-grabbing only against a background of expectations about artefacts, including the assumption that they do *not* have mental capacities (Boyer and Walker 2000: 135; authors' italics).

This is an attractive theory and seems generically plausible. But explaining the success of retaining or transmitting spiritual or religious notions according to the cognitive salience of their elements independently of the sociocultural worlds where they exist is not a satisfying exercise for me. This for the simple reason that it is an explanation that fails to explain such things as the cultural diversity of spiritual ideas and why certain of them are particularly catching to some social groups while being indifferent to others. Further, it does not contemplate the non-representational aspects of spiritual knowledge. I want to put into practice here an anthropology that addresses issues such as these. The object of this anthropology is the embedding of material and ideal things in people's living and in the historical processes that frame their living, while the object of hard cognitivist anthropology is the universal properties of the human mind-brain.

Christian Rationalism in Cape Verde

Christian Rationalism is a spiritualist doctrine from Brazil with a great many followers in Cape Verde.[2] It is firmly rooted in the islands of São Vicente (where it arrived in 1911) and Boa Vista, and has followers as well on four other islands. The main activities at Christian Rationalist centres are the 'séances of psychic cleansing', which are free of charge and open to the public. The séances take place on Mondays, Wednesdays and Fridays at 8pm. As soon as the clock on the wall begins to strike the hour, the doors close, the room darkens, bells ring and everyone looks at the group seated around a large rectangular table. At its head sits the 'president' and at the opposite end sits the 'respondent', whose role is to pronounce at certain moments an invocation called 'irradiation' to the 'Great Focus', the Creating Force of the universe. The mediums sit on both sides of the table, together with other 'militants' called the 'supports'.[3] There are also two chairs at the foot of the table which are reserved for sick people suffering from 'psychic disorders' that the president judges especially serious. In Christian Rationalist vocabulary, 'psychic' is synonymous with 'spiritual'.

In purpose-built centres, the table is on a raised level. Those attending sit on rows of long benches on the lower level, men on the left and women, always in far larger numbers, on the right. The spatial separation between the people who carry out the psychic works on the plateau around the table and the people who sit on the lower level roughly corresponds to a social divide. The latter come chiefly from the poorer classes, while the former are typically members of the petite bourgeoisie – shopkeepers, businessmen, skilled workers, civil servants, schoolteachers, nurses, doctors, housewives. Of course, things are not as clear cut as this. Furthermore, there are variations in social composition among the centres.

The séances last about one hour and are divided into two parts. First, the mediums incorporate the 'inferior' or 'backward spirits' that arrive clinging to people to whom they have been instilling morbid

thoughts and inciting to depraved behaviour. These spirits never identify themselves but often disclose that they belong to 'phalanges' under
the command of sorcerers. The 'higher spiritism' of Christian Rationalist centres thus bears out the realness of the 'lower spiritism' of
witchcraft and 'black magic'. The president talks with the inferior spirits in teacherlike tones and explains that it is out of ignorance that
they remain in Earth's atmosphere doing evil instead of ascending to
the astral plane where they should be waiting for their next incarnation. These conversations are invariably convincing. Resigned and
enlightened, the troubling spirits are then dispatched to their worlds
thus improving the lives of those they had been harassing. Christian
Rationalists say that their centres are schools. Students are the backward spirits along with the 'less enlightened' people seated on the rows
of benches. Teachers are the president of the table and what are
known as the 'superior spirits', who intervene during the second part
of the séance and give doctrinal talks. Included among them are very
distinguished spirits of deceased Cape Verdeans regardless of whether
they sympathized or not with the doctrine, as well as a number of spirits of people who were outstanding members of the movement during
their lifetime either in Brazil, Cape Verde or elsewhere.

The founder of Christian Rationalism was Luiz de Mattos, a Portuguese who emigrated very young to Brazil and became an affluent
businessman in the town of Santos in the 1880s. In 1910, at the age
of fifty, Luiz de Mattos began to attend a Spiritist Centre in Santos after
he had a heart attack that had left him greatly shaken. He soon
became the president of this centre. During the second half of the
nineteenth century, Spiritism, a doctrine codified by the French edu-
cator Allan Kardec in the 1850s, gained huge popularity among the
middle classes in the urban centres of Brazil, especially in the Southeast states. It was a new doctrine about life beyond the material. It
claimed to have a scientific basis and spoke of reincarnation as a
mechanism for spiritual evolution, of the plurality of inhabited worlds
and the reciprocal influence between disembodied spirits and human
beings. Spiritism also grew very popular because of the cures it offered.

Eventually, Luiz de Mattos disagreed with the head of the Brazilian
Spiritist Federation and started work on his own variation of Spiritism,
which he first called Christian Rational and Scientific Spiritism. The
main office of this new movement, the Centro Redentor of Rio de
Janeiro, was opened on Christmas Day 1912. The first doctrinal book
appeared two years later. Luiz de Mattos' Spiritism gradually moved
away from Kardecism, removing all references to the Gospels and the
Virgin Mary and giving less importance to charity while developing his
own terminology and his own procedure for spiritual works. The term
'Christian Rationalism' was first used in 1925, a year before Luiz de

Mattos died, but was only to become the official name of the doctrine and the movement in the 1940s.

Christian Rational and Scientific Spiritism came to Cape Verde in 1911, brought by Augusto Messias de Burgo (alias Maninho de Burgo), a Cape Verdean who lived by then most of his time in Brazil and worked as a medium at Luiz de Mattos' centre. However, the person primarily responsible for implanting the movement in Cape Verde was Henrique Morazzo, a naval constructor of Italian descent. Morazzo joined Spiritism when he was very young after Maninho de Burgo cured him of tuberculosis during one of the medium's visits to his homeland. He travelled to Rio de Janeiro two or three times between 1917 and 1919 in order to meet Luiz de Mattos and take part in psychic cleansing works that were carried out at the Centro Redentor. In 1927 he managed to persuade the government of the Cape Verde province to authorize a centre which he had set up in Mindelo, capital of São Vicente. Five years later, at the onset of Salazar's dictatorship, a new governor decided to have the Centro Caridade e Amor closed, alleging that séances could cause children mental disturbances and were likely places for contagious diseases to spread. Despite this, Morazzo and a number of followers carried on organizing spiritist séances in the homes of fellow sympathizers and in Morazzo's own home towards the end of his life.

The Centro Redentor of Rio de Janeiro cut relations with Morazzo in the 1920s due to complaints about his being a womanizer. Morazzo continued with séances on his own account, but the official link between the São Vicente spiritists and the movement's main office in Brazil from 1934 onwards was the primary school teacher João Miranda, who organized a centre in his house. In 1960 Miranda retired and left for Portugal. Morazzo died in 1967. Their followers maintained the practice of psychic cleansing and kept on circulating Christian Rationalist literature. Between 1960 and 1974 they had to live with the political police surveillance and recurring denouncements made by the local priest to the civil authorities. Séances were conducted in secret and on an irregular basis. With national independence, Christian Rationalism came out of clandestinity.

Christian Rationalism expanded only modestly in Brazil, remaining hardly noticeable against the luxuriant background of the country's religious and spiritualist movements. In contrast, it spread very quickly in Cape Verde where there were 23 centres in 2001. Moreover, the spreading of Christian Rationalism outside Brazil has been almost exclusively due to Cape Verdeans. They have taken the doctrine with them to countries in Africa, Europe and North America where they emigrated. About 90 per cent of the letters to the Centro Redentor of Rio de Janeiro asking for advice and information are sent by Cape

Verdeans from all over the world. Hence, outside Brazil Christian Rationalism has almost become a Cape Verdean movement.

Christian Rationalist Cosmology and Ontology

According to Christian Rationalist doctrine, the universe is built on two basic elements: 'Force' or 'Universal Intelligence', which is active, and 'Matter', which is passive. Life as we know it results from the action of Force over Matter. Human beings are made up of a 'body' (an assemblage of material elements), 'spirit' (a particle of the Universal Intelligence) and 'perispirit' (the 'ethereal double' of the physical body to which it is linked by 'fluidic chords' and animated by the spirit's 'vibrations'). Spirits, when discarnate, inhabit 33 'astral worlds' or 'planes' according to their level of evolution. Spirits evolve from the first to the thirty-third plane through successive incarnations on physical bodies. Apart from exceptional cases, only those that are between the first and seventeenth worlds incarnate as human beings on Earth; from then onwards incarnations take place on other more 'diaphanous' planets. Evolution is a universal law; a spirit never retrogrades although the evolutionary process can be slower or faster according to how each spirit lived its life while incarnate. The worst that can happen is that a spirit may 'miss out' an incarnation – that is to say, disincarnate without having advanced even one step along the path.

The less evolved a spirit is, the more 'materialized' it is, with the result that when it disincarnates it often is too weighty to ascend to the astral world where it should wait for the following incarnation and remains in the Earth's atmosphere instead. Disincarnate spirits in this situation form what is known as the 'Inferior Astral' world. Spirits on the Inferior Astral act upon human beings and much of the evil man suffers or inflicts on others is due to them. 'Obsession' is the generic name for the bad influence the inferior spirits exercise on human beings, and it can appear in different degrees and forms, ranging from manias, phobias, eccentric behaviour and apathy to madness. An upright life regulated by the moral code as transmitted by Christian Rationalism is the path an incarnate spirit should take in order to evolve more quickly. It is also the most effective albeit not infallible way to avoid obsession. This is because of the universal law according to which like attracts like and opposites repel opposites: people who lead immoral lives attract the 'miasmas' of obsessing spirits who exacerbate their immorality; people leading upright lives attract the beneficial 'effluvia' of more evolved sprits that reinforce their uprightness and shelter them from the influence of the Inferior Astral. These higher spirits, also known as 'diaphanous spirits' or 'spirits of light' according to their level of evolution, form the 'Superior Astral' world.

The public séances of psychic cleansing that take place in Christian Rationalist centres are aimed at attracting the forces of the Superior Astral and channelling them to find solutions to problems affecting people present at the centre as well as those absent. As mentioned above, séances also seek to conduct to their respective astral worlds inferior spirits who on disincarnating have remained on Earth tormenting the living. Inferior and superior spirits manifest themselves at séances through 'incorporation mediums'. They are given this name because they are able to allow spirits to temporarily inhabit their bodies. Incorporation mediums are also called 'instruments', and are compared to telegraphic devices or radio receptors.

Instruments are always women in São Vicente. Seated around the large rectangular table, the mediums learn to externalize the 'vibrations' of spirits that act through them only by means of words and repress other forms of bodily manifestation. They also learn how to keep their own spirit in a state of semi-consciousness so that they can be in command of the alien spirit that temporarily cohabits their body when, if it is a coarse spirit, it tries to use bad language or manifest itself by means of gestures, for instance. This apprenticeship is for the most part acquired by reading, observing experienced mediums at work and attending occasional meetings with the centre's president and mediums. When sporadically a medium loses control of the manifestation because of her lack of experience or concentration or else because the spirit acting upon her at the time is especially violent, the president immediately ends the communication.

For Christian Rationalists, mediumship generally speaking does not necessarily mean what anthropologists usually call spirit possession. One can be 'intuited' by spirits without being acted upon by them. But even when someone's behaviour is understood to be the result of direct spirit agency, Christian Rationalists avoid using the word 'possession'. The reason for this is that in the Christian cultural tradition, in which Christian Rationalism is embedded, 'possession' immediately calls to mind the idea of demonic takeover (see Kramer 1993 [1987]: 60). It happens that Christian Rationalists reject the existence of the devil, as they reject the existence of Heaven and Hell. This is why they prefer to say that people are 'acted upon' by spirits, good or evil, rather than possessed. Here I will adopt their terminology, not only to be faithful to native categories, but also because the idea of being acted upon accurately describes what is at stake. Being acted upon implies losing one's agency (either completely or partially, and either in a deliberate or involuntary way) and handing it over to spirits.

Learning Mediumship

Mediums who worked at the seven Christian Rationalist centres on São Vicente were all women and generally middle-aged. In the past, until the 1940s or so, some men had also been mediums, but even then they were always few in number and from that time onwards the séance presidents have not allowed men to develop incorporation mediumship at their centres. It so happens that a large number of women that manifest signs of mediumnic faculty (they have visions, hear voices and experience other perturbations that they and others close to them interpret as signs of spirits' agency) begin to reveal them as a result of conjugal crises. It also happens that most mediums at Christian Rationalist centres are middle-class women who, following these crises, begin to attend séances (or attend them more regularly) and show that they are willing to develop this faculty as instruments in the service of the Superior Astral.

When I showed my interest in speaking with mediums, I immediately faced an obstacle. According to the regulations as set down by the Centro Redentor of Rio de Janeiro which must be kept to by all the centres in the world, mediums are forbidden from speaking about their faculty outside the centres.[4] Mediums should read doctrinal books and listen carefully to colleagues when they manifest spirits and presidents when they talk on doctrine. This is enough for their thoughts to tune in and know what to do when the moment comes and they are acted upon by a spirit. Too much cogitation or talk on the mechanisms of mediumship could lead to the medium thoughts interfering with the spirits' manifestations or even simulating them. Worse than that, it could even make the mediums doubtful about their faculty.

In order to circumvent the regulation that forbids instruments from speaking about their gift, I was advised by one of the presidents to look for former mediums who were no longer active because of age or other circumstances and eventually I came to have a close relationship with three with whom I spoke several times and formally interviewed. They had all worked in Christian Rationalist centres for many years and they all continued to follow the doctrine and attend séances. I will now concentrate on one of them and her story, focusing on the circumstances that led to her becoming a medium.[5]

When I met Dona Cândida in 2001 she was sixty-four years old although she looked a lot less. She was careful and discreet in dress and usually wore a blouse and a skirt that went below her knees. She had her long dark hair always pulled back. Dona Cândida owned a hairdressers in a middle-class neighbourhood. Like so many other people in São Vicente, Cândida was born on the neighbouring island of Santo Antão. Cândida's family was relatively well-off. Her father had several properties in Ribeira de Paul and also worked as a solicitor. Daughter of respectable people, Cândida was brought up by an aunt in Ribeira Grande, the small capital of Santo Antão. She received her first communion there when she was six, she attended primary school, went to catechism every Sunday, sang in the choir and learned to embroider and cross-stitch with Miss Felismina, the priest's sister. Her dream and destiny was to be wife, mother and housewife.

Cândida had never shown an interest in spiritism at that time. It was not that she did not know about it. The subject was often spoken about but always with a certain reserve. To speak a lot about spirits, especially low spirits, might attract them. Henrique Morazzo's centre had been operating on a regular basis since the end of the 1910s, and many people who lived in Santo Antão would, when in great distress, take the boat to the neighbouring island for psychic cleansing with Nhô Henrique. A close relative of Cândida's once went there for a treatment and had a few books published by the Centro Redentor of Rio de Janeiro in her house. In 1947, when Cândida was ten years old, Lela Martins, a farm-owner from Vale do Paul, opened the first Christian Rationalist Centre in Santo Antão. Consequently, Cândida had been familiar since childhood with the existence of spirits, Christian Rationalist literature (especially *Life Beyond the Material* [*A Vida Fora da Matéria*], an educational book with dozens of illustrations of all kinds of *psychic* phenomena) and recourse to psychic cleansing séances in the case of spiritual harassment.

At the age of twenty-one, Cândida got married and went to live in São Vicente with her husband. He was a sailor and his three-year-old son by another woman came to live with them. They had a romantic attachment for a while but it did not last long. Cândida's husband returned to his old ways. When he was not at sea, he would spend his time on the island out drinking all night with his friends and return home in a sorry state and stinking of rum. Cândida began to suffer with all this. She also began to suspect there were other women. And it was in the midst of this suffering that Christian Rationalism arrived. At least, this is the account she gave me of the circumstances that led her to enter a spiritist centre for the first time.

> I came to Christian Rationalism rather subtly. One evening my husband went out at night and came back in the early hours. He knocked at the door for he hadn't taken the keys. He knocked and I got up, like half ... between waking and sleeping. I went to open the door. Then, I was suddenly acted upon. I mean, I became ... When I tried to call out my husband's name, I saw a phenomenon in him. With him there was a group of people whose faces I didn't know. I saw them, but they weren't people I could identify. When I opened my mouth to ask him why he had come home with these people, my tongue was acted upon, my tongue was tied in my mouth. I

couldn't utter a single word. I then fainted and fell down on the floor. I was pregnant of my first child. I was at the time twenty-two years old and a bit.

He picked me up from the floor, lay me on the bed and began to call my name. I couldn't do it, I couldn't come ... He then shouted out to a neighbour and told her to help me, that I was in great distress. He shouted from my door to her door, because our doors were that close. So, I was acted upon during that morning. I wanted to sleep but I couldn't. Whenever I was about to fall asleep, I would get frightened and called out for my husband. I mean, in my subconscious I wanted to call him. But he didn't reply because I couldn't manage to get the words out, my tongue was tied in my mouth.

So, the next day he took me to Senhor João Miranda, who was the president of a centre, and carried out séances. [...] He took me there, at night. They did the cleansing. Then, at the end of the séance, I went back home, normal. I started to attend during the end of my pregnancy, until my son was born. Then, when he was born, I stopped going to the centre.

Cândida came to Christian Rationalism as a patient with severe manifestations of what she herself and those close to her understood as a psychic or spiritual disturbance. In her story, Cândida herself associated the appearance of the first signs of an awakened mediumnic faculty with a prolonged period of conjugal anxiety. The most common reason for a first visit to a spiritist centre is to find relief for incapaciting acute or chronic conditions of physical or psychic discomfort that are believed to have a spiritual origin. People do not first come to a Christian Rationalist centre in a state of ignorance. They know that there are evil spirits about ready to take advantage of people's weaknesses, they know that people can be intuited or even acted upon by them and lose control of themselves, and they know that when this happens, they had better go and seek help in a spiritist centre. What they still do not have is that 'knowledge all made out of experience' (to use Camões' famous phrase) that some of them come to acquire. That sense of revelation, of intimate certainty, which is usually called belief only springs when getting ideas about spiritual entities and being moved by them come together.

After the birth of her first child, Cândida stopped going to João Miranda's centre. This is what most women do during their first months of motherhood. A year later, her husband went back to sea and she remained in São Vicente taking care of her son and step-son, and living off the money he sent them. After a few months, her step-son, who was five years old at the time, 'began to get agitated and distressed. He said he could see people at the end of the house, and that someone was calling him to join him or her'. One of Cândida's sisters advised her to start attending séances again as she was convinced that the boy's visions were provoked by lower spirits. At that time, Miranda had just closed his centre and had left for Lisbon. Cândida then began to attend Morazzo's séances.

Despite the clandestine nature of spiritist meetings by that time, Cândida regularly attended Morazzo's centre for five years together with her step-son. The boy's fears gradually faded away. At the end of 1965, Morazzo suffered a thrombosis and stopped having séances at home. At that time, about two thousand people out of a population of twenty-five thousand regularly attended his centre. Cândida then ceased going there. Morazzo's closest companions dispersed and each of them gave short psychic cleansing séances in their homes or in places lent by sympathizers. Cândida also kept on doing her own psychic cleansing at home with her children, who by this time were four. Every evening at eight o'clock, they would get together around the parlour table, and Cândida would say out loud for five minutes the irradiation to the Great Focus she already knew by heart. Her husband continued to work on a Dutch ship and spend half the time on the island and the other half away at sea.

At the start of the 1970s, twelve years after she had first gone to João Miranda's centre as a patient, 33-year-old Cândida had become increasingly interested in Christian Rationalism. She found in that 'science' not only a doctrinal system that gave meaning to the various 'psychic' experiences that regularly troubled her, such as visions and nightmares, but also a moral system that bolstered her decision to remain married despite her husband's philandering, which caused her so much suffering.

At this time, Cândida began to work as a 'checker' at the centre of Mário Mimoso, a shopkeeper born in Santo Antão and a former member of Morazzo's group. She was having nightmares all the time.

> It very often seemed I was about to drown at sea and afterwards I would wake up with a start. Very often it seemed in the dream that I was pushed off a rock and there I'd go rolling down that rock. When I'd get to the foot of the mountain, I'd wake up exhausted. Then, there would be some cattle running after me, a number of them would chase after me and I'd zigzag my way and I'd move away just as they were about to get to me, and the creature would go one way and I another.

Cândida wrote about these dreams to the Centro Redentor of Rio de Janeiro. She received a letter back saying that she obviously possessed a strong mediumnic faculty and that she should make it known to the president of the centre so that he could sit her down at the table in order to develop her mediumship properly. Cândida's younger boy, however, was still only six months old. He could not be left at home with his siblings while she went to the séances at the end of the day. So she kept the letter. A year later, as these dreams continued to trouble her, Cândida took the letter and showed it to Mário Mimoso. The president sat her down at the table, on the fourth chair, which is for developing mediums, and a few days later Cândida began to exhibit manifestations.

> It would happen ... I mean ... I felt I couldn't move my hands, they remained motionless on top of the table. I seemed frozen. My whole body was tied down and I'd just utter whatever came to my head. And I'd say things that were not anything that had gone through my mind. I could neither see nor feel nor anything else. And I'd just stay there, I had already begun to receive when my turn came. I mean, the person there had already transmitted, the second was receiving and about to transmit and when it is my turn, I would transmit. But during that work, my hands seemed to be made of ice. They were cold, swollen, it seemed I had swollen hands, that I couldn't close my hands, neither open nor close them. At the end of the séance, they [the checkers] would shake people and then they would become normal.

Cândida worked as a medium for over twenty years, first with Mimoso and then in another centre in town. When she opened her hairdressing salon, her schedule was no longer compatible with her work as a medium. She continues to attend séances but gets there at the last minute and does not have the time a medium needs to prepare herself. During our conversations, she always insisted on the feeling of serenity with which she leaves the séances and the good they do to so many people who arrive at the centres truly obsessed, demented.

Class, Gender and Christian Rationalist Morality

Mediumship at Christian Rationalist centres is not open to any woman. Christian Rationalist rules recommend that only literate women should be trained as mediums, although there are exceptions. At séances, mediums externalize the spirits that inhabit their bodies through their words. They must have good control of language and speak properly otherwise they could sound silly and ridiculous and bring public discredit to themselves and Christian Rationalism. This is consequently a restriction for many women whose mediumnic sensibility is acknowledged by the presidents but lack the necessary education to access mediumship. In Cape Verde, where Portuguese is the official language and the one spoken at formal events, including religious services and spiritist séances, a great emphasis is put on the mediums' ability to speak Portuguese fluently. In social terms, this means that lower class women, most of whom are solely proficient in Creole, are in general excluded from careers in mediumship.[6]

In addition to speaking Portuguese fluently, women who aspire to be mediums should be calm and serene, have few material worries and lead a modest life. Christian Rationalists say that in order to be a proper medium, a woman should be married; if not, she must at least like to stay at home and do domestic chores (*se não for casada, que seja caseira*). Together with the necessary command of the Portuguese language, these conditions narrow even further the range of candidates. Young girls do not generally fill the requirements nor have the desire to develop as proper mediums even if they feel they have or are said to possess that gift. Women in their twenties and early thirties are usually too busy having babies and raising them. Women with full-time jobs as well as families to take care of do not have the time and cannot free themselves from everyday concerns. Old women, on the other hand, often lack the health to attend the séances on a daily basis as required.[7] Therefore it is no surprise that most mediums are women in their 40s and 50s – either widowed or single or, much more commonly, housewives without a job or else with light or part-time occupations and children old enough not to need them too much.

These rather matter-of-fact circumstances relating to literacy, gender patterns and women's life cycle prevalent in São Vicente partially explain the narrow class and age range of most women who develop as mediums at Christian Rationalist centres. But, important as they are, practical issues are not all that is at stake here. In addition to a cosmology and an ontology, Christian Rationalist literature conveys a set of morals. And it happens that many of these fit like a glove the ethos of middle-class women. They intimately echo their life experiences, concerns and expectations. We could say that Christian Rationalist morality comprehends a number of ideas that are very likely to be connected by middle-class women with their own lives. If this connectedness is achieved, referential images and notions become experientially real as well.

What kind of referents and morality am I speaking of? I will concentrate here solely on those moral stances that have to do with family and gender relations, and more specifically with a certain ideal of womanhood. We can take as an illustration of this ideal the following passages from the basic book of Christian Rationalism: 'As a rule, if the spirit incarnates as a woman, its aim is motherhood. [...] The maternal instinct arises in women in the dawn of infancy. To be a mother – devoted to her mission with body and soul – is the noblest accomplishment of a woman on Earth' (Centro Redentor 1986: 164-65).

Many Christian Rationalist publications emphasize women's natural vocation as devoted mothers and wives. Maria Cottas, the deceased wife of António Cottas, the former president of Centro Redentor, published a number of chronicles in the centre's monthly newspaper *A Razão* (*Reason*), many of which were reprinted in widely read edificatory books. Maria Cottas wrote on correct behaviour for women; how, for instance, they should act and dress with modesty and resign themselves to the fact that their husbands will succumb to material vices typical to men – such as quarrelling, losing their tempers and womanizing. Women must be strong enough to close their eyes to their partners' disgraceful behaviour or gently call them to reason. They must act as real ladies, even if their companions do not treat them as such. They must never forget that they were born to be the anchors of their families.

Not all Cape Verdean mediums' life histories are like Cândida's. However, in the many accounts I heard of mediums and their lives, the awakening of a mediumnic faculty is frequently linked to marital crises. This is no surprise for those who are familiar with the anthropological literature about spirit possession. According to Lewis's classic study, the prime targets of malign spirits are usually married women: 'the stock epidemiological situation is that of the hard-pressed wife, struggling to survive and feed her children in this harsh environment, and liable to some degree of neglect, real or imagined, on the part of her husband' (Lewis 1989: 67). In several societies, spirit possession is incorporated in women's cults that usually have a peripheral character from the dominant male point of view.

Lewis contrasts these 'peripheral possession cults', which are in the hands of women and some outcast men, with 'central morality cults', 'where possession is a precondition for the full exercise of the religious vocation' and 'those selected by the deities are typically men' (1989: 158). Spirits that possess men in central cults are themselves central moral deities, while spirits that possess women in peripheral cults are usually marginal amoral beings. Between these two extreme poles, Lewis acknowledges the existence of an intermediary kind of cults that he characterizes as follows: 'where an established male priesthood, which does not depend upon ecstatic illumination for its authority, controls the central morality cult, women and men of subordinate social categories may be allowed a limited franchise as inspired auxiliaries' (1989: 159).

This is roughly what happens at Christian Rationalist séances. The presidents are for the most part men, while the mediums are always women. As in the case of the Welsh spiritualist circles studied by Skultans (1974), although in a slightly different scenario, men take an active role as educators and healers, while women act more passively as 'instruments' and let themselves be 'acted upon'. Their participation in the séances is absolutely necessary: without them, spirits could not come and manifest themselves. But during most of the séance, while the mediums transmit the words of inferior spirits, it is the president who takes command of the operations. In addition to the morality transmitted in Christian Rationalist literature, the actual performance of psychic cleansing puts into practice the male's role of command and the female's role of submission. Christian Rationalist séances thus enact middle-class male and female roles as ideally conceived.

Of course, things are not this straightforward from a woman's point of view. Those who work as mediums derive great satisfaction from it and achieve a sense of fulfilment that both Cândida and the other ex-mediums I interviewed always mentioned. Mediumship strengthens their conviction that adhering to the ideal of middle-class womanhood is the correct choice, the right and proper path to take, and gives them a sense of moral superiority over men – starting off with their own menfolk.[8]

Concluding Remarks on Spiritual Knowledge

> If you say: 'I can imagine myself being a disembodied spirit. Wittgenstein, can you imagine yourself as a disembodied spirit?' – I'd say: 'I'm sorry. I [so far] connect nothing with these words.'
>
> I connect all sorts of complicated things with these words. (Wittgenstein 1966: 65)

During my fieldwork in São Vicente, I often found myself in the awkward position that Wittgenstein writes of in this passage. I used to go to psychic cleansing séances once a week and nearly every day I would talk with other attenders and Christian Rationalist militants. The inevitable question came every now and again: 'Do you really believe in that science?' Whether the question was phrased in these words or in a more roundabout manner, what people wanted to know was if I could *really figure* the spiritual phenomena whose bodily and verbal exteriorization I observed at the séances. That is to say, if I could figure them as real.

My answer then was always the same, and continues the same even after these years. I would say that I was studying Christian Rationalism, that I read carefully and had an understanding of the books, that I also grasped, at least up to a point, what so many people meant when they patiently recounted cases of spiritual influence they had experienced or witnessed. But I could not honestly say that I believed in that science or even in the objective reality of spirits. First, I could not uncritically accept the label of 'science' that Christian Rationalists gave their doctrine and its practices. But this was a minor problem – and an issue I will not discuss here.[9] The main problem (my problem, I must emphasize) is that I could not relate myself meaningfully with Christian Rationalist literature, nor with the personal or second-hand accounts of spiritual phenomena that meant to confirm it. I was unable to bring these things into my life. They did not affect my life in the way I was to learn they affected the lives of so many other people.

In Wittgenstein's terms, I could only connect what I heard and saw at spiritist séances with all sorts of complicated things. I associated the problems that were described by the spirits of the Inferior Astral with the lives of the people seated on the centre's long benches – but not with mine. I associated the description of how a man was rescued after clinging to a half-submerged tree during the terrible Mozambican floods in February 2000, a rescue carried out by the spirits of mediums at a centre during a special séance of 'spirit doubling', with images shown the day before on television.[10] I associated the manifestation of the superior spirit of Baptista de Sousa, who came down at the end of a séance to give his doctrinal lecture, with the social memories of this cherished doctor in São Vicente.

I was trained to understand human phenomena in sociological terms; that is to say, to connect them to those human constructs called society and culture, and not to those called spirits or divinity. I was thus basically sceptical about the truth of Christian Rationalism and spirits' existence in general – and I still am. But I also know through experience that, as Lewis wrote, 'scepticism clearly is not necessarily a full-time intellectual or emotional occupation. It is often simply a function of an individual's lack of direct involvement in particular circumstances' (1996: 20–21). By bringing together narratives of spiritual experiences such as those presented here with some anthropological and sociological literature, I came to the conclusion (a provisional one, like all conclusions) that all knowledge which I will call, in the absence of a better term, *spiritual knowledge*, has something in common.

I have a strong reason to prefer the expression *spiritual knowledge* to *religious knowledge*. The type of knowledge that I will try to describe pertains to religions themselves though not exclusively. It is also typical of magic, witchcraft and spiritual movements that do not define themselves as religious, such as Christian Rationalism. In any case, it is knowledge (1) that entails ideas concerning spiritual powers or entities and (2) also involves an important non-conceptual dimension. It is the properties of this non-conceptual dimension and how it links up with ideas relative to spiritual objects that I would like to briefly examine now.

I take as my starting point for this discussion Weber's ideas about 'religious experience'. Weber was not a religious man. But unlike modernist intellectuals who viewed this as emancipation, he considered his non-religiosity a handicap. He declared himself 'religiously unmusical'. Religious experience as such, he wrote,

> [...] is of course irrational, like every experience. In its highest, mystical form it is [...] distinguished by its absolute incommunicability. *It has a specific character and appears as knowledge, but cannot be adequately reproduced*

by means of our lingual and conceptual apparatus. It is further true that every religious experience loses some of its content in the attempts of rational formulation, the further the conceptual formulation goes, the more so (Weber 1930 [1920]: 233, n. 66; my italics).

He also wrote that 'all theology represents an intellectual *rationalisation* of the possession of sacred values', but that 'whoever does not "possess" faith, or the other holy states, cannot have theology as a substitute for them, least of all any other science' (1948 [1919]: 153–54; author's italics). In other words, there is something in spiritual knowledge that cannot be accounted for by means of conceptual formulation and rationalization. Weber did not know exactly what to call it. He called it 'faith', but he also wrote of it as 'possession', in the sense of possessed or embodied knowledge, distinct from conceptual knowledge. We can learn concepts and theories about spiritual forces and beings, but spiritual knowledge cannot be based *only* on this kind of learning, in the same way as learning ideas about meditation is not the same thing as learning to meditate (see Spickard 1993: 116).

Weber's acknowledgement of the non-representational dimension of religious experience can be approached in some aspects to many other non-intellectualist accounts of spiritual knowledge and its acquisition, starting with Lévy-Bruhl's (1998 [1949]) later writings on 'mystical knowledge', followed by Smith's (1991 [1962]) view of religion as an interplay between 'faith' and 'cumulative traditions', and more recently, by studies such as those by Favret-Saada (1977, 1990), Claverie (1990, 2003), Lambek (1993) and Stromberg (1993). The comprehension of spiritual influence certainly presumes concepts and representations, but is not reducible to them. You cannot be affected by that of which you have no concept.[11] But you can learn ideas about spirits and yet not learn how to put yourself in conditions to be affected by them.

Talking about affection, I am bringing into play Deleuze's outline of a theory of knowledge that postulates that concepts are not to be understood as simple ideas. They involve two further dimensions besides the properly 'conceptual' one: a 'perceptual' and an 'affectual' dimension. 'Percepts', as Deleuze defines them, are not mere perceptions, but 'packets of sensations and relations that survive those who experience them' (1990: 187). 'Affects', on the other hand, have an emotional quality. Deleuze defines them as 'becomings [*devenirs*] that overflow those who pass through them – who become other' (1990: 187). These three dimensions are not mutually exclusive, and they are all involved in any knowledge act. But the weight of each varies, and this variation may imply considerable differences between styles of knowledge. Following Goldman's reading of Deleuze, what Lévy-Bruhl called 'mystical experiences' refer to styles of knowledge in which 'affection' plays a major role (see Goldman 1994: 378).

A certain kind of incomprehension arises when we are unable to connect *our selves* with words we hear or actions we witness. We may then marvel at them, we may laugh at them, we may forget them and keep on walking. We may also make an effort to interpret them, start working out ways of giving them meaning, connecting them to all sorts of complicated things. On the other hand, there are words and actions that touch us deeply. Learning or relearning them makes us experience things in a new way – it is knowledge that affects us. Affection then becomes the very basis of its facticity. And could there be a firmer basis than our selves?

Affection, however, is not a purely subjective way of knowing. Our lives are lives of relationships. Knowledge in which affection plays a major role is intersubjectively constructed, like any other kind of knowledge; it is achieved through communication, by means of exchanging ideas and experiences. Claverie (1990, 2003) demonstrates this very well when she describes how the facticity of Our Lady (the sense of her effective existence and of her effective intervention in human affairs) is produced and strengthened through conversations and the sharing of spiritual experiences between pilgrims who go to the Bosnian sanctuary of Medjugorje, a site of recent Marian apparitions. For knowledge grounded on affection not to be pure delirium, there has to be both shared referents (e.g. 'Our Lady') and shared experiences of connectedness to them (e.g. 'She changed my life'). Returning to my own ethnography, both Cândida's and other mediums' accounts of how they learned proper mediumship at Christian Rationalist centres were elucidative as to the importance of talking about their experiences of being acted upon with presidents and fellow mediums. Together with the reading of some books, this partaking of experiences was critical in dissipating their doubts and strengthening their sense of participation in the spiritual works.

This can be related with Stromberg´s (1993) analysis of conversion narratives among Californian evangelical Christians. For Stromberg, the act of narrating one's religious conversion operates a transformation of a religious 'referential language' (evangelical doctrine and imagery) into a 'constitutive' one – a language that renders experiences of self-transformation meaningful to the person in question and to others. If I understand him properly, Stromberg's notion of the constitutive is akin to Deleuze's notion of affects as new ways of experiencing. In Deleuzian terms, we could say that when concept acquisition goes together with powerful affection, the experiential reality of concepts gets strengthened. This is also something Michael Lambek (1993) argues when he conceives every act of knowledge as a dialectical movement between two poles or moments, 'embodiment' and 'objectification'. 'Embodiment provides the ultimate ground for legitimating objective knowledge, rendering it experientially real and confirming its presence in and for the bearer or recipient. Objectification makes embodied knowledge graspable by others, loosening its attachment to the immediate crucible of its production and reinscribing it in the public domain' (1993: 307).

To conclude, then, and going back to our Cape Verdean ethnography, we could say that the content of Christian Rationalist objectified knowledge makes it particularly apt to become internalized knowledge by middle-class women, a knowledge rendered experientially real for them. Adopting Stromberg's terms, we could say that Christian Rationalism conveys a referential language whose themes and imagery are likely to awaken a sense of significance among those women, thus becoming a constitutive language for them that brings about a deep inner feeling of the realness of the doctrine.

Notes

1. This text derives from a doctoral thesis completed at the Institute of Social Sciences, University of Lisbon. Fieldwork and archival research were funded by the Portuguese Institute for International Scientific and Technological Co-operation (ICCTI) and the Foundation for Science and Technology (FCT). I am heartily grateful to David Berliner, Filipe Verde, João de Pina-Cabral, Luís Batalha, Ramon Sarró and Wilson Trajano Filho, whose careful reading and criticism encouraged me to improve and shorten previous versions. I am equally indebted to Carole Garton for her patience and proficiency in translating this text into English. Translations from citations originally in French and Portuguese are my responsibility.

2. The archipelago of Cape Verde is made up of nine inhabited islands in the Atlantic Ocean south of the Tropic of Cancer and about 600 kilometres off the west coast of Africa. These hitherto desert islands were absorbed into the Portuguese Crown in the early 1460s. They started being occupied by settlers from Portugal and slaves brought from Senegambia and over time evolved into a Creole society. Cape Verde was a Portuguese colony for five hundred years. It became an independent country in the aftermath of the April 25 Revolution in 1974 which brought to an end forty years of dictatorship in Portugal, twelve years of colonial war and the Portuguese African Empire. A population of about 430,000 live in the archipelago nowadays, a number that is close to that of the Cape Verdean diaspora.

3. 'Militants' (*militantes*) is the name given to the more committed followers of the doctrine, those who participate actively in the spiritual works or contribute with a monthly fee to their centres as associate members. 'Supports' (*esteios*) are given this name because their task consists in upholding the energy of the Superior Forces during the séances by concentrating their thoughts on them.

4. See for instance Centro Redentor (1989: 110). Mediums are also prohibited from exercising their faculty outside the centre.

5. In order to protect this woman's privacy, her name is fictitious.

6. The coexistence of the Creole and Portuguese languages in contemporary Cape Verde, and the use of the latter by spirits both at Christian Rationalist séances and

in unexpected episodes of spirit possession are discussed at some length in Vasconcelos (2005).

7. In addition to the public séances of psychic cleansing held on Mondays, Wednesdays and Fridays, the mediums must also participate in the private séances of 'spirit doubling' taking place on Tuesdays and Thursdays.

8. For a similar conclusion in a very different cultural context see Lambek (1993: 334).

9. I discuss this question and historically contextualize the scientific claims of Spiritism in Vasconcelos (2003).

10. The 'private séances of psychic doubling' take place on Tuesdays and Thursdays at 8pm. Participation in these séances is restricted to the staff of the centre. I was able to attend three of these séances as a guest.

11. I am, of course, speaking of being affected as a cognitive act, and not as the (perceived or ignored) effect on a subject of some cause external to him. In this second, objectivist sense, it has been proved that we can be affected by things of which we do not hold the concepts (such as viruses, gravity or radiation) and it has not been proved that we can be affected by some other things we conceive (such as the grace of God or evil eye).

Chapter 9

COPYRIGHT AND AUTHORSHIP
RITUAL SPEECH AND THE NEW MARKET OF WORDS IN TORAJA

Aurora Donzelli

Introduction

During the last one hundred years, the religious life of the Toraja high-landers of South Sulawesi (Indonesia) has undergone a considerable process of transformation.[1] Conversion to Christianity, which started at the beginning of the twentieth century with the arrival in the high-lands of the Calvinist missionaries from the Dutch Reformed Alliance, engendered important changes in Toraja ritual practices and in their symbolic meanings. The process of religious and socio-cultural change relating to colonial penetration and missionization unfolded through a series of radical fractures and enduring continuities. As I have more thoroughly described elsewhere (Donzelli 2003, 2004), the encounter between the Dutch missionaries and the highlanders resulted in multiple reciprocal processes of mimesis endowed with different degrees of reflexivity.[2] Hence, on the one hand, the Toraja transformed their ritual practices of buffalo slaughtering and meat distribution in order to make them fit into the Calvinist (and capitalistic) ethic endorsed by the Dutch missionaries; on the other hand, the Dutch moulded their attempts at proselytizing on the local system of practices and beliefs. Thus, in spite of the gradual – and yet inexorable – process of conversion to Christianity, the 'traditional' system of religious practices and rituals deeply pervades the contemporary Christian liturgy, resulting in locally differentiated and hybrid forms of orthopraxis.

How did this process of 'crossed mimesis' (Pemberton 1994), triggered by the colonial encounter, intermingle with changes in the forms
of religious learning? In the following pages, I will try to answer this
question and to address the broader issue of the shifts in the transmission of religious knowledge, grounding my discussion on the ethnographic analysis of a narrower and more specific topic, namely, the
locally shared ideas about how ritual speech is learnt.[3] As we shall see,
the focus of this chapter lies at the intersection between the multiple
fractures and continuities that – during the last one hundred years –
have been underlying the transmission of religious knowledge and
practice among the inhabitants of the Toraja uplands. While the core
of the local aesthetic notions concerning ritual speech has remained
largely unchanged throughout the process of religious transformation, the way of representing the transmission of linguistic competence from older to younger generations of ritual spokesmen seems to
be undergoing an interesting metamorphosis: competence in ritual
speech is increasingly described not as a naturally acquired gift, but as
the outcome of an intentional and self-conscious learning process.

As I will argue, these new ways of portraying the process through
which speechmakers acquire their verbal expertise are deeply related
to the process of monetization of the local ritual economy, which
started at the beginning of the twentieth century with the introduction, in both mortuary and fertility rituals, of fund-raising auctions
and microcredit associations connected to traditional animal slaughtering and meat distribution. The economic and symbolic changes produced by these new monetary institutions and grass-root capitalist
organizations laid the groundwork for the introduction of monetary
compensations for ritual speechmakers, which led to a gradual process
of professionalization of the traditional ritual specialists. The following
pages are devoted to analysing the relevance of these processes for the
development a new form of reflexivity within the Toraja discourse on
ritual speech apprenticeship.

Local Ideas on the Role of Intentions in Teaching and
Learning Ritual Speech

Notwithstanding the vast ethnographic literature devoted to ritual
speech and to the study of its changes in the light of missionization
and religious conversion within the Indonesian archipelago (George
1990; Keane 1997b; Kuipers 1998; Siregar 1979), little attention has
so far been paid to a systematic analysis of how the process of learning
ritual registers is represented and discussed by the local speakers. In
fact, as I will try to demonstrate, the discourses on ritual speech

apprenticeship deserve deeper investigation. As will become apparent in the following pages, speakers' beliefs about the process of learning ritual language can enrich our understanding of the social and historical world they inhabit, as well as shed light on the process of religious change and on the related shifts in cultural transmission.

Becoming a religious specialist in Toraja entails acquiring competence in a highly formulaic and densely metaphoric ritual register, which is locally referred to as *kada kada to dolo* ('words of the ancestors'), *basa tominaa* ('language of the tominaa') or *kada kada tominaa* ('words of the tominaa'), after the name of the ritual specialist and spokesman, the 'tominaa', which in the Toraja language literally means 'the one who is wise and knowledgeable'. Toraja ritual speech, like elsewhere in eastern Indonesia (see Fox 1988; Keane 1997a; Kuipers 1990, 1993), is constituted by predetermined sets of paired elements.[4] The ritual spokesmen's ability thus consists of drawing on fixed and pre-existing sets of couplets and combining them in verbal performances in which the respect of genre conventions intersects with their capacity of improvisation. Ritual couplets are believed to have been handed down by the ancestors and to be thus endowed with an unchanging nature.

The conventional and formulaic structure of ritual couplets, together with the idea of their ancestral origins, constitutes the ideological and practical backbone for the reproduction of ritual speech authority. In other words, the shared belief that ritual couplets, conceived as the words of the ancestors, refer to a source of authority that transcends the context of performance is reproduced – in actual ritual events – through the deployment of formal linguistic features that 'detach discourse from the immediate constraints of utterance and attach it to a shared, coherent, and authoritative tradition' (Kuipers 1998: 71). As has been pointed out by cross-cultural and cross-linguistic analysis (Bloch 1975; Du Bois 1986, 1993), certain structural properties of ritual speech such as shifter avoidance and suppression of deictic elements are common to several ritual modes of speaking. In Toraja (and elsewhere), the actual use of these linguistic features intertwines with the speakers' ideas on the nature and origin of ritual speech and results in powerful technologies for the reproduction of linguistic (and social) authority. In simpler terms, the omission in ritual speech of linguistic elements (such as personal pronouns and words like 'here', 'there', 'now' and 'then') that refer to the immediate pragmatic context and presuppose knowledge of the time and place in which they are uttered, contribute to conferring to ritual speech a textual dimension.[5] The deployment of these 'decontextualizing features' reproduces the belief in the unchanging and ancestral nature of ritual speech and, at the same time, 'de-emphasize[s] the particularity of the immediate occasion and the agency of the performer' (Keane 1997a: 117).

Besides its ancestral nature, another building block of the authority of Toraja ritual register is constituted by the socially shared belief in its semantic opacity, which makes it supposedly unintelligible to non-experts.[6] Access to the symbolic capital embodied by ritual language has traditionally been restricted to ritual specialists (tominaas) and to high-ranking individuals who share the tominaa's knowledge of ritual couplets and metaphors. However, in spite of the non-evenly distributed knowledge of basa tominaa, the general way of representing its apprenticeship tends to downplay learning efforts and difficulties. Apparently at odds with the emphasis on its semantic obscurity and social exclusivity, the acquisition of performative competence in basa tominaa is locally framed as a sort of *unintentional mimesis*. In Toraja, as Keane (1997a: 154) observed for Anakalang (in the neighbouring island of Sumba), ritual experts 'say they never actively learn their skills', and claim instead that 'it is knowledge that comes to them'. This tendency to downplay wilfulness on the part of the apprentice is probably linked to the structure of linguistic authority I sketched above. The deployment – at the level of performance – of linguistic features aimed at bracketing the speaker's authorship and disclaiming responsibility for what he is saying is therefore paralleled by an 'unintentionalist' ideology of learning.

According to several accounts provided by 'traditional' (or 'traditionalist') tominaas with whom I worked in Toraja, mastery of ritual speech is generally believed to be naturally transmitted from fathers to sons. When, for example, I asked Tato' Dena' (one of the most respected and famous tominaas in the whole Toraja regency) how and when he had leant his verbal skills, he answered that he had never studied or willingly decided to learn how to use ritual speech. He had just become competent through listening to his father's or to other tominaas' performances and letting his natural talent develop spontaneously. As he once told me, he became tominaa in 1976, replacing his father who had died the previous year. But, in his view, it is hard to predict who, if any, of his sons will take his place after his own death. As he explained to me, he could not decide who would inherit his skills and become his successor, even though he confessed that he would be happy if it were one of his sons. He expressed his preference with the words: 'may my soul colour them [his sons]' ('semoga jiwa saya bisa mewarnai mereka').[7] Tellingly, he framed his hope through the use of the modal marker 'semoga' (roughly corresponding to the English 'hopefully' or 'may'), which allows him to disclaim his personal agency and removes any sense of direct and personal causation.

Tato' Dena', like many other ritual specialists I met, claims that his verbal skills, which entail memorizing long sequences of couplets to be declaimed in performances that at times may last a whole night, are not the outcome of some form of systematic and wilful training. In the local view, to be a ritual spokesman, one has to be gifted and to have a natural talent. At times I experienced a veiled contempt towards those whose performances are judged to betray the signs of a previous training. Once my landlord – a Toraja nobleman and talented orator – passing by while I was replaying a video recording of a wedding ritual speech, casually commented that the performer was not very skilful. When I asked him why, he sharply answered that it was clear that the man (a prominent representative of the new generation of ritual speech specialists I will describe below) 'had learnt every sentence he was uttering by heart' (*hafal setengah mati*).

In the last decades, however, the traditional denial of a voluntary apprenticeship of basa tominaa has started to intermingle with a new orientation to linguistic secrecy and a new understanding of the process of learning ritual speech. As a consequence of the growing commodification of the local ritual system and of the related introduction of monetary compensations for ritual performers, the traditional verbal dexterity, once the exclusive prerogative of the tominaa, has now become the expertise of a new type of speechmaker, as well as a remunerative occupation. Interestingly, the newly bred generation of ritual speech specialists, variously labelled *protokol* or *hansip*,[8] is marked by a novel attitude concerning the process of apprenticeship and transmission of ritual speech knowledge. Contrary to the traditional belief that knowledge of ritual speech is never the object of an intentional and wilful process of active learning, the protokols tend to emphasize the role of the apprentice's agency and volition in the learning process.[9]

As is apparent in the narrative by Tato' Dena' referred to above, being a tominaa is not only a matter of linguistic expertise but it also entails being in charge of an important religious role within the community. On the contrary, being a protokol requires good mastery of the ancestral language, but it does not imply having knowledge of ritual practices or being an adherent of the traditional religion. In this essay, I will not deal with the more general issue related to the process of secularization of ritual expertise; rather I will focus on the shifts in the patterns of linguistic authorship and on the transformations in the framework of authority related to the new representations of the process of ritual speech apprenticeship.

The emergent generation of ritual specialists displays a new way of conceiving the notion of authorship in ritual speech, which results in a tendency to emphasize personal oratorical styles. As we will see, their attitudes gesture towards a form of *stylistic copyright* in which the

emphasis on individual styles fades into a conception of personal ownership of ritual words and formulas. The spreading tendency among
speechmakers of emphasizing personal stylistic markers is connected
to their agentive and reflexive attitude towards the knowledge of ritual
speech. As I argue, in order to make full sense of what at first sight can
seem negligible details in the ways in which the new generation[10] of
ritual spokesmen describe their verbal expertise, we need to analyse
the historical process that led to the changes in the local ritual economy, which in turn are responsible for the important transformations
in the local market of knowledge and for the related shifts in the local
'epistemologies of secrecy' (Berliner 2005). It is of this history that I
shall now provide a brief account.[11]

The Mission, the State and the *Aluk To Dolo*

Like other eastern regions of the Indonesian archipelago, it was only
relatively late that the inner territories of the island of Sulawesi were
absorbed into the Dutch colonial system. The penetration of the Dutch
army into the Toraja highlands and the establishment of the colonial
administration in 1906 was shortly followed by the arrival of Dutch
Calvinist missionaries from the *Gereformeerde Zendingsbond* ('Dutch
Reformed Alliance'), who were sent to Toraja as early as 1913 to create a Christian 'buffer' to counter Islamic expansion from the Bugis
lowlands (Bigalke 2005). Initially slow, conversion to Christianity has
seen an incredible acceleration in the last four or five decades. Nowadays, most people inhabiting the regency of Tana Toraja are Christian
(88.8 per cent), with only a minority (4.07 per cent) remaining faithful to the local ancestral religion (Badan Pusat Statistik 2001).[12]

Prior to the diffusion of world religions in the region, the local system of religious beliefs was based on a cult of the ancestors and on a
ritual system marked by a dualistic structure: 'smoke descending rituals' (*aluk rambu solo'*) (mortuary rites) and 'smoke ascending rituals'
(*aluk rambu tuka'*) (rituals promoting fertility and prosperity). Both
types of rituals involve the slaughtering of cattle (mostly pigs and buffaloes) and the distribution of the animals' meat through a complex
web of affinal and consanguine ties.[13] It was only in the 1950s that
this autochthonous system of religious practices and beliefs started
being identified with the term *aluk to dolo* ('the way of the ancestors').
The wider popularity of the expression 'aluk to dolo' over other alternative terms suggests a local incorporation of the teleological bias
inscribed in the modernizing project endorsed by the missionaries. The
term reflects the temporal framework underlying the missionaries'
accounts in which the Toraja system of practices and beliefs was

'allochronically' (Fabian 1983) labelled as *pikiran kekafirannya yang lama* ('old pagan thoughts') (Belksma quoted in van den End 1994: 144) or *agama lama* ('old religion') (Belksma quoted in van den End 1994: 261), as opposed to the 'new religion' (*agama baru*) (van der Veen, quoted in van den End 1994: 132).

In more recent times, this allochronic and marginalizing represen-tation of Toraja indigenous religion has played an important role within the post-colonial policies of recognition. According to the *Pancasila*, the Indonesian state ideology established after independence from Dutch and Japanese colonial rule, what officially counts as reli-gion (*agama*) is restricted to the four major world religions (Islam, Christianity, Buddhism, Hinduism, while all the local, non-monothe-istic, minority confessions are denied the status of religion and result in being derogatorily labelled *kepercayaan* ('beliefs')).[14] Whoever falls outside the officially recognized faiths is classified as animist (*animis*) and pagan (*kafir*). Followers of the numerous indigenous religions within the nation-state borders are thus confronted with the alterna-tive of having their systems of religious practices and beliefs recog-nized under one of these four major labels or being considered as 'people who do not yet have a religion' (*orang yang belum beragama*).[15]

While since the early post-colonial years (i.e. late 1940s), Indone-sian state policy has presented monotheism 'as a keystone of solid progress-oriented citizenship' (George 1990: 6), the pressure to con-vert to one of the official religions became particularly strong in the mid-1960s, with the new political phase of the 'New Order' (1965–98), which coincided with the coming to power of Suharto. Among the several reasons that account for this, was the strong asso-ciation between atheism and communism, which, after the 1965 *putsch* and the following massacres of communists or suspected com-munists, became the main target of Suharto's political discourse.[16] It was precisely in the early years of the New Order that the Toraja local elites, drawing on the allochronic representation of their local religion as traditional crafted by the Dutch and on the exoticized image of their culture produced by the international tourist market, obtained the formal recognition of their local religion as a branch of Balinese Hinduism: in 1969, aluk to dolo was granted by the Indonesian Department of Religion the status of official religion.[17]

Evangelization and the Dutch Mimetic Subversion of the Toraja Ritual Economy

Not surprisingly, the Calvinist form of Christianity endorsed by the Dutch Reformed Alliance stood at odds with Toraja rituals in which an important role is played – especially at funeral ceremonies – by the exchange and slaughter of buffaloes and pigs, and the subsequent distribution of their meat according to distinctions of rank. As is apparent in the letters and reports written by the missionaries in the early decades of the twentieth century (van den End 1994), ritual animal sacrifices and mortuary meat division were considered as wasteful extravagances, exclusively motivated by a vain competition for prestige.[18]

As I argued elsewhere (Donzelli 2003, 2004), the evangelizing efforts of the Dutch missionaries concentrated not so much on converting the souls of the Toraja but rather on 're-semanticizing' their rituals. In order to contrast the Toraja 'wasteful pagan feasts', the missionaries, in the early decades of the twentieth century, introduced the custom of holding fund-raising auctions (*lelang*) at the ceremonies (van den End 1994: 124). Their goal was a sort of capitalistic re-functionalization of ritual expenditure through which 'irrational' and 'wasteful' animal slaughter could be converted into occasions to collect funds to promote social development and religious conversion. The Calvinist propaganda against Toraja 'wasteful' ritual slaughtering underwent a process of appropriation by several groups of the local elite. Archival sources (Tana Toraja Archive, bundles no. 636, 106, 1128, 274, 1454, 1450, 383, 248) testify that missionaries' emphasis on the need to promote development resulted, between the 1930s and 1950s, in the founding of local saving and loan organizations aimed at promoting social progress. Funds for the constitution of these microcredit associations were mostly achieved through donations of animals, which instead of being ritually slaughtered, were sold. The meat auction and the microcredit associations introduced at the beginning of the twentieth century mediated between local practices of meat distribution and the missionaries' concern for optimizing ritual expenditure and finalizing it to promote the development and diffusion of Christianity. Furthermore, they constituted important practical and symbolic structures for the ideological and material penetration of a cash economy within ritual and initiated the practice of setting aside some pigs and buffaloes from the funerals that, instead of being sacrificed, started being sold to collect donations for building schools and other infrastructure.

The Monetary-Driven Professionalization of Ritual Performers

Nowadays it has become customary throughout Tana Toraja not to *mantunu* ('kill' – literally 'to smoke') all the animals: some of the cattle are *dipatorro* ('spared'), set aside and either given to the church or the village council or converted into cash and used to pay the several kinds of ritual specialists and performers who are hired for the event. A vivid account of the way in which a significant share of animals contributed by affinal and consanguineal relatives for the ritual is converted into cash is given by a conversation I had in Nanggala with several members of a family who had recently held the funeral of one of their *nene'* (elder family member), a woman of semi-noble rank who had been buried with a ceremony of medium grandeur. When I last visited this family (August 2004) almost one year had passed since they had celebrated the funeral. Now that the hectic days of the ceremony were past, I thought it was the right moment to make some straightforward inquiries on how they had managed the ritual expenditure, a topic, which – in my experience – can be indelicate to touch upon at the time of the actual negotiations. As I sat with them on the rice-barn platform in front of their house, I drew the conversation to the number of buffaloes that were actually slaughtered compared to those that were set aside and given to the church or the village council[19] or that were used to compensate the several kinds of ritual specialists and performers who had been hired for the occasion:

Grandchild (of the deceased): Eh for the funeral of the woman that we celebrated last year, [we slaughtered] more than 30, 36 [buffaloes]... more or less ... no? ... more than 40 ... Together with those that were given to the *lembang* ('village'), the church, the to *ma'badong* ('those who performed the ma'badong' – funerary chant), to the *to massuling* ('those who played the flute'), to the *to ma'marakka* ('those who performed the *marakka'* – another kind of funerary chant) ...

Son (of the deceased): Yes and also the to *ma'dolanni* ('those in charge of escorting the groups of guests to the reception shelter') [were paid].

Grandchild: not all [the buffaloes] were slaughtered (*tae' nasang na ditunu*) ... because if that had been the case ...

Grandchild's wife: ... They would have all gone [i.e. all the buffaloes would have been slaughtered and none would have been spared for paying the bills].

Grandchild: Those that actually exited ... [those] that were slaughtered (*ditinggorona*) were only 36.

Son: ... Yes and there was one buffalo [that had been used] to pay the *tau-tau* (mortuary effigy) maker.

Grandchild: But that [the one given to the person who carved the mortuary effigy] was not even included in the calculation, those that we calculated are only: one for the village council, one for the church, one for the ma'badong, one for the village savings organization (*kas tondok*), one for the flute players, one for those who performed the war-dance ... All [these buffaloes] were converted into money (*diuangkan*) corresponding to the value of a *sangpala* (a male buffalo whose horn-size measures roughly 15 cm).

As this account testifies, the introduction of monetary forms of compensation for ritual specialists and performers plays a significant role in the way in which people deal with ritual expenditure in contemporary Toraja. The increasing professionalization of the performers of the most typical funeral choral chant (ma'badong) offers a good example of the more general process of ritual commodification triggered by the ongoing introduction of cash into the ritual economy. Funeral ceremonies in Toraja generally entail the performance of mortuary chants in which the deceased is praised and mourned. The ma'badong chant is performed in groups of forty to sixty people who, holding their hands in a circle, sing and move their feet and hands according to different combinations of patterns. The ma'badong is generally performed spontaneously at night during the period that precedes the funeral by groups of villagers who gather in the evenings at the house where the funeral will take place. However, in the last decades, along with these more casual and informal forms of ma'badong chanting performed by the neighbours, it has become increasingly common to hire professional groups who perform the ma'badong during the one or two days scheduled for the *penerimaan tamu* ('reception of guests').[20] Unlike the spontaneous performances, ma'badong professional choirs are composed only of men and are staged during the day. As Daniel Sakka, the leader (*ambe'*) of one of the most well-known professional choirs in the district of Nanggala (who perfomed also at the funeral spoken about in the excerpt above), explained to me in August 2004, the honorarium (*ongkos*) for the ma'badong group in the Nanggala area is set on the value of a sangpala, that is, a male buffalo with horn-size of 15 cm, whose price at the time of the interview was around four million rupiahs (four hundred euros). Besides this, the family who hires the group is expected to provide its sixty members with food and matching clothes (generally a dark t-shirt bearing the name of the deceased and a white sarong). The family who organizes the funeral has the option of paying directly in cash or with a buffalo, in the latter case the animal is sold and the money is divided between all the group members.

The Protokol and the New Market of Ritual Knowledge

While ma'badong performances are generally limited to no more than a couple of hours, the protokol's job is more demanding both in terms of time and responsibility. He has to perform different orations throughout the funeral (that generally lasts several days) and, during the guest-reception days, he is in charge of welcoming the procession of guests (who can easily number several thousand) with appropriate honorific couplets. The role of the protokol within a funeral is much more relevant than that of the ma'badong performers and so is his individual salary. If you hire a professional speechmaker, you will be charged between one and three million (one hundred to three hundred euros) for a funeral, while the fee for a brief performance at a wedding party ranges between five hundred thousand (fifty euros) and one million rupiahs (one hundred euros), which is a remarkable amount of money given that a monthly salary of one million is considered comfortable for a family living in a village.[21]

The monetary compensation to which protokols are entitled differentiates them from the more traditional spokesmen and becomes a critical element of their social identity. The salary they are given also constitutes a basis for judging their expertise against that of other protokols. Different protokols have different prices: higher fees imply acknowledgement of their greater skills and thus higher prestige. This is apparent in the way one protokol once described to me his own value:

> I already have a price list (*tarip*) ... obviously there are many others who are cheaper. But people still prefer to pay a higher price to hire me ... because when they hear my voice from afar ... they already know: 'oh this is Sam's voice!'... I have already met many people who do not know my face but know my voice!

Furthermore, being given a salary makes the protokol eligible to be hired easily and quickly and makes them more mobile. On the contrary, asking a tominaa to officiate at a ritual requires pre-existing relations. The tominaa will not need to be paid an honorarium (although he will be given meat and probably even cash gifts), but his availability is much more unpredictable and subject to his other ritual engagements and to his bonds of clientele towards the notables he is connected to. Protokols, on the other hand, can be thought of in terms of freelance professionals. They are the ones who are generally hired by the communities of Toraja migrants who live outside Toraja and who lack the necessary social network to mobilize a tominaa. Protokols can be hired from far away places, and sometimes travel even to Jakarta or to Kendari (in the distant southeast peninsula of Sulawesi) to perform at wedding parties or funerals.

But most strikingly, unlike tominaas, protokols emphasize their commitment to the study of ritual speech. Samuel Barumbung, for example, a young protokol in his early 30s, described the time he devotes to cultivating his knowledge of ritual speech with the Indonesian term *pengkajian*, which generally refers to academic and intellectual research. As he explained to me,[22] his decision of 'doing research' (*mengkaji*) on ritual speech grew out of his linguistic studies at Hasanuddin University in the city of Makassar. More than ten years ago, while he was an undergraduate student in the linguistics department, he happened to go back to Toraja to attend a wedding ceremony. It was on this occasion that he noted that many speechmakers were committing serious mistakes in the usage of the ritual couplets. It was the awareness of the others' mistakes that prompted him to choose basa tominaa as the topic of his BA dissertation. However, shortly before graduating, he decided to replace his dissertation on Toraja ritual speech with another dissertation based on the analysis of the lyrics of the songs of Iwan Fals, a popular Indonesian folk singer.

As he explained to me, his decision to keep secret his research on what he terms 'the Toraja literature' (*sastera Toraja*), was due to a copyright concern: he feared that if he had submitted his 'real' dissertation in which he had provided a thorough documentation of the 'real' basa tominaa, somebody else could have used it 'without recognizing his copyright' (*hak cipta saya tidak diakui*). In order to prevent this risk, he wrote a second dissertation on a much more trivial topic (the lyrics of an Indonesian pop-star) as a sort of camouflage of his real research.

Samuel's narrative epitomizes a new attitude towards linguistic secrecy. As I mentioned in the introduction, communicative exclusivity has always been a quintessential ingredient of basa tominaa authority. As with the case of many other types of ritual registers elsewhere, the use of a highly specialized and esoteric code, mostly incomprehensible to common people, serves to reproduce the authority of the political and religious elite. From this perspective, ritual speech works as a sort of ciphered language whose esoteric meanings are perfectly transparent to those who own the interpretative key, but totally obscure to all the others. Thus, while – within the local linguistic order – basa tominaa is canonically understood as a code whose interpretation is hierarchically restricted to a limited social group, Samuel's account alludes to a new configuration of the 'traditional' notion of secrecy embedded in ritual speech expertise. Samuel's concern for his own copyright and his efforts in preserving it allude to more individualized notions of communicative exclusivity, remarkably different from those encoded in the traditional form of linguistic oligarchy grounded in a shared (although elitist) regime of secrecy.

In addition to this novel and individualized way of framing linguistic secrecy, other distinctive features of the protokol's attitudes towards the transmission of ritual speech expertise are constituted by their self-perception as professionals and their display of a prominent reflexive awareness of their verbal skills, as well as of traditional matters in general. This self-conscious attitude towards 'tradition' is effectively conveyed by the way in which another young and famous protokol with whom I worked during my last period of fieldwork described his professional commitment to the study of ritual speech:

I try to convey the messages from the ancestors regarding the original Toraja customs and traditions (*kebiasaan dan adat istiadat asli toraja*) ... My attempt is to provide an understanding through the language of the chiefs and the wise ones in order to make the people appreciate the real Toraja language (*bahasa toraja yang benar-benar bahasa toraja*) ... [And to provide] an understanding concerning the Toraja cultural philosophy (*philosophi kebudayaan toraja*) ... the true Toraja life-style ... and to provide an understanding of the difference between the authentic Toraja culture and the Toraja culture [that derives] from acculturation ... besides being an emcee, I am an activist! (*saya adalah seorang aktivis!*) ... I am an active researcher of the Toraja tradition (*saya seorang pengkaji adat toraja*).

Notions and Practices of Stylistic Copyright

As these narratives clearly suggest, the recent development of a new market of words has important consequences for the shaping of new local notions of linguistic authority and personal creativity among speechmakers. Once, as I was engaged in transcribing the speech of an authoritative tominaa from the southern part of Toraja, I was struck by some comments made by a protokol who had stopped by at my house. The text on which I was working consisted in ritual formulas that were traditionally used to strengthen the *sumanga'* (life energy) of small children. Peeping at my computer screen the protokol could not help but making some remarks. The text offered a beautiful example of parallelistic structure:

1. *kurarako rarana bai ma'kuli' pindan*
   I sign you with the blood of a white haired pig

2. *kutera'ko lomba'na bonde ma' ka'pun inaa*
   I mark you with the blood of a pig full of wisdom

I noted that the third line had somehow caught the protokol's attention:

3. *nenne' panoto' ba'tang tumimbu*
   May the strength always pervade (enter in) (your) body

Pointing out to me the last word, he said: 'well actually, as far as I am concerned (*kalau saya*), I use *tidukun* instead of *tumimbu*'.[23] Both words mean 'to enter', but replacing one with another is enough to turn the text into a slightly different version. He then moved to the closing couplet:

5. *Nenne' panoto' tontong papatuinaa undaka' eanan sanda makamban*
   May the strength always enable (you) to search for richness of every kind

6. *Sola barang apa sanda' ammu susi todiba'gi tento dikataanni*
   and goods of any kind like the one who has been granted inheritance

and explained to me that he would rather replace the last word 'dikataanni' with 'ditage'tageranni' (although both words mean 'to give').

These remarks are quite representative of a general attitude of commenting on other speechmakers' performances that I encountered while revising my transcriptions with protokols who had not originally performed the text I had transcribed. All the protokols with whom I worked displayed a consistent tendency to suggest possible alternatives to ritual couplets appearing in the texts and openly voiced their personal stylistic preferences, an attitude that I never observed among the 'old school' of the tominaas. Despite the fact that these comments concern apparently negligible stylistic details, they embody a new tendency towards a personalistic re-articulation of ritual speech formulaic structure. The protokols' explicit emphasis on their individual styles produces interesting shifts in local patterns of linguistic authority. Although they do not go as far as claiming to be the 'authors' of the words of the ancestors, their claim of originality in the use of the ritual repertoire endows them with a higher degree of agency than that of mere 'animators' of the ancestors' words.[24]

The notion of copyright – in Indonesian *hak-cipta* (literally, 'right of invention') – often evoked by my interlocutors, stands as a sharp paradox to traditional ideas concerning Toraja ritual register. As I mentioned earlier, the authority of basa tominaa is traditionally grounded in an ideology of invariance. Like many other instances of ritual and esoteric registers, the belief in the ancestral origin and unchanging nature of tominaa language is reproduced, in the context of performance, through verbal behaviours aimed at downplaying personal authorship of ritual words. This idea is reinforced, at the level of learning ideologies, through a way of representing ritual speech apprenticeship as a process of unintentional mimesis.

The protokols' emphasis on the originality of their own repertoire of ritual speech formulas and on their individual choices in selecting specific genres in certain performances conveys the idea of stylistic copyright and embodies a remarkable change in the local notions of linguistic authorship.

In a similar way to what happens in other forms of formulaic oral performance (Finnegan 1988; Keane 1997a; Lord 1960; Zurbuchen 1987), ritual speaking in Toraja is based on a dynamic tension between conventionality and improvisation. As suggested by the negative evaluation of those performers 'who learn their speeches by heart', in spite of the emphasis – placed by local metalinguistic discourse – on the fixed, unchanging and ancestral nature of the ritual couplets, the speakers' ability to improvise and to use couplets innovatively is highly appreciated by the audience.[25] Furthermore, notwithstanding the general claim that ritual speech is unintelligible, people are generally able to identify the personal features that mark the oratorical styles of individual performers. Hence, within the highly formulaic character of the compositional techniques employed by Toraja speechmakers, personal styles have always played an important role. However, what is really distinctive in the language ideologies that developed around this new type of speechmakers is the explicit and reflexive emphasis on their individual styles and the related rearticulation of linguistic secrecy through a new form of verbal economy grounded on a notion of copyright.

As linguistic anthropologists long ago suggested, within processes of language learning much more is at stake than the acquisition of communicative competence. Apprenticeship of verbal skills related to special registers also entails socialization to a specific cultural and professional ethos. The notion of copyright explicitly evoked or tacitly implied in my interlocutors' accounts and their departure from the traditional attitude towards learning as an indeliberate and unpredictable process are full of implications.

The shift in the local ideology of learning and the heightened awareness of personal stylistic markers could suggest a transformation in the local notions of personhood and action, as well as in the forms of historical imagination underlying socially shared frames of linguistic authority. While the traditional representation of basa tominaa as an authoritative and esoteric language handed down by the ancestors is still widely shared by both speechmakers and their audiences, the way of construing the 'speaking subjects' (Keane 1997c) of these ancestral words, is undergoing a remarkable historical shift. The wilful and intentional way of framing the learning process and the reflexive commitment to the study of ritual speech at the same time derive and constitute a particular form of historical consciousness grounded in the voluntarism that pervades the local idea of modernity.

Toraja vernacular theories of modernity have been strongly influenced by the rhetoric of development (*pembangunan*), which substantiated the missionaries' ways of framing religious conversion, as well as the public discourse during the post-colonial New Order regime. Notions and practices of temporality in contemporary Toraja are marked by the coexistence of a teleological narrative of development – understood as a process of building, of 'creating something which was formerly non-existent' (Heryanto 1988: 16), with a retrospectively oriented form of historical consciousness based on the cult of the ancestors (or, at least, on their authority). The proactive and agentive style of the new speechmakers is clearly to be ascribed to the former of these coexisting structures of historical consciousness, in which the notion of development based on 'reliance on a conscious human will' (Heryanto 1988: 16) is pivotal. The cultural and economic dynamics I have sketched in this chapter open up views on a novel notion of the speaking subject and shed light on the historical construction of the concept of agency in the Toraja highlands.[26] In these processes a great role is played by different conceptions and practices of ritual speech knowledge. My aim here has been to show how learning postures contribute to shaping the way in which people inhabit the world.

Acknowledgements

This chapter is based on several periods of ethnographic and archival research conducted in Sulawesi between 2002 and 2006 under the auspicies of the Lembaga Ilmu Pengetahuan Indonesia and the Universitas Hasanuddin in Makassar. Fieldwork was funded by the Department of Epistemology and Hermeneutics of Formation of the University of Milan-Bicocca (2002–03 and 2004), by the Institute of Social Sciences of the University of Lisbon and by the Portuguese Foundation for Science and Technology (2005–06). An earlier version of this essay was presented at the International Symposium on 'Learning Religion: Anthropological Approaches' held in September 2005 at the Institute of Social Sciences of the University of Lisbon. I am grateful to the organizers (David Berliner and Ramon Sarró) and to those who participated in the discussion. In particular, I would like to acknowledge Carlos Fausto, Charles Hirschkind, Michael Houseman and Carlo Severi for their useful remarks. Gonçalo Duro dos Santos read the manuscript at different stages of preparation and provided very helpful comments. Finally, a special thanks goes the several speechmakers with whom I have worked in Toraja in these years: Dahlan Kembong Bangnga Padang, Pong Jeni, Samuel Barumbung and Ne' Sando'.

Notes

1. The Toraja administrative region (*Kabupaten Tana Toraja*) nowadays comprises an area of roughly 3,200 square kilometres, inhabited – according to local statistics (Badan Pusat Statistik 1999) – by 381,260 people. Toraja society is primarily agrarian: aside from wet-rice farming, the local population also cultivates small

gardens of sweet potato, cassava and other cash crops such as vanilla, clove and coffee. The social structure is marked by an interesting combination of a remarkably inclusive kinship system (in which descent is traced bilaterally) and a notably rigid stratification in ranked descent groups.

2. A key aspect common to all cross-cultural encounters consists of their potential to induce reflexivity (Keane 1997c). Shortly after their arrival in 1913, the Dutch missionaries set up an official commission aimed at establishing a theological distinction between *adat* ('traditional culture') and *aluk* ('pagan beliefs'). The commission became an important arena for debating the role and the semiotic meaning of the different material objects used during rituals. It may be argued that the asymmetrical relationship between different forms of tacit and explicit reflexivity engendered by the cross-cultural encounter between the Dutch Calvinist missionaries and the people dwelling in the Toraja uplands has greatly contributed to the reproduction of the discursive hegemony of the colonizers. While the Toraja cultural and ritual systems became matters of explicit and thorough discussion, Dutch cultural and religious assumptions were not talked about.

3. The importance of the analysis of the ideologies of learning for the study of the transmission of religious knowledge has also been foregrounded by Michael Lambek (this volume).

4. Sandarupa's (1989, 2004) work provides exceptionally fine-grained accounts of how Toraja ritual speech parallelism unfolds within verbal performance.

5. Students of ritual and formal speech refer to this semiotic process by the term 'entextualization' (Bauman and Briggs 1990; Silverstein and Urban 1996).

6. Elsewhere (Donzelli 2007), I provide a more detailed analysis of the implications of the linguistic ideologies of ritual speech unintelligibility for the Toraja historical consciousness and the reproduction of social hierarchy. On the socially shared belief concerning ritual speech unintelligibility, see also Coville (1988, 2004); Sandarupa (1989, 2004); and Volkman and Zerner (1988: 284).

7. Conversation with Tato' Dena', 19 September 2004.

8. A borrowing from the English 'emcee' (MC).

9. Protokols do not represent the only new group of ritual speech experts. Acquiring mastery of basa tominaa is considered an important requirement for anyone willing to become a Christian priest. Since 1913 when the Calvinist Mission first arrived in Toraja, there has been a pervasive appropriation of ritual speech from the side of the Church. Basa tominaa, after being properly purged of its pagan elements, is no longer considered as an esoteric language to be used in animistic rituals but is nowadays employed in Christian ceremonies. Here I focus only on the differences in the learning postures I observed among the tominaas (adherents of the ancestral religion) and the protokols (who for the great majority are Christian). However, it is worth mentioning that I often noted among Christian priests who engage in the study of ritual speech an attitude similar (though slightly less narcissistic) to that of the protokols described here.

10. My use of the term 'generation' could be misleading, in that protokols are not necessarily younger than more traditional types of speechmakers.

11. The historical sources I have used comprise, along with first-hand interviews conducted in the Toraja area, the late colonial and early post-colonial archival material from the Tana Toraja Archive in Makassar, which I was able to examine directly in 2002–03 and 2004. Access to earlier sources was made possible thanks to Thom van den End's (1994) edited collection of letters and reports written by missionaries and colonial administrators during the first half of the twentieth century.

12. There is, however, a small percentage of Muslim adherents (7.11 per cent), mostly located in the southern districts. While the advent of Christianity is dated to the

turn of the twentieth century, for the diffusion of Islam it is not possible to identify an equally precise beginning. Islamic penetration was more gradual and less remarkable since it occurred as a consequence of long-term contacts with the neighbouring Bugis lowlanders who have been Muslim since the seventeenth century. This chapter is mostly focused on the changes connected to Christianization. The Toraja Muslims and the role of Islam in the peasants' revolts and religious uprisings of the 1950s and 1960s constitute interesting topics of inquiry on which little has yet been written (see Donzelli 2004).

13. For thorough accounts of the web of affinal and consanguineal ties at play in funeral and house ceremonies, see Waterson (1993).

14. According to this official repartition, Catholicism and Protestantism are considered as two different religions.

15. The temporal adverb *belum* ('not yet') alludes to the construction of a development scale based on a dichotomy between backward people who do not yet have a religion and developed people who follow an official and 'true' religion.

16. '(L)ack of affiliation with a world religion' was thus equated with a potential indicator of communist political sympathies, in addition to being stigmatized as a 'sign of primitiveness' (Sillander 2004: 74).

17. Not all the minority religious communities received the same recognition at the same time. For example the Bentians, a Dayak people of east Kalimantan, had their religion officially recognized under the umbrella of Hinduism only in 1980 (Sillander 2004: 74). While the ancestral religion (*ada' mappuro*) practised in Pitu Ulunna Salu, a region not far from Toraja in the 'hinterlands of Sulawesi's southwest coast' (George 1990: 6) has not yet been recognized by the Indonesian government. The success obtained by the Toraja in the political recognition of their cultural and religious specificities is partly due to the capabilities of the local elites to exert political pressure and to use symbolic resources to achieve the status of privileged minorities. But it also needs to be related to the late 1960s resurgence of the old Toraja ruling class. As Crystal (1974) effectively argued, in the late 1960s, the old guard of the Toraja aristocracy took advantage of the raising hegemony of the Golkar Party (which became the state party during Suharto's regime) at the expense of its long-standing political rival, that is, the local middle class (and its political expression in the Christian Party – Parkindo), which had played a leading role during the 1940s and 1950s.

18. The Dutch missionaries' view of Toraja ritual practices as wasteful and irrational was greatly motivated by their failure to understand that Toraja ritual slaughtering is embedded in a complex system of investments and circulation of wealth connected to funerals.

19. It should be added that aside from these donations, livestock meant to be used at rituals (be it sacrificed or spared) is also subjected to taxation. Those who bring the animal to the ritual field are required to pay to the District administration fifty thousand rupiahs (five euros) for pigs (roughly a tenth of the market price of an average male pig) and one hundred thousand rupiahs (ten euros) for each buffalo. Prices of buffaloes vary remarkably according to the size, horn shape and colour of the eyes, fur and spots. In 2004, prices at the Rantepao buffalo market ranged from four to five million rupiahs (four to five hundred euros) for a standard black male up to eighty million (eight thousand euros) for the most expensive spotted buffalo.

20. Several elder ma'badong performers I interviewed in 2004 agreed that the introduction of monetary compensations dates back at least as early as the 1960s. Several of these accounts emphasized that in the 'old days' people performed without requiring any payment.

21. Figures dating to 2002–04.
22. Interview with Sam Barumbung, January 2006.
23. 'Tumimbu' comes from the root 'timbu', while 'tidukun' comes from the root 'dukung'.
24. I am referring here to Goffman's (1981) notion of speech roles. Goffman (1981) identified three main speech roles: animator, author, principal, and showed how individuals can take different alignments with respect to their utterances.
25. The positive value of personal creativity in the usage of ritual couplets is also noted by Webb Keane (1997a: 111) in Sumba.
26. Keane (1997c) shows how the concept of agency is an historical and cultural product and provides an illuminating analysis of the role of religious conversion in the historical construction of the idea of agency in Anakalang (Sumba), although he does not address the issue of ritual speech apprenticeship.

Chapter 10

LEARNING FAITH
YOUNG CHRISTIANS AND CATECHISM

Laurence Hérault

Opening the door of a church hall where a catechism meeting is taking place is like discovering activities which can conjure up childhood memories for those who have experienced a Christian education. You can see a catechist telling attentive or annoyed children the story of Jesus' birth. You can find another one praying with concentrated, mischievous or rowdy teenagers. You can observe a priest explaining the meaning of the Holy Eucharist to a group of children excited by an approaching communion festival. You also can discover a pastor trying to answer difficult questions simply and openly: 'Who is God's father?', 'Have miracles ever really taken place?'. At first glance, these multiple and varied activities which gather adults and young people in the name of a supernatural being, God, seem quite common and ordinary. Anthropological studies have generally overlooked them, perhaps because of their 'banality', as this discipline has been more interested in the more 'marginal', 'folk', or popular expressions of Christianity. In fact, pilgrimages, worship of saints, spectacular ceremonies of the Holy Week or Christian rites of passage have attracted anthropologists much more than the Sunday mass or catechism. However, these ordinary activities constitute a significant part of the faithful existence and are therefore essential for the comprehension of the Christian experience. Moreover, this so common catechism appears to be an interesting place for those who want to explore religious learning and question the way the contemporary Christian can engage in faith and constitute his or her membership in a Church.

Contemporary Catechism: A New Way of Teaching and Learning

Contemporary Christian catechists often say that their work consists in 'transmitting the faith'. This self-proclaimed definition is quite consensual as it goes beyond the denominational 'boundaries'. However, the apparent simplicity of the project poorly conceals the complexity of this catechetic enterprise. How can something originating in personal choice, such as faith, be transmitted? How do catechists go about this? What do they do when they claim to be 'transmitting' faith? The ordinary sense of the verb, which evokes the transfer of a good, or the gift of something previously received, suggests that catechism consists of handing down religious knowledge to children so that they can be seen as Christian heirs (Protestants, Catholics, Orthodox, etc.). This conception of transmission implies the existence of formal religious knowledge which can be stated, heard, understood and memorized: 'God created the heavens and the earth', 'Jesus has risen', 'Mary gave birth to God's son', 'The blessed Trinity is one God in three divine persons', etc. It seems that such statements have been spread over space and time for millenaries. Being Christian would consist of acquiring such knowledge and believing in it, becoming thus a link in a long transmission chain of multiple statements and associated practices. 'Old-style catechisms' were actually based on the memorizing and reciting of such dogmatic assertions in order to train young Christians. The catechism handbooks were presented in a dialogue form borrowed from the first catechisms of the Reformation. The master would put forth questions and the pupil would memorize the appropriate answers. This pedagogic process seemed to be developed in order to teach each member of a particular confession the dogmatic knowledge of his Church and to help him resist against the 'errors' spread by others. This presentation of the Christian faith in a dialogue form was continued successfully until the middle of the twentieth century. Many people who learned 'the highest truths of the Faith' (Freppel 1875: 4) by heart can still testify to it today.

Second Lesson
Q. What is God?
A. God is an infinitely perfect spirit, creator of Heaven and the Earth. He is sovereign Lord of all things.
Q. Why do you say God is infinitely perfect?
A. I say God is infinitely perfect because he has all the perfections and his perfections are without end.
(...)
Q. Where is God?
A. God is everywhere

Q. Does God know all things?
A. Yes, God knows all things, sees all things, even our most secret thoughts.
(Freppel 1875: 35)

Fifth Lesson
Q. What is the Holy Eucharist?
A. The Holy Eucharist is the sacrament which really and truly contains the body and blood, soul and divinity of our Lord Jesus Christ under the appearances of bread and wine.
Q. Is the body of our Lord Jesus Christ in the Eucharist the same body He had on Earth and He has in heaven?
A. Yes, it is the real body of our Lord Jesus Christ, the same body He had on Earth and He has in heaven.
Q. What do you mean by the appearances of bread and wine?
A. By the appearances of bread and wine, I mean whatever appears to the senses; the colour, the figure and the taste of bread and wine (Freppel 1875: 71).

This dogmatic catechetic programme has proven to be very problematic. In fact, catechists and theologians have criticized it for several decades mainly on three points: the maladjustment of this catechism to the modern-day context, its inadequate vision of the learning process, and finally the amalgam it implicitly makes between faith and belief. The first point takes into account the process of secularization, or rather dechristianization, observed in Western societies. According to those critics, this process modifies, to some extent, the 'catechetic deal'. The 'old catechism' took place in a favourable environment where children came into contact with faith that was very much 'alive' in their local community and their family. Thus this catechism was a way to clarify this faith already present and active for children. On the contrary, contemporary catechism, for the most part aimed at children without real religious references or practices, has embarked upon a new challenge. It must pay particular attention to 'the awakening of faith' and tries to give children their first 'experience of God'. This discovery of God and of the alliance he proposes to human beings is from now on essential: 'catechism aims at allowing children to come into contact with the God revealed by Jesus Christ and to live in his Spirit' (Lalanne and de Vinols 1998: 19); 'the catechists prepare children to experience this, to recognise themselves as children of God' (Lalanne and de Vinols 1998: 24).

Contemporary catechists, who are aware of the work of the social and human sciences, also criticize the 'old' practice's intention to indoctrinate children especially with its fixed and rigid vision of the roles and places of each participant. The catechist was seen as an erudite, as scholar, an active and skilful master teaching ignorant, passive and flexible children 'what one must believe' in order to be a Christian. Faced with this practice thought to be illusory or aberrant, but especially vain and unproductive, the current theologians and catechists insist on the children's free will and involvement: 'The object of learning is not knowledge, but the personal existence of the participants. The didactic problem does not consist in transmitting knowledge but in working out a procedure which allows for personal reflection and choice' (Baumann 1993: 92).[1] The pedagogy implemented must therefore 'allow [the children] to express themselves and give them ways to appropriate faith, while rendering them responsible for their choice' (Lalanne and de Vinols 1998: V).

This new formulation of the people's involvement in catechism is also related to the third criticism mentioned above: the tendency to assimilate faith and belief. For the catechists, faith cannot be reduced to truths that one must believe in. According to them, it is incorrect to confuse knowledge of the dogma and personal commitment expected of the faithful. The faithful cannot and should not be confused with the 'believer' as is normally thought.[2] Faith is not an expression which limits itself to religious statements, i.e., which can be defined as repeated information. As de Certeau underlines, when 'believing' is understood as a speech, something which one can hold and/or profess, it stops being that which it fundamentally is. In other words, it is a relational involvement between different beings. According to him, 'believing' must be understood as an ability to make, something which gets to do (de Certeau 1981).[3] Having faith is not knowing a creed but being able to establish a relationship with God and other human beings; a relationship which is experienced as a revelation, a transformation of the self, of one's life and one's way of viewing the world. Consequently, contemporary catechism reorients its pedagogy. It refuses dogmatic teaching in order to privilege religious training which offers the opportunity to discover a message which is not simply information but which aims at transforming the individual.[4] The project of the 'transmission of faith' consists thus of giving children the possibility to commit themselves in a partnership with God. They are asked to acquire the specific competence needed for the establishment of such a relational contract.

In order to show how catechists attempt to make this alliance with God understandable and active for the children, I will focus on Communion. The apprenticeship of Communion is, in fact, an interesting situation because of its place in the Christian's life. To live and build oneself as communicant is to live as a faithful person. The Last Supper where Jesus Christ shared bread and wine with his disciples precisely announced a 'new alliance' with God; its enactment during current worship actualizes the personal and collective meeting with

Jesus. Teaching children Communion gives them the opportunity to discover hopeful faith. In the following pages, I will compare the training of this sacrament in two Churches, the Roman Catholic Church and the Reformed Evangelical Church of Neuchâtel, in Switzerland where I observed catechism sessions over a period of a year in 1997–98.[5]

Protestant and Catholic Catechetic Eucharistic Programmes

The Catholic First Communion is prepared in the third year of catechism (9–10 year olds) and includes an especially adapted 'communion course'. It consists of ten weekly sessions of catechism, two preparatory meetings and a three-day retreat. This course ends with two celebrations: a ceremony of 'First Communion' with parents and catechists and, a few weeks later, a 'Feast of Communion' with parishioners and the children's relatives. In the Reformed Church, the Lord's Supper is presented to all children from infancy to teenage years. Access to the first communion is individualized and can be conducted at different ages according to parents' wishes.

From an organizational viewpoint, these two programmes are heterogeneous. The Catholic programme appears relatively strong and intense. It is clearly located, taking place at one particular time of the catechism course. It is consistent and well structured, precisely defining the content of the course and the respective interventions of the catechists and the priest. Finally it is intensive, giving the basics in a few months, and also integrated as it is conducted in connection with a first practice of the communion. In comparison, the Protestant programme presents itself more flexibly. It is spread out, being located in multiple parts of the catechetic course. It is adaptable not only to the changing maturity of the children but also to the circumstances of Christian community life (it takes into account, for example, the parochial sensitivity on the matter of Eucharist and can also take place when some 'interesting' ceremonies, baptism or family service, occur). It is also extensive, gradually giving or renewing knowledge and know-how needed for participation in the Lord's Supper. Finally it is independent as its accomplishment does not grant automatic access to the practice of Communion.

This difference in the organization of the Eucharistic learning experience seems to be related to the divergent theologies of the Lord's Supper. For the Catholics, the Eucharist holds a central and fundamental place in Christian life. It is seen as the source and summit of the ecclesial life. For their part, the Protestants relativize the value of the sacrament. Far from being the centre of the Christian life, it rather has the appearance of being auxiliary to the preaching, i.e., it is understood as a useful complement for the transmission of the Word. The theological divergences with regard to the Lord's Supper relate, however, not only to the 'value' granted to the sacrament but concern other dimensions: in particular, the delicate problem of the mode of the divine presence. Both Churches recognize a special presence of Jesus Christ in this sacrament, but they differ about the way He is present. The Roman Catholic theology understands the presence of Christ in the Eucharist as a real presence not only an actual but a substantial presence, a sort of extension of the incarnation. In this view, the consecration Word in the Eucharistic liturgy operates a 'transubstantiation', i.e., a change in the elements (bread and wine). As the fifth lesson of the catechism quoted above says, bread and wine truly become the body and blood of Jesus Christ. Their appearances are not changed but their reality is. The Reformed theology of the Eucharist, particularly Calvinist, understands the sacrament as a sign and denies a true corporal presence of Christ. His body and blood do not come 'to inhabit' the elements. The bread and the wine which are manipulated in memory of Him remain unchanged during the liturgy.

However, regarding this discussion, the contents of the programmes are not as dissimilar as one might expect. Contemporary catechism does not adopt a doctrinal presentation of this sacrament. Young Catholics do not hear the term 'transubstantiation' and do not have any more detailed explanations than young Protestants about the mode of Christ's presence. In fact, the ways of presenting things are rather similar. Sometimes the same texts or the same expressions are used to evoke the presence of Christ and catechists' handbooks remind them that the assertion of the presence is more significant than explanations given about the way it occurs.

> While trying to explain the presence of Christ, Christians exhausted themselves and became divided over the centuries. Even though the mode of its presence is inexplicable, inexpressible. It is like a mystery, an inconceivable reality to our spirits which, however, drives us to live. Let us not waste time searching for an inadequate explanation. What is rather expected from us is to proclaim the truth of his presence while letting ourselves be enlightened by the light of the Holy Spirit (*Agence Romande d'Education chrétienne* 1984, B: 21).

> You should not embark upon a search for explanations ... to know how that occurs ... If you do that, you are on the wrong path (...). What is important is to help [the youths] understand that this meeting occurs in the heart (meeting for the preparation of the Catholic catechists. 17 February 1998).

This point is interesting because it raises the question of the denominational difference in the current catechetic project. By privileging the discovery of faith, is doctrinal prospect forgotten? In fact, it is really present but not where one might expect it. Furthermore, it provides another window on the denominational divergence. What is learned are two ways of considering the partnership created through the sacrament rather than two disputing dogmas. Therefore, to learn and to understand communion is not to grasp a deep or a concealed sense of the sacrament but rather to grasp the way it is possible to share in it. Two points seem particularly significant here. The first one is the apprenticeship of the Lord's Supper and, in particular, the relations between the Last Supper and the current achievements of the Eucharist. The second one includes the exercises and rehearsals concerning the practice of Communion.

Learning the Lord's Supper's Partnership

One of the significant things the children have to learn is that Communion is not an ordinary act of sharing and eating. It is also an act which mobilizes various kinds of participants establishing particular relationships between them. This discovery of the specificity of Communion is achieved first of all through a presentation of *two* Lord's Suppers. The first Lord's Supper, the one realized by Jesus Christ the day before his death (the 'biblical Supper') is distinguished from the second one which is performed by contemporary Christians (the 'liturgical Supper').

The importance of the first Last Supper for the understanding of what Communion consists of is obvious. According to Goffman's terminology, this supper provides the primary framework for the knowledge needed to understand or apprehend the current modalized Eucharist. Consequently, catechists present the context of the last meal of Christ to the children and underline the fact that it announces his death and his resurrection. Thus, it constitutes one of the main signs of the new alliance established with God through Jesus Christ. This is not only taught through 'informative' statements but also appears in the ways the 'biblical Supper' and the 'liturgical Supper' are presented to the children.

First of all, during catechism sessions, 'the biblical Supper' is always presented in a narrative form. It can be read, often several times, told by an adult or presented as a movie. However, it is never performed by children. This is surprising in the context of catechism where stage performances of New Testament episodes are an appreciated pedagogic tool for memorizing and understanding biblical accounts.

In the case of the Eucharistic teaching, I did not find any such stage performance in the observed sessions or in the handbooks used by the catechists.

In contrast with the 'biblical Supper', the 'liturgical Supper' is never read or told to the children. They observe, experience, or even perform it. Direct personal contact with this Lord's Supper is significant. So much so that a Protestant handbook stresses the fact that children must be taken to observe and to participate in such a cult before attending a gathering where Communion will be presented, if they have never attended a service with Communion before (*Agence Romande d'Education chrétienne* 1984, C: 3). This teaching method best underlines the relationship between the biblical Last Supper and the liturgical Lord's Supper. The first is and should be only a 'narrative', whereas the latter is and should be only a 'performance'. In other words, one is presented as a definitively closed historical event, the other as a recurring ceremony. This difference is underlined here in order to make the children aware of the fact that participation in Communion is not a stage performance of the last meal of the Christ but a performance of the Lord's Supper. The faithful do not mimic what Jesus did, but re-enact it. This fundamental dimension is developed by working with the participants about their role and their place.

From one event to the other, these participants differ. In the 'biblical Supper', there are three types of participants: Jesus Christ, the apostles and the food (bread and wine). In the 'liturgical Supper' these are Jesus, the faithful and the elements (bread and wine). Learning about the Eucharistic aims not only at establishing a bond between these participants but especially stresses their presence within both frameworks. A first link is established, by delegation, between the apostles and the faithful. The twelve apostles were Christ's first faithful followers. When Jesus addressed them, he was also addressing the contemporary faithful. The children have already mastered this identification between Jesus' fellows and current Christians, so it is not underlined in the learning sessions. Christ's presence in the first Supper is thought of as a historical fact that the Bible testifies. His presence in the 'liturgical Supper' seems a priori more difficult to apprehend because of his 'double nature'. The question is not only of introducing a historical personality in a current context but also of a supernatural being in an ordinary situation. To understand what this insertion is like, one has to remember that present-day communions are modalizations, i.e., non-literal actions literally accomplished. The interest of these particular acts lies in this space of transcription as Bateson has shown in his analysis of play as fiction. It is possible to use this analysis, like Piette (1997, 1999) did to understand the subtlety and the productivity of the divine presence in the Eucharistic liturgy. Basing his argument on the capital character of the '*not really'* highlighted by Bateson concerning playful biting, Piette shows that the presence of the Christ stated by theology is 'a presence of Jesus that is not presence and an absence that is not absence either' (1997: 144). In other words, Jesus is present and absent at the same time. The participation in the Lord's Supper, which the children must do, thus requires the understanding of this particular dimension of the Communion, i.e., the non-literal reality of the interaction with Jesus Christ. This constructive and fictional dimension of the ceremonial framework leads to a specific learning process of the divine presence where the reality of this one is not connected to a particular operation that is 'rationally' explainable but to the importance of the Word and to the agency of the Eucharistic elements.

In a Catholic session, the catechist read a text where children learned that in the Eucharist there is '*nothing magic, nothing mechanical, nor electronic*', that this presence is like that of love: '*love isn't visible if I don't make a gesture or say a word*'. Then she concluded by saying: '*we cannot explain everything, it is a mystery*' and recalled the promise made by Jesus:

Catechist: '*Is Jesus present when we are here?*'
Several: '*Yes!* '
Catechist: '*Yes. We have read the Word: whenever two or three [people] come together in my name, I am there with them*'.

In a handbook used by Protestant catechists the same idea is found: 'if children ask you questions about the mode of the presence, you should not panic (...) do not avoid telling them that many attempts have been made to explain this, but all were unsatisfactory because this presence is inexplicable. The only way of answering is to say that God stands by his promises' (*Agence Romande d'Education chrétienne* 1984, B: 26).

Concurrently, the uselessness of the ordinary senses to apprehend the divine presence is frequently and variously stated. Jesus cannot be seen, heard, touched, or even tasted even though he is there. In one session, for example, the catechist gave non-consecrated hosts to the children with instructions on the way of eating them. While the children expressed their feelings, the catechist pointed out: '*when you receive the bread during the Lord's Supper, it has the same taste, but you will know that it is Jesus*'. In a later meeting, the priest also underlined this point: '*when I say the words, it is the Christ but the taste does not change. We know in our hearts that it is the body of Christ*'. This Catholic teaching obviously refers to the conception of the real presence peculiar to this Church but does not appear, however, as a clarification of the Catholic dogma. One can see that as soon as the teaching mentions the body of Christ it refuses to go into the details. Consequently what is taught is less the idea that the host is truly (and really) the body of Christ than the idea that the host is the object which certifies this presence and reveals its particular content. In this sense, the Catholic learning is not very different from the Protestant one. Both insist upon the fact that the bread and wine testify to the presence-absence of Christ. Significant work is, moreover, developed about the agency of these objects which attest that Christ is present *and* absent at the same time.

Ordinary presences-absences are recalled in order to underline the mediating role of these objects. In a Catholic meeting, the catechist asked the children to try to remember the absence of one of their close relatives or loved ones and how they coped with that experience. Several underlined the void they felt and how they maintained the presence of the absent one: '*my father was always in my heart*'. For others, pyjamas or pictures ensured the delegation. From these accounts, objects '*which make us think of Jesus*' were sought. The Bible, the cross and also the bread and wine were found. In a Protestant session, a poster representing a blurry figure of Jesus holding a clear cup of wine and loaf of bread was shown. The visibility of bread and wine was underlined by the catechist in order to show the children that they are the guarantee of Jesus' presence. This guarantee is obviously due to the way Jesus initiated the use of these foodstuffs during the Last Supper. Like the presence of ordinary 'absents', the divine presence shows itself through objects which Jesus had himself chosen to testify to his role in the alliance between God and human beings. In fact, the agency of these elements is so essential that bread and wine have an important place in all catechism sessions. They are always present and used in one form or another: pictures are exposed on walls or presented as jigsaw puzzles; individual or collective drawings are made during the session; hosts are tasted; a loaf of bread and a wine cup or bottle are presented on the table; sometimes bread is even kneaded and grape juice squeezed with the children.

These two elements are also very closely associated with the *institution narrative*. For example, in a Protestant course, the first meeting included a reading of the account of the Last Supper in front of an already set table (tablecloth, loaf of bread and bottle of wine). During the second meeting, the same reading was done while some children put bread and wine onto the table. In the third meeting the reading and the setting of the table were repeated but in a more solemn way (enacted roles, procession, etc.). Through this *mise en scène*, the bread and the wine handled by Jesus and instituted as revelations of himself ('this is my body, this is my blood') are identified with the bread and the wine manipulated by the children. In this way, the young Christians learn that bread and wine ensure the link between the inaugural Supper and the subsequent ones.

Through these various procedures, catechism sessions draw attention to the fundamental differences *and* similarities between the two Suppers. Beyond a simple focus on the mode of the divine presence, the participants in either Lord's Supper are not only specified but connected to each other. What is thus presented to the children is a first draft of these partners' relationships. Jesus institutes a particular use of bread and wine (to break, share and eat) and incites human beings to repeat His act ('do this in remembrance of me'). Bread and wine translate the divine commitment ('this is my body given for you') and ensure the commensality amongst the faithful. People who gather in the name of Jesus actualize the instituted usage and invite God into their lives. This Eucharistic partnership is shown diagrammatically in Figure 10.1.

With this partnership, each participant acquires a new status and new relationships are set into place. God is presented as Lord and Father. Human beings who are faithful, show themselves as children, as brothers and sisters. Foodstuffs which are 'transformed' into Christ's body and blood become the guarantee of an alliance. Learning Communion is learning how to commit or bind oneself in such a relational network, how to find a place in it and experience the encounter with God. In order to experience that and their faith, the children must also learn the conditions of felicity of this Eucharistic relationship. In other words, they learn to understand their role and acquire the necessary competence needed to be faithful.

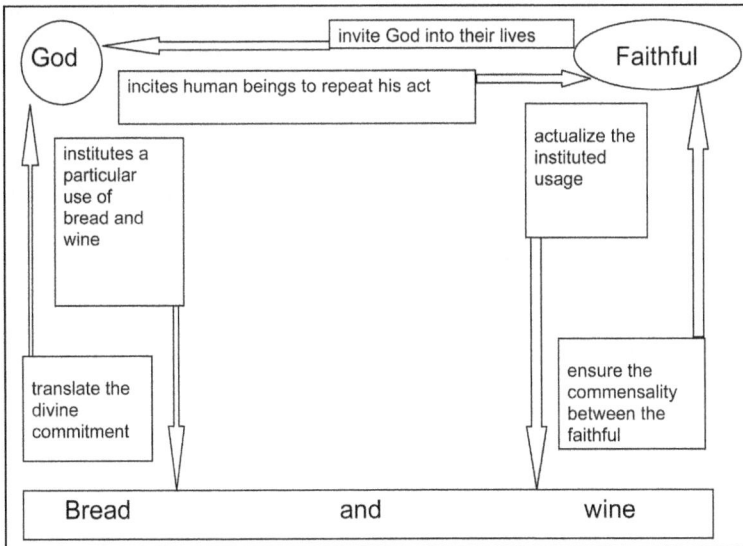

Figure 10.1: The Eucharistic partnership

Practising Communion: Learning to Master Ritual Action

This learning experience takes place mainly through exercises and rehearsals of the Eucharistic act and in particular through a comparison between the genuine Communion and the 'training' or 'practice' Communion. In both Churches, exercises where children handled the bread and wine were observed. They take place both in catechism sessions and in rehearsals preceding celebrations intended for children.[6] The aim of these rehearsals is to ensure that the children master their role. Priests, pastors and catechists train children in situ and give them a series of instructions and rules related to the actions they take part in. For instance, they may repeat processions in the church, songs, prayers, readings, Communion and all liturgical sequences.

Regarding Communion, the exercises of the Eucharistic gestures are carefully differentiated from the genuine Communion. Careful attention is made to point out this difference to the children. The catechists not only insist upon the place where the acts are performed (for example common room vs church), but also on the way liturgical actions are accomplished (they are split up into small sequences and repeated several times with many interruptions). This particular treatment of liturgy is done not only in order to train the children but also to make the words and actions completely inoperative or ineffective. The first significant element of this treatment is, in fact, the exclusion of the divine actor from the exercise. This exclusion is carried out through the fragmentation of the Eucharistic actions and the non-performance of the prayers where the divine action is required. In a Protestant rehearsal, for example, the *institution narrative* was present but without the prayers which usually accompany it (in particular anamnesis, memorial, epiclesis). The pastor pointed out this absence to the children: '*during the service, I will say the prayer to invite the Holy Spirit*'. Moreover, he did not train the children to make the gesture of the Communion. In the Catholic rehearsals, the presentation of the offerings at the altar (offertory), the distribution and the eating of hosts were present but without the associated prayers, in particular without the Eucharistic prayer, i.e., the prayer of Thanksgiving and consecration of the elements, which normally comes before the communion. The consequences of this absence were implied when the priest underlined the effect of the words of consecration for the children: '*when I say the words, it is Christ*' (so now it is not).

This exclusion of the divine is obviously fundamental because it reveals the significant role of the supernatural being. He is the author of the Last Supper and the main actor of the Eucharist. The actions performed can be regarded as a Eucharist only when He is invoked, when one asks for His presence, when one repeats the words which He pronounced on the eve of His death. Without the repetition of His institution act and without His renewed presence there is no Communion; only a rehearsal. This absence and its consequences are not only explored in rehearsals but also in previous catechism sessions. The Catholic course of Communion included a meeting where the children tasted non-consecrated hosts. The person in charge of the course put particular emphasis (with the catechists) on the contrast between the two 'types' of hosts. '*You must make the difference carefully, but often the children do it easily*'. In fact, at the sight of hosts presented in a cup, the children were delighted and several immediately underlined that they were different from those used during the mass: '*they are false*', '*they are not blessed*'. Another one asked: '*is it cardboard?*'. Underlining the children's observations, the catechist explained, '*the priest didn't make the prayer for the Spirit to come*'.

In rehearsals, we can also observe the way children learn to constitute the ritual nature of bread and their own involvement in the ritual action. The Eucharistic bread is not only the guarantee of the divine presence because of its institution by Jesus but also because, in the Lord's Supper, it is different from ordinary bread in its form and/or in its use. The children have to acquire the ability required for this extra-ordinary use. Young Catholics have to master a particular object, the host, and all young Christians are asked to handle and properly ingest bread and/or wine in order for these to be seen as signs of the alliance with God. The young Catholics are thus generally invited to taste the host beforehand. In the course observed in Neuchâtel, when the children tasted the host, the catechist invited them to express their feelings. '*It's like plastic but even so, it's good, it's digestive*'; '*It's a bit strange, it's not real bread, it's crusty*'; '*It's good, I like it. It's like candy sheets*'; '*I like it and I don't. The taste is good but it's kind of like dough*'; '*when it melts, it's pasty*'. The catechist asked whether they are disappointed and two boys said they were. In order to underline the difference with ordinary bread, she then inquired: '*can we live on that?*'. Patrick, one of the disappointed boys, answered to the point: '*if I had to live on that for a whole day, I'd just die!*'.

During the retirement preceding the first Communion, more elaborate training of the Eucharistic gestures takes place especially during the rehearsals of the ceremony. The priest oversees the learning of these gestures (teaching the children exactly what they should do): '*I will show you how to receive the bread. Normally, except for left-handers, you receive the bread in the left hand.* [he puts his left hand over his right hand and children do the same] *Don't hold your hands like this* [he brings his hands on the level of his thighs], *that would mean: 'I don't want it'. Nor in top like that* [he puts his hands above his head], *that would mean: 'I don't know what is happening to me'. Put your hands at the level of your heart and they shouldn't be stiff* '. The children put their hands in position and the priest goes among them to correct their gesture: height, suppleness of the arms, etc. The exercise is then repeated with hosts and the priest corrects them once again: '*don't raise your hands in advance. You must keep your hands together. The gesture is important because that helps you understand what you are doing'*.

Protestant children do not have to discover the taste of a special bread (the host) because ordinary bread is split and shared by the minister during the Lord's Supper. Moreover, if the situation of Communion is often present in catechism sessions, catechists do not always train children to make Eucharistic gestures but only tell them how to perform them. It seems that when bread and wine are used in a session, they are handled in order to avoid the complete Eucharistic sequence (breaking, sharing and eating). For example, in a previously described session, a whole loaf of bread and a corked bottle of wine were brought to the table and manipulated several times but neither shared nor eaten. In another session, the usual liturgical unfolding was reversed: the loaf was cut up into slices beforehand and given to children at the beginning of the session. Then catechists asked them to reassemble the loaf like a jigsaw puzzle. Sometimes, however, there is a genuine training of the Eucharistic gestures. A pastor told me that when she prepares children for Communion, she shows and makes them experience some ways of receiving the bread and drinking from the cup. However, she does not distribute either bread or grape juice. She emphasizes the gestures where the communicant receives the bread (with one hand or with both forming a cup where the minister puts the piece of bread) and discourages those gestures where he takes the bread from the hands of the minister (gesture observed among adult communicants). Regarding the grape juice, she stresses that they must drink only a small quantity. The significant element here seems to be that the children understand well that the Eucharistic use is one which does not only connect the handling and the consumption of the bread *and* the wine but which moreover must be *complete* in order to be recognized as such.

The difference observed here between Protestants and Catholics has less to do with the elements consumed (host vs bread and grape juice) than the specific role of the faithful during Communion. Although the Catholics tend to pay particular attention to the correct handling of the host, it appears that the reality of the Communion act resides less in the appropriate gestures than in the very nature of the host. The multiple regulations and corrections of the Eucharistic gestures show that the faithful (like Jesus) *produce* the host. At the same time, this production appears secondary. The reality of the Eucharistic act does not result from a correct communicant's performance but rather from the nature of the host. Children learn, in fact, that the host's state makes the communicant. When they eat non-consecrated hosts, they are training. When they take consecrated ones, they receive Communion whatever the quality of their performance. For the Protestants, the state of bread is also different during the training sessions and the genuine Communion. This difference is, above all, due to the faithful. The bread of catechism is the whole loaf while the bread of the Lord's Supper is broken and consumed. Here, the difference between exercise and Communion is determined by human action. In the first case, children do not make the gestures or if they do, they perform them with empty hands. In the second, they perform them entirely. Young Catholics learn that to receive Communion is to ingest a consecrated host (and vice versa). Whereas young Protestants learn that to receive Communion is to break, share and ingest bread and wine (and vice versa). This difference between Protestant and Catholic training is fundamental. At this point, the specific denominational apprehension of the Communion is determined.

According to the way the partnership is defined, each participant takes an equal place and role in Eucharist. Each one takes part in the constitution of the relationship and shares in the production of the other ones as partners.[7] However, the apprenticeship of Communion shows a hierarchical collaboration. First, in both Churches, children learn that the author and the main actor of the Lord's Supper is Jesus. Without His act of institution and His renewed presence, there is no Communion. When God leaves the scene, there is no Eucharist. On the other hand, the roles of the other participants are taught in different ways in each Church. The importance of their respective involvement is, to some extent, reversed. Catholic exercises suggest that the main actor, next to God, is the host, as rehearsals, although rigorous, minimize human competence to the benefit of the host. In other words, even if a child adequately handles a piece of unleavened bread this does not make it the body of Christ. But the state of the host, consecrated or not, draws the boundary between the communicant and the non-communicant. Protestant exercises seem to indicate that faithful hold the second role. The child who is training should not perform the necessary gestures completely because to perform them adequately and totally already signifies that he receives the Communion. In the Catholic training, human action is minimized in such a way that the Christian seems to be the passive beneficiary of the actions of his partners, God and the host. In the Protestant initiation, bread and wine are the passive matters; ordinary commodities of the divine intention and of the human projects rather than genuine partners. In this sense, what the catechists teach children is a hierarchical mastery of ritual action rather than a belief or a non-belief in transubstantiation. This teaching shows us that it is less important to know how the divine presence occurred in Eucharist than to understand the specific register of the roles which a Church imposes and proposes to the faithful and to the liturgical objects. The dogmatic divergence which usually focuses on the mode of God's presence, appears here rather through a differentiated learning regarding both the human involvement and the role of objects in ritual action. Are communicants the producers or the receivers of the Eucharistic action? Are the Eucharistic bread and wine regarded as partners? This understanding of the control of the action is essential for the *felicity* of the Eucharistic act but it broadly relates to the involvement, expected and hoped for, of the children, in faith. The contemporary project of transmission of faith which neglects all dogmatic teaching does not dissolve the denominational particularities. On the contrary, it puts them at the centre of the partnership that Christian children are invited to establish with God.

Notes

1. See also Dubied (1992).
2. For a criticism of the notion of belief, see, in particular, Pouillon (1979), Favret-Saada (1977), Lenclud (1990), Claverie (1990), and Latour (1996).
3. 'Le croire se mesure aux liens plus ou moins étroits qu'il entretient avec ce qu'il fait faire et/ou s'attend à voir faire' (de Certeau 1981: 8).
4. See also Latour (1990, 2000).
5. I would like to thank the Fyssen Foundation for the financial support that it provided for this research and the Institute of Ethnology, University of Neuchâtel, that welcomed me throughout my stay.
6. For Catholics, this is the First Communion. For Protestants a special service is centered on Lord's Supper where children can receive Communion.
7. Latour's sociology of the 'factisches', which explores another definition of action, could be used here insofar as each participant '*fait faire*' to the others what it will become. Cf. in particular Latour (2000).

Chapter 11

WHAT IS INTERESTING ABOUT CHINESE RELIGION

Charles Stafford

As a child, I spent about four hours every week attending church services with my parents, who were devout Christians. During those hours, I might have focused my attention on any number of things. But I have a strong recollection of staring, on successive Sunday mornings, at the light fixtures on the ceiling of our church. I found myself stranded, to borrow Harvey Whitehouse's expression, in a rather dull 'mode of religiosity'. The services bored me and I would sometimes lie next to my mother, flat on my back on the pew, staring upwards. There I saw fluorescent lights with grid-like covers which resembled, or so I thought, Nabisco Sugar Wafers (a popular brand of biscuit at the time). I may have noticed the similarity because I was hungry, counting the minutes until we could go home and eat Sunday lunch.

I mention this anecdote because it raises an important question about what religion is, and more specifically about what goes through our minds while participating in it. And I am drawn to this question, in part, because when I first started conducting research on Chinese religion in a Taiwanese village almost twenty years ago (cf. Stafford 1995, 2000) I was struck by how *interesting* everything seemed by comparison with the boring religion of my childhood.

This was not simply the effect of it being new to me. Much of what happened would surely have grabbed the attention of almost anybody from anywhere. Certainly no-one was required to listen to long-winded sermons or to sit in temples for hours at a time. Instead they could watch, among other things, the bloody spectacle of spirit mediumship. Or they could participate in deeply theatrical, indeed operatic, rituals for 'sending off' the dead. Almost every activity was punctuated by attention-grabbing volleys of firecrackers and by the frenetic crashing of drums, gongs and cymbals. Rather liberally, I thought, the villagers (including children) seemed to be allowed to concentrate on whatever they liked, while safely ignoring the rest.

And it did turn out, as one might have expected, that there are some boring things about Chinese religion too. I soon learned, for instance, that most villagers had no interest whatever in watching priests carry out routine tasks. It's not that what priests do is unimportant – on the contrary. But more than once during fieldwork I ended up as the sole observer of their work, sitting in a corner of the temple while everybody else got on with more interesting things, such as playing cards or gossiping or working. The people I have known in rural communities, however devout, have also seemed largely indifferent to Daoist or Buddhist philosophy, and only rarely bothered to talk about doctrine, as such. In fact, quite a few of the people I met did not even know the names of the gods they worshipped on a regular basis, except for the most famous ones such as Guan Yin or Mazu. Not much mental effort was wasted by them on such matters.

Of course, the level of interest in specific aspects of religion and ritual varied from person to person and between social groups, and it must also have varied over time. For instance, children seemed to enjoy the puppet and variety shows put on to amuse the gods during temple festivals. But I was told by many people that children's attendance at such events had, in reality, declined markedly after the arrival in the village of televisions and video players. They claimed that religious entertainments were now sometimes watched only by the gods. Meanwhile, one of my friends, a young man who had been injured in a car accident, suddenly became fascinated by Daoist esoterica. Perhaps he would become a priest? He spent hours poring over religious texts which few other villagers even knew existed.

*   *   *

Surely the question of attention – that is, what people pay attention to and what they ignore – should be a central one for the anthropology of religious *learning*. We can imagine religious or moral lessons being 'acquired' in any number of ways, including both explicitly (e.g. through hearing sermons) and implicitly (e.g. through observing – perhaps without much noticing it – the body language of the elders). But in order for individuals to develop new understandings of how things are, i.e. in order for learning to take place, there clearly has to be a cognitive effort of some kind. This raises the difficult question of exactly what motivates this effort and exactly what it is directed *at*. A good religious text might well force you to rethink your understanding of sin through subtle argumentation, and by demanding – somehow – that you concentrate your thoughts on this famously difficult topic. But what if your mind is elsewhere? What does it take for a text (or sermon, or ritual) to lead you to think new thoughts?

In *Day of Shining Red* (which is based on fieldwork amongst the Gnau of Papua New Guinea), Gilbert Lewis discusses the question of attention. Among other things, he suggests that the 'alerting quality of ritual' may influence both participants and anthropologists. With respect to the latter he says that:

> The fixity, the public attention, the colour and excitement or solemnity that go with such performances are what captures the anthropologist's attention. He responds to this peculiar quality in ritual performances. It can guide him as to where to concentrate his efforts at interpretation (Lewis 1980: 7).

So the anthropologist follows, at least to some extent, the gaze of his informants. But what of the Gnau? What guides them in concentrating *their* efforts and thoughts? Lewis wanted to avoid imposing his own understandings of ritual onto Gnau practices (not least because they have no words at all for 'rite' or 'ritual'); so he adopted the simple fieldwork technique of leaving a tape recorder running while they prepared, over a period of days, for an important event (even when he, himself, had wandered away to observe something else). This generated data of a kind – specifically: a large quantity of unsolicited direct speech from his informants – about Gnau priorities when it comes to ritual (Lewis 1980: 39–40). In principle, this should reveal something, at least indirectly, about what they are bothering to *think* about.

But as Lewis makes clear, this evidence cannot, on its own, solve the anthropological problem of interpreting and understanding ritual. Nor can it answer, on its own, the question of what the Gnau learn through participation in initiation ceremonies, house-building rites, etc. One problem is that even if they talk a great deal about certain aspects of ritual, it cannot be assumed that their most significant cognitive efforts are related to those things. After all, a number of anthropologists, most famously Levi-Strauss, have suggested that informants' explicit and/or conscious understandings of rituals, myths and other cultural forms – the kinds of things they could talk about if asked – are somewhat beside the point. By way of exposure to cultural forms people may come to master many complex things (including underlying cultural logics or 'grammars') which they typically would never – and in most cases could never – put into words.

One virtue of this approach to cultural transmission is that it highlights the central significance of implicit – perhaps 'unconscious'? –

knowledge (cf. Bourdieu 1977 [1972]; Bloch 1998: 3–21). One defect, however, is that in doing so it relies on models of thinking and learning which are not well supported by the known facts of human psychology (Sperber 1975, 1985: 64–93, 1996; Bloch 1998, 2005). Following on from this, in recent years cognitive anthropologists have begun to formulate classic anthropological questions about cultural/religious learning in new – and hopefully more psychologically plausible – ways. As part of this shift, the question of attention has, in one way or another, been very much at the foreground.

Notably, Pascal Boyer (inspired in part by Sperber's (1996: 56–76) epidemiological model of cultural transmission) has produced a cognitive account of (among other things) the 'catchiness' of certain types of religious representations (Boyer 1994, 2001b). Boyer notes that humans are inclined to pay attention to and process – and thus recall and pass on – representations which fit well with our intuitive expectations (e.g. spirits whose psychological dispositions are quite like those of humans) while simultaneously violating some of them (e.g. spirits who contravene some of the laws of physics). That we are inclined to *register* such representations can be shown experimentally (Boyer and Ramble 2001). Of course, Boyer's point is not that individuals necessarily sit around consciously registering and commenting on the intuitive and counter-intuitive properties of the spirits they worship. The point instead is that we as a species – at an aggregate level, over time – have intuitively *selected* certain religious representations as interesting and memorable, thus ensuring them a place in our history. (Note the contrast with my childhood anecdote, above, in which the question of selective attention was formulated very differently – almost as a matter of individual volition.)

Harvey Whitehouse, for his part, stresses that the process of selection and remembering outlined by Boyer may be tied not only to cognitive mechanisms but also to sociocultural factors – including, for instance, the frequency with which representations are transmitted within particular traditions. Whitehouse has written extensively on the very significant contrasts between different 'modes of religiosity'. For example, in some traditions rituals are repeated frequently – they may be boring, but they cannot really be avoided, nor can one exactly avoid the representations and doctrines embedded in them. Whereas in other traditions, rituals are sporadic, even once-in-a-generation, events. They may involve dramatic (sometimes life-threatening) experiences which not only capture the imagination of participants, but stay with them as vivid (unforgettable) memories throughout life (Whitehouse 1995, 2000, 2004).

This takes me back where I started: religious phenomena vary greatly in the extent to which they demand our attention, and in the means through which they do so. But it is also true (as both Boyer and Whitehouse observe, and as I noted above) that individual participants vary a good deal in the extent to which they find the same religious phenomena compelling. What is 'interesting' for us at an aggregate level, over time, may not correlate very closely to individual experiences of religion. Undoubtedly many people, rather like my childhood self, are inclined to ignore the proceedings as often as possible.

However – and for the purposes of the present discussion this is a crucial point – our attempts to do just this (e.g. to stare at light fixtures rather than listen to sermons) are confounded in one important respect by our nature as human beings. In brief, we typically find it difficult, sometimes almost impossible, to ignore the psychological states of the people around us, and to shut out the attempts they are making, verbally and non-verbally, to communicate with us. On the contrary, there is usually little else in the world that we find more fascinating. This is because we are natural psychologists (Bloch forthcoming; Humphrey 2002 [1986]), and also because our default assumption – for better or worse – is that almost any human communication directed at us will, in some way, be 'relevant' (Sperber and Wilson 1995 [1986]). Following on from this, I want to suggest that when we 'learn religion' we are often, to a very significant extent, focusing our actual attention and efforts on the psychology of the humans around us.

*   *   *

But let me go back to the question of what is interesting about Chinese religion. In answering this, the evidence I rely on is primarily ethnographic, and not entirely unlike the randomly tape-recorded evidence used by Lewis for the Gnau. I assume that something is interesting if people *appear* to pay attention to it, if they stay in the vicinity in order to watch something happen rather than walking away from it, and/or if they bother to talk about it spontaneously. Sometimes they might themselves explicitly refer to an issue or event as being 'interesting' (*you yisi*) or 'fun' (*hao wan*); but for the most part I make inferences about levels of interest based on my own observations.

Readers should again bear in mind the significant distinction between something being interesting and it being important. As I pointed out above, most people would say that priestly work is important – it's just that the rest of us do not really need to think much about it. And here I want to focus precisely on those areas of religious life in which people *do* appear to invest a good deal of mental energy, on the assumption that attention is correlated to learning in some way. But in proceeding along these lines, I still want to hold in mind two points which emerged in the previous section: (1) that important cultural knowledge may be transmitted at an implicit level, and therefore not be very obvious/accessible to either informants or to those who observe them; (2) that 'paying attention' to things in one's environment may be motivated not only by factors such as personal interest, but also by the underlying realities of evolved human psychology.

What is interesting about Chinese religion? First, as you might expect, people are generally very keen on the social paraphernalia of religion: the gossip about how events are funded, for example, or the rivalries between temples. In short, they elaborate on the social business somewhat outside the boundary of religion, in the strict sense. Of course this boundary is a matter of definition. But people generally pay more attention to the noisy banquet happening outside a temple, for example, than to the ritual being held inside. Or, to cite another example, when they attend weddings they usually seem rather indifferent to the symbolism of marriage, per se, whereas they are endlessly fascinated by questions such as how much everything costs, and who helped to pay for it.

Second – and again, as you might expect – people are keen on stories about gods and other spirits. In Taiwan, to be sure, there is widespread interest in the story of the goddess Mazu. As a child, Mazu went into a trance and saw her father and brothers drowning at sea, after which she tried to rescue them in a miraculous fashion. She scooped up her brothers in her hands, and her father in her mouth. In one tragic version of the story, however, her mother wakens Mazu from the trance, causing her to open her mouth and drop her father back to his death. Divine narratives of this kind are told in various ways, now including televised versions which are effectively soap operas with period costumes and special effects. I should also mention that in the context of local spirit medium sessions – in which mediums speak and act as if they were gods – these divine stories come to life in two significant ways. On the one hand, what happens in the spirit world moves out of the fixed realm of received legend and becomes less predictable. This, it seems, is very interesting. On the other hand, the gods start to behave almost as if they had become regular members of the local community. This, it seems, is also very interesting. They scold villagers for their shortcomings, give them highly personal advice about even trivial matters, and joke with them about the ironies of recent events. They handle difficult cases of childhood illness and misfortune, and mothers therefore listen to the words they say with great attentiveness. In sum: the gods are localized, and become inserted into the unpredictable soap opera of local life.

Third, people are keen on the parts of Chinese religion in which, in one way or another, belief is called into question. I should point out that in Chinese popular religion this is *not* something which happens during routine, everyday worship. On most occasions, people are simply required to offer incense to gods and ancestors, as a mark of respect, or to show up at banquets without really being forced to say or show that they believe in the literal existence of spirits, or in the ability of spirits to act in this world, or in the possibility of an afterlife, etc. It's almost as if you can think and believe what you like, so long as the correct rites are performed (see below). However there are, in fact, a number of practices within this tradition which can be said to push the question of belief quite hard – and my point is that people tend to find these practices especially compelling. Spirit mediums again provide a good illustration. In Taiwan, at least, much of what they do – e.g. writing classical Chinese in spite of never having learnt it – is explicitly about convincing doubters to believe. The foregrounding of doubt is also aggressively there when individual worshippers are asked to submit to their own possession experiences, e.g. by walking through fire under divine protection, or by carrying (in front of their neighbours and friends) sedan chairs which are (supposedly) being violently rocked by the gods. Can it really be true?

Fourth – and in some respects this focus may seem more surprising than the others I have mentioned – participants in Chinese popular religion are notably keen on the numerical aspects of what they are doing. As I have discussed elsewhere, when preparing for things like temple festivals they often talk spontaneously about quantities, rather than qualities, of things. They talk about numbers of sticks of incense, numbers of times to bow before the gods, numbers of tables at banquets, numbers of dishes of food on each banquet table, numbers of families represented at the rite, etc. Meanwhile, Chinese cosmology is also explicitly numerical – even mathematical – in orientation, thus making it possible for people to literally 'calculate' their fates. All of this is consistent with the general 'numericization' of Chinese and Taiwanese society and culture, and is built on the conviction that numbers say something profound about the universe and about the flow of human life within it (cf. Stafford 2003, 2007).

*　　*　　*

To briefly recapitulate: I have so far highlighted four areas or dimensions of religious life which seem to capture the interest and attention of the people I have known in rural Taiwan and China – the social side of religion (including things like banquets); religious stories (if you like, the divine soap opera); the parts of religion in which belief is challenged; and numbers. This list is not meant to be comprehensive. Religion is, of course, a hugely complex phenomenon, and people pay attention to all manner of things. However, I would suggest that if we could somehow install timers in the brains of my religiously active informants, we would find that a significant proportion of their 'thinking time' was focused on the areas I have mentioned above.

So what, if anything, might bring these four – rather diverse – things together?

One possibility, albeit somewhat counter-intuitive, is that people are interested in the parts of religion which are the most like ordinary life. As I have said, they focus on 'real world' activities around the edges of religion, such as fund-raising and neighbourly gossip and banquets. This is all pretty much like fund-raising and gossip and banqueting in relation to anything else; it doesn't seem to be religion, per se, that people find fascinating about it. A similar argument could be made about the stories of the gods. Of course, these involve remarkable events. But part of what is truly engaging about them, needless to say, is that they deal with issues (loyalty, disloyalty, love, death) familiar to everybody. This familiarity effect is heightened when spirit mediums insert, as I have described, the narratives of the gods into the soap opera of ordinary human life (e.g. as when they battle demons in order to save local children from illnesses). It's almost as if the more the gods are like us, and the more they are actually living in our midst, as part of *our* story, the more we can be bothered to focus sustained attention on them.

And what about the parts of religion in which belief is challenged? At first glance, these practices (such as fire-walking) seem designed to highlight precisely the extraordinary, rather than this-worldly, nature of religion and of divine power. But they also surely test the possibility that religion is, after all, literally true, and that it is therefore part of the ordinary world – among the things we can really see and touch. Again: the closer it is to life, the more we can be bothered to pay attention. Then, finally, there is the focus on numbers, which at first glance seems the odd one out. However, it should be stressed that real life in rural China and Taiwan (i.e. everyday experience in the domains of kinship, economics, politics, etc.) is equally heavily numericized – to the apparently endless fascination of ordinary people. In other words, this numerical orientation is not something restricted to religion and cosmology. On the contrary, when people 'talk in numbers' during religious activities, it is scarcely different from what they do every day, as a matter of routine (e.g. in playing the lottery, or haggling over purchases).

But if it is true that what is interesting about Chinese religion is that it is like real life, we are of course left with the old question of why it should need to exist at all as a separate domain. Why, for example, do religious stories need to include bizarre elements if what we are really keen on is their ordinariness? Bearing this in mind, let me try a slightly different tack, while still holding onto the idea that there is something real-world about most religious preoccupations. I want to suggest: (1) that people are interested in these four aspects of Chinese popular religion at least in part because they are *psychologically* compelling; and (2) that when people 'learn religion' – more specifically, when they concentrate on what is happening in the religious sphere – they are *'learning psychology'* in several interesting senses.

These suggestions rest on the claim of Humphrey and others, already mentioned above, that all humans are 'psychologists', in the sense that we have implicit and sometimes explicit theories about how people think (Humphrey 2002 [1986]). We are, more precisely, innately predisposed to be extremely *interested*, from early childhood, in the question of human thought not least because knowledge in this domain is a prerequisite of human intersubjectivity and communication. We are intuitively inclined to assess the psychology of those around us (including spiritual others), i.e. to 'read their minds' in order to ascribe intentions (and other psychological states) to them. The significance of this for religion in particular has been discussed by a number of authors (cf. Bloch forthcoming, Boyer 2000b, Barrett 2004).

But exactly what, from the point of view of folk psychologists, is interesting about Chinese religion? What can they be said to learn from participating in it?

One obvious answer, much discussed by anthropologists, is that religious narratives might teach them something – perhaps in a coded way – about what it is to be human, about the complex nature of human existential dilemmas, and so on (for an interesting discussion along these lines see Sangren 2003). But it could be argued that these mythical 'psychology lessons' are sometimes less subtle than the understandings ordinary humans derive from their everyday experience of other people in the world. Indeed, what is perhaps most psychologically remarkable about religious narratives, at least from the point of view of non-believers, is not their wise content – something replicated in stories of many kinds – but rather the fact that the people around us behave as if they were factual. In other words, for many of us the most striking psychological feature of religion is the apparent suspension of disbelief amongst participants. This is a domain of life in which, after all, huge collective efforts are made (temples are built, wars fought, etc.) and yet doing such things *genuinely* in the name of the gods requires participants to behave in quite remarkable ways. They must make emotional commitments to spirits that cannot be shown to exist.

But is the suspension of disbelief the kind of thing folk psychologists – believers and non-believers alike – are themselves likely to find striking? As I have already mentioned, Chinese religion is noted for placing a priority on ritual practice – that is, for precisely *not* worrying much about the problem of belief. James L. Watson, in a widely cited article (1988), suggested more specifically that Chinese religion is characterized by a tendency to consider 'correct practice' (orthopraxy) much more important than 'correct belief' (orthodoxy). But this raises again the complex question of the relationship between something being interesting and it being important. Watson argues, and I would agree with him, that the correct performance of rituals is a priority in China. But what this actually means, in practice, is that people want the rituals to happen – not that they have any desire, for the most part, to actually think about them in detail. Further to Watson's argument, I would suggest that while practice is indeed important, belief is somehow far more interesting for most ordinary people. And if one considers the whole gamut of Chinese religious practices (especially the more ecstatic elements revolving around spirit possession and ritualized violence at festivals, rather than solemn ancestral rites) there are a number of contexts in which belief – and disbelief – is heavily foregrounded.

One should also bear in mind that Chinese and Taiwanese religion today is rife with different types of scepticism. For instance, many people say that ancestors can and perhaps even should be 'memorialized' simply out of respect, and that the same can even hold true for gods, who are really nothing more than a special subset of dead people. But for them this is not religion, per se. And while mild sceptics (memorializers) of this kind may not believe in an afterlife or in the literal existence of spirits, they can still happily participate in rituals with their neighbours. Others, by contrast, are more aggressive in rejecting religious claims altogether and will, for example, make fun of spirit mediums and their clients as victims of superstition – while sometimes still being prepared, nonetheless, to make respectful offerings to the gods and ancestors. Nobody living in a village in modern China or Taiwan could be unaware of the widespread doubts about religious claims, which have been broadcast for years as a matter of government policy. Possibly as a result of this, very few of them, no matter how devout, are what could be called literalists: believers in the literal truth of religion. And the few people who *are* literalists – e.g. those who get too carried away with the idea that the gods are here right now, moving around the village on a daily basis – are seen to be somewhat strange. Everybody else (certainly the mild and aggressive sceptics, but also the majority of devout worshippers, including spirit mediums and their clients) seems likely to be aware that something psychologically interesting is going on.

In suggesting this, I take the lead of Dan Sperber, who in a famous essay criticized anthropologists who make the 'unwarranted empirical assumption' that:

... religious and other apparently irrational beliefs are not distinguished from ordinary knowledge in the believer's mind (either consciously or unconsciously) ... Even if the subjects failed to report a difference between their views on witches and their views on cows, even if they asserted both views in similar fashion, it would not follow that they hold them in the same way (Sperber 1985: 48).

If a distinction of this kind (say, gods versus cows) exists in the minds of Chinese believers too – and I would be very surprised if it did not, regardless of what happens elsewhere – then it should be interesting for them to participate in something like fire-walking, in which physical risks are being taken by fellow villagers on the basis of what they, themselves, know on some level to be a peculiar and possibly even dubious type of knowledge. During fire-walking episodes, they have repeated opportunities to observe and guess at the psychological states of other participants, and also to reflect on their own psychological states, for instance by asking themselves if they, too, are not participating in some kind of play-acting. Are the gods really there? And if not, why on earth are we going to so much trouble? If the gods are not really there, will I be burnt by walking through fire? My assumption is that with age and experience the answers to such questions, and indeed the questions themselves, might become increasingly complex and shrewd. And the 'suspension of disbelief' problem is, of course, only one of the many psychological issues to be confronted.

*   *   *

I have been arguing that my informants appear to be interested in aspects of religion which are psychologically compelling and instructive. It is perhaps relatively easy to make such a claim based on (1) their interest in the social paraphernalia of religion (which is just the normal human drama of gossip, rivalry, comradeship, etc.); (2) their interest in the 'soap opera' of the gods' lives (ditto); and (3) their interest in belief-challenging (and thus psychologically interesting) religious practices.

But what about the numbers? Numbers, at least from a Western point of view, seem not only to be almost intrinsically dull (as opposed to attention-grabbing) but also, more importantly, to have nothing very obvious to do with human psychology, emotion, intention, etc. I should probably clarify again that I'm not, in any case, claiming that people are only interested in aspects of religion which are psychologically compelling. Still, as I have pointed out, from the perspective of the Chinese tradition as a whole, numerical knowledge is certainly not considered to be dull. On the contrary, numbers are held to say something intrinsically interesting and important about the universe and about human life. But specifically within the religious domain, numbers have an added advantage. Briefly, in divination and other numerological practices they are a way, precisely, of trying to evade human intentionality – that is, of escaping the potential traps which might be set for us by the people around us. In theory (if not always in practice) the logical rigour of numerical reasoning enables people to construct a narrative of human experience – and of arbitrary fate – which is *not* distorted by the vagaries and dissimulations of human thought and language. In some respects it is the antidote, and a very effective one at that, for everything else religious.

*   *   *

I began this paper with a story about myself as a child, staring at light fixtures on the ceiling of the church, imagining them as Nabisco Sugar Wafers, perhaps because I was hungry. From my experience of living in Taiwanese and Chinese villages, I know that in these places the intellectual engagement of children with their religious environments is equally patchy and selective. An important point, of course, is that this intellectual freedom (or diffidence, as the case may be) is made possible by people like priests and elderly women who manage to sustain religion, as a collective artefact, long enough for younger generations to actually, eventually focus their attention on it. Much of the time, however, the mind wanders, and it is often difficult to say exactly what children are thinking about or learning as religion passes them by. In my experience, for many of them religion is primarily a domain associated with food and firecrackers, rather than anything else. But food and firecrackers are also psychologically interesting, the former because food connects the emotions of domestic and communal commensality to the world of spirits, and the latter because firecrackers help introduce an air of violence, danger and intense excitement into what might otherwise be boring public events. Over time, children (partly drawn in by the food and the firecrackers) are given repeated opportunities to observe and participate in the aspects of religion which I have discussed in this paper – the social paraphernalia, the stories, the parts of religion where belief is challenged, the numbers – all of which might provide them with 'psychology lessons' of different kinds.

However, I would like to stress, by way of conclusion, that my aim is not to provide a deeply reductionist account of religion, in which its sole function is to teach us this or that. Nor do I think for a minute that psychological accounts of religion are intrinsically preferable to historical, sociological and ethnographic ones. But examining religious participation in terms of what it teaches participants about human thought may be an interesting, and potentially productive, avenue for research.

Of course, the actual developmental story, the empirical story of how children engage with religion, and the ways in which it may be psychologically instructive for them to do so, is beyond the scope of this very short chapter. But a good starting point – beyond the ethnography of children's religious experience – might be found in the thought-provoking work of the psychologist Paul Harris. Harris's recent research examines what he calls 'the work of the imagination', including the realms of make-believe, role-play and religion (Harris 2000). His leading idea is that the ability of children to entertain hypothetical possibilities (including thinking about impossible, but nevertheless imaginable, outcomes) plays an important part in children's cognitive development. Among other things, he explores the possibility – clearly a crucial one in terms of the argument put forward in this paper – that sharing imaginative projects with others helps children learn about how people think. As Michael Tomasello and his colleagues have noted, religion is but one illustration of the wider human ability to produce highly elaborate schemes and projects (including, ultimately, social institutions) through shared intentionality (Tomasello *et al.* 2005). This skill at shared intentionality is one of the reasons that we, as humans, are instinctively drawn to observe and participate in religion, and are also motivated to learn lessons from it as a living product of human thought.

Chapter 12

THE SOUND OF WITCHCRAFT
NOISE AS MEDIATION IN RELIGIOUS TRANSMISSION

Michael Rowlands

Once, when I was living in Bamenda, a small provincial town in Cameroon, I stayed in a house next to one of the new *Bonagen* (pidgin for Born Again) churches that had recently been founded in Mankon Old Town. It was a mistake. The noise kept me awake many nights and the hustle and bustle of living in the neighbourhood quite wore me out. I can remember thinking at the time, how this contrasted with the sedate atmosphere of the Catholic church and its complex of buildings set on top of a hill where I could go and have my car fixed and be given a cup of coffee in the seminary rest house. In experiencing the contrast, I admit to my own prejudice in which I was associating noise with disorder but also with social effervescence; ok for a while but gradually it gets you down. But it also made me realize that sound and in particular its amplification, had an impact in Mankon-Bamenda that was something more than relative ideas of order and disorder. After all, the association of noise with liveliness and social excitement is a widely recognized relationship between Christianity and popular entertainment in Africa (cf. Collins 2004). It is also distinguished by spontaneity and informality and in particular relevance; the capacity for sound to have an effect, to act as a medium of answerability. Finally, I came to realize that, as recognized elsewhere in Pentecostalism, noise in the *Bonagen* churches in Bamenda is associated with wealth and success and is seen as a means of unblocking or removing the obstacles that impede personal progress and prosperity. But the means of achieving this depends on the materiality of the noise produced which, in turn, is deeply embedded in a praxeology of speech and sound that is distinctive to living and dying in Bamenda.

In the *Bonagen* churches in Bamenda, as elsewhere in this part of Africa, the association of noise with worship is a literal following of the narrative of the Pentecost. In the text of the Acts of the Apostles (2: 1–13) it says twice that the Christ's disciples heard 'a great noise', 'a sound from heaven as of a mighty rushing wind and it filled the entire house where they were sitting'. They were filled with the Holy Ghost and began to speak with other tongues, 'as the Spirit gave them utterance'. The inspiration of speaking in other but the same tongue, which brings a diversity of peoples together in the same congregation, is a consequence of being possessed by the noise of the Holy Spirit. An important connection made by the congregations in Bamenda, is between the sound of the Holy Spirit, as the blowing breath of God, and the performance of miracles, i.e. if you want miracles you have to make a noise. Noise production in Bamenda is efficacious by adapting to Pentecostal innovation through drawing heavily on local procedural knowledge. In this chapter I will argue that such adaptation has to be related in particular to music, death celebrations and noise in a 'traditional' setting. Both settings share in common, I suggest, a reliance on noise to create a sense of shared feeling and experience and a belief that this contributes to the removal of the impediments which block the realization of personal success and prosperity. They also show how the senses play a role in learning and the transmission of knowledge. This is obvious in respect to the fact that music and singing is often pedagogical, but what we have to add to this is how the materiality of sound has to be understood as part of the transmission process. Indeed, we show how sound is part of the 'message' itself, inasmuch as sound plays a cosmological role and helps shape social experience.

The relationship between music, noise and religious transmission is something more therefore than the creation of 'soundscapes' and more like what Anzieu (1985), Lecourt (1990) and Warnier (2001, 2006) have variously described as 'acoustic envelopes'. From such a praxeological and cognitive point of view, noise and music produce an envelope in which people are included or excluded or if they are inside the bubble but do not belong (as in my case), it produces a cognitive contradiction and they find it unbearable. So, sound and noise and music are means of inclusion and exclusion, both cognitively and physically, that address issues of 'belonging' but also mark what it is to be outside the 'envelope' and to be vulnerable to anxiety, fear and terror.

Acoustic Envelopes

The usual point made about sound is the absence of boundaries in space (Lecourt 1990). There is no respite from sonority, except deafness and death. Also it lacks substance – sound-objects are the constructs of composers and analysts and yet like images, a capacity to hear relies on simultaneity of expression. Yet whilst there is a continuum between no sound and loud sound, in most situations there is a boundary that appears at the point where an encounter occurs between the experiences of the subject, the sound out there and the 'gestalt' effect. Acoustic envelopes, in Anzieu's sense, are therefore a consequence of hearing and perception, including everything that goes together to influence sonorous experience (Anzieu 1985). Anzieu used the term 'sonorous bath' to describe this and he also uses the bathing metaphor to introduce the idea of weightlessness – the feeling of being lulled, born along, transported in the movement that he also calls the 'qualities of holding' (Anzieu 1985; Lecourt 1990). The sonorous bath is therefore the sharing of sounds, music, words, noises, vibrations and silences that we are introduced to from birth – a veritable acoustic womb. Warnier distinguishes between sounds associated with one's own body and self recognition and an undifferentiated 'sound bath' which is close to but clearly differentiated from oneself (Warnier forthcoming). Anzieu claims that the infant builds and inhabits three different acoustic bubbles within six weeks of birth: those of the self, those made by the noises of the nurturing subject – this may be several persons – who are out there, can approach and go away, and the last is made by a sort of 'gestalt' combination of the other two (Anzieu 1985). In Bamenda, from birth the sonorous bath is maternal in terms of the combination of sounds, voices, women singing to babies and the close touch of being carried on the body. Men will sing sweet lullabies to babies in contrast to the use of harder and more abstract voices when addressing other grown males. Acoustic envelopes are therefore like bubbles produced by noise and music to which you either belong or are excluded by the process of growing up within them. In the Pentecostal sense of the importance of 'speaking with one voice', it is literally loudness of speech that asserts this particular desirable state and therefore creates the bubble within which the unity of vocal possession or the capacity to speak in other tongues comes about. It is therefore not surprising to find that 'noise' in some sense is deeply embedded both within the psychic origins of birth as a highly maternalized soundscape and also as a highly inclusionary participatory act that acts to define the outside and the nature of the excluded.

Even though sound is a kind of continuum, the capacity to hear without contradiction is an aspect of being brought up or socialized within these sonic envelopes. Yet contradictions occur because we inhabit an envelope, however temporarily, not of our making. Also participation within it becomes restricted or formalized in such a way that cognitive participation may denote degrees of exclusion. To follow this point further, which is rather crucial for understanding religious transmission, I am drawn to Attali's model of the political economy of noise; that the form taken by these acoustic envelopes is also an indication of how violence is channelled: it reminds people from what forms of order they wish to escape or from which forms of disorder they wish to hide (Attali 1985: 6–11). Attali associates noise with Adorno's (1982) argument that music precedes and anticipates change – it is the disruptive effects of noise that opens up the potential for change to occur (Attali 1985: 43). At least this is the prejudice of a certain view of the history of popular music in which modern jazz and blues, described by Pentecostals as Satan's music, is said to derive from and anticipate a fusion with hot gospel and soul music or how resistance to the commercialization of rock music is said to have led punk bands to emphasize musical discordance in order to disrupt what had become the placid enjoyment of rock music as a music of repetition. Adorno, when he described modern avant-garde music espousing difficulty and complexity as cultural resistance to mimetic music, also claimed to uncover in these actions the hidden contradictions in bourgeois culture/society (Adorno1982; cf. Leppert 2002: 243–45).

As an example of exclusion within an acoustic envelope, the minimizing of sound as choral or liturgical music in the Western sacred tradition, created an envelope within which the majority of a congregation could hear but not perform. Such a sonic dichotomy did not always remain unquestioned; collective and vigorous choral singing, for example, became a characteristic feature of Welsh Methodism, as it broke from the orthodox Anglican church in the late eighteenth century in Britain. At first unable to build churches, meetings of thousands of people took place in fields to hear the visiting sermons and loudness was celebrated as a proper sign of worship. If we contrast noise to silence as resistance to formalization, we arrive at a certain continuity of thought about the capacity of religious and popular music to anticipate change. As Chris Hann mentions in a recent article, there have been numerous debates in Western orthodox Christianity as to the proper place for music in worshipping God (Hann 2003). Hann would claim that Weber's description of the increasing minimization of Western classical music as a product of a process of rationalization, had already been played out in the religious sphere. Within Christianity, one of the differences between the Eastern and Western churches is that in the former the entire liturgy should be sung as an integral part of worship whilst in the western tradition, the

introduction of instruments, solo singing and singing in the vernacular decontextualized music from worship (Hann 2003). In similar
vein, Adorno described the introduction of the phonograph record as
removing music from the realm of live performance and losing the
immediacy of collective participation. Yet with this process of petrification, comes a certain justification in the hope that 'once fixed in this
way, the last remnant of a universal language will be preserved' (cf.
Leppert 2002: 237).

We have detected two processes – formalization and petrification –
by which the contradictions implicit in acoustic envelopes can be realized. The former is mirrored in Bloch's discussion of formal oratory
and traditional authority as a means of transforming dangerous and
uncertain presents into fixed eternal and orderly pasts (Bloch 1975:
15). In his case, fixed loudness patterns and limited choices of intona-
tions are associated with formalized speech acts (Bloch 1975: 13). The
latter extends Adorno's riposte to Walter Benjamin that the technology for preserving and reproducing music rather than being a liberat-
ing force, will lead to isolated and passive listening; the i-pod acoustic
envelope whose individual listeners are in a sound bubble of their own
making, rather than sharing in a collective musical performance
(Adorno 2002: 243–45).

Belonging to a *Bonagen* church in Bamenda, whilst it involves
hearing in a different acoustic sphere from those of kin groups and the
practices of ancestral rituals, it is not contradictory to them. They both
depend on similar principles linking beliefs to the audible and a commitment to collective performance. Yet amplification implies the possibility of petrification and exclusion. Amplified noise shows the power
of the Holy Spirit and is deemed effective through the capacity of
sound to produce miracles. In one popular Nigerian Pentecostal video
film entitled 'The Beginning and the End', we see the preacher entering
a village which he visits in order to defeat the local sorcerer 'at home'.
He is preceded by men carrying powerful loudspeakers and he walks
along the paths of the village shouting at the top of his voice into a
microphone. The implication is that the witchcraft being sought is
silent. The people, believed to be possessed by the devil, will not make
any noise unless threatened. It is the noise from the loudspeakers that
will provoke and torment those possessed by the devil or witchcraft.
When the reverend shouts at the sick person or the bewitched, the victims in the film start yelling because the Devil possessing them is being
tormented by the noise. In this way, through the power of his amplified
voice, the pastor performs three miracles during this visit. His assis-
tants add to the noise and all of them place their hands on the sick or
mad person they have come to cure. All of this is done in a completely
orderly fashion; a matter of dressing in best clothes, following orderly

religious observation in terms of the length of time in prayer/singing/ shouting determining material and personal success/well-being. The fact that this goes along with high decibels and an impressive sound system implies that 'loudness' has a particular salience in both Pentecostal and kinship-based acoustic envelopes.

In Bamenda, 'loud speech', angry speech or unguarded comments are seen as inherently powerful and dangerous. Richard Dillon, for example, quotes a Meta case in which affines were arguing over bridewealth payments and one of them abruptly stopped and said: 'we should not talk so much; all these strong things we are saying might affect somebody' (Dillon 1990: 71). As he goes on to argue, the notion of 'mystical danger' stemming from a strong statement depends not only on the accuracy of the speech but also to whom it is addressed. Although the subject of the complaint is the husband and his patrilineage, it is believed that the *njawm* ('strong statement of correct words') of the MF will directly affect his daughter's children since they share his body substances. Speech in Bamenda, of a correct kind and loudness, is directly related to and activates physical effects that can cause a kin relative to become ill or to die. In Dillon's case, he also describes how the speech gains what he calls 'mystical power' by being spoken over an ancestral drinking horn and that it accumulates in it. The older the drinking horn, the more 'strong statements' that have been uttered over it, the more powerful it is.

The way different (church, state, kin-related) acoustic envelopes overlap and interpenetrate is also a consequence of attempts to limit access to the means of making different kinds of sounds. We have records at least since the 1930s to show that the tensions between the missions and the chiefs or Fons in Bamenda were often expressed over rights to play music in church and the recruiting of women in particular to form church choirs. The Fons would try to ban the playing of double gongs and xylophones in the churches and refuse the use of new styles of music and instruments at their annual dances. The fact that both draw heavily on local procedural knowledge of noise production means that such tensions have to be related to music, death celebration and noise in a 'traditional' setting.

Noise and Ritual Power

Funerals in Bamenda relate the living to the dead through the medium of sound. In this section, I am concerned with 'death celebrations'; those occasions, the first about a year after death, when a commemoration is held in the compound of the deceased. The decision when to hold 'a dance' is usually made after consulting a diviner and it may well coincide with the celebration of several ancestors who might otherwise feel neglected, particularly if a series of misfortunes had occurred recently that had sparked off feelings of anxiety. It may also be the occasion when the successor to the deceased title might be named since neglect of doing this is often the fault identified by a diviner. The prominence of the celebration is judged by the numbers attracted to it, the number of masked dance groups attending, whether they come from other villages and the status of the deceased. As with mortuary rites, death celebrations extend over several days and combine dancing and feasting, with the performance of masked dance groups. But 'music of the day' is separated from 'music of the night' with the latter both more secret and also more dangerous in terms of what can happen to those who both see and hear it in inappropriate ways. In the language of acoustic envelopes, music of the day is inclusive and harmonious whilst music of the night is heard as cacophonous, excluding and threatening; people usually stay inside their houses and, while they can 'hear' the music, they do not 'see it' and will remain outside of it. These two forms of music/noise also differ in the use of musical instruments with a combination of xylophone and drum ensembles and ankle rattles played in the day and the use of shrill sounding whistles or voice disguisers and double iron gongs at night.

Whilst death celebrations vary in detail, most comprise the following stages stretched out over 3–4 days and nights:

- *First day* – is when family/patrilineage group members meet in the compound of the deceased. They will bring and prepare food and drink. Local people wait for family/lineage members to come from elsewhere in Cameroon or arrive from abroad before anything more can be done so it can be a long drawn out wait into the night. An important requirement is that all should come to the compound without resentment or anger against other family members since this will lead to failure of the sacrifices to ancestors. People will sit and eat/drink and make statements about whether they are all 'speaking with the same mouth'.
- *Second day* – should be the formal meeting of family and patrilineage heads to discuss problems and in particular resolve disputes. No-one can make offerings to the compound shrines if they are angry with other family members. It will be noted whether some members have not turned up – whether those who have will have brought enough food, money, etc. with them for the celebration. Loud speech and angry words, unless resolved, can lead to people leaving and a decision whether to carry on with the event.
- *Second night* – family heads will meet in the night to sacrifice to lineage ancestors, discuss and resolve conflicts and decide on the

name of a successor. If decision is agreed, the successor will be 'captured' and prepared, i.e. he is stripped and his body smeared with a combination of palm oil and camwood, he will be given special 'foods'/medicines to eat and he will be dressed in a special blue/white cloth. The successor spends the rest of the night in the house with the ancestral altar. At some point, a visit by a 'masked' figure from the palace will come to remove the medicines that had been planted in the compound by the dead elder.

- *Third day* – is the day of the main dance when other patrilineage heads and the Fon will come to the compound. Masked dance groups may arrive from other quarters and villages. The majority of the food and drink is dispersed. Arrival of the Fon initiates the formal dance and the firing of dane guns. The successor is brought out and presented to the Fon. The latter will offer his cup of wine to him and drinking wine poured into his cupped hands makes the successor a person of shared substance with the Fon. It means he can touch the body of the king, address words to him directly and, if necessary, help prepare food for him or participate in palace rituals. The day ends with the dance of the Fon who joins everyone in a large circle, holding rattle spears in his hand, guns firing, feet stamping and the rousing loud sound of xylophones, drums, rattles and gongs.

Each of these stages can be elaborated in the details of gifts/recipients; food and sharing; treatment of the body; visual impact of the masked dancers and the instruments played and offerings given. Each masked group competes with the others for visual impact, the energy of the dancing and the quality of the music; the stamping of feet is exaggerated by the rhythm of ankle rattles; the speed of the xylophone/drum ensembles is intended to encourage the masked dancers to greater efforts. Depending on the status and wealth of the person remembered, masked dance groups and women's choirs will come from other quarters in Mankon or from other 'Fondoms' to celebrate the death. The aim is to create a single sonic envelope that is shared by all the participants: people are inside it and feel comfortable and will share in the benefits that flow from satisfied ancestors.

The significance of the musical instruments employed emerges most clearly when contrasted with the 'noise of the night' and its exclusionary intent. On the night of the second or third day, depending on when a message is sent to inform the palace that the name of a successor has been agreed, a group will leave one of the houses in the palace associated with a 'regulatory society' or *kwi'fo*. Here is a short summary of my participation in such a visit to a compound of a notable in Mankon-Bamenda organizing a death celebration:

We met at the palace in the house of *kwi'fo*, where each member brought raffia wine to share. Drinking had started by 11.30pm or so and soon the group began to play their music. Each man had either a whistle, a drum or a double gong. It takes an hour or more of playing and drinking for the whole group to assemble and finally be ready to move from the house. The idea, explained to me, is that we should walk to the compound of the deceased trying not to meet anyone on the way. The music we play will frighten any women and children but we will take the more obscure paths. As we walk in single file, *mabu* – a figure from the palace masked with a raffia cagoule precedes us – and the music of *kwi'fo* is played. Anyone who hears the music should rush indoors and shut the windows and doors. The music is strident; in particular I wince at the sharp whistle blowing. I ask about it and am told that *kwi'fo* is crying the death. When we reach the compound, nobody comes out to meet us. It is dark and silent. Only then do I realize that one of the group is from the patrilineage of the deceased but is not a title holder. He, with the head of the group, goes to the house of the deceased and goes inside. I stay with the others outside and we continue to play the music of *kwi'fo*. The two men come from the house holding a bag and one carrying a knife. We leave the compound and take the fastest and direct route back to the *kwi'fo* house in the palace. There I am able to ask about the bag and am told it contained a *kwi'fo* 'thing' – and I am told this had been taken from under one of the stones set in the hearth of the house of the deceased.

Unlike the masquerades of the day, *kwi'fo* members wear no masks. A single figure, mabu, who wears a cagoule made from raffia fibre, comes from the palace and escorts the group to the compound of the notable. The visit to the compound of the deceased involves no spectacle; if anything the reverse. *Kwi'fo* music should terrify; it will be heard but is played in order to prevent people seeing the men playing the instruments or having any physical contact with the group. Jokes are made about how women will rush off the path or out of the compound if there is any chance of them 'seeing' *kwi'fo*. Yet the music, while cacophonous, is not particularly loud nor is it played very quickly. But it is associated with violence. In the past, *takinge* – the executioner figure who carried out *kwi'fo* judgements, a figure whose head is also covered in a cagoule of raffia matting and carries a bag with a club inside – would leave from the *kwi'fo* house. A masked figure *mabu* would go ahead of it, playing strident notes on a whistle/voice disguiser. In both cases, it is *mabu* that creates the sound envelope within which all the figures are included, so that other people may hear it but stay outside and hide. The violence of *kwi'fo* is also associated with its origins as coming from outside the kingdom of Mankon. Hence its association with violence and death is the antithesis of the lineage heads and the Fon and by extension the authority of ancestors and the principle of the death celebration.

The 'noise of the night' and 'music of the day' are therefore alternative modes of religiosity, emotional states and feeling. They are formed as a consequence of the exclusionary and inclusionary nature of their respective sonic envelopes. In turn this sense of inclusion and exclusion is literally and physically experienced as alternative sources of religiosity; the noise of the forest or the wild being contrasted with the music of the compound and of ancestors. The shrill sound of the whistle/voice disguiser used by *mabu* associates it with the night and with the noises of the bush at night; the music both copies and participates in the shrill sounds of the wild. It is why the explanation given to me that the music of *kwi'fo* played at night is 'crying the death', is probably a gloss for my benefit, since *kwi'fo* cannot participate in the music of the day and the festivities of the compound. The intention is to create a sonic envelope that includes the powerful sound elements of animal and non-animal elements in the bush and will exclude people of the compound of the deceased or those encountered along the way. On other occasions, the same figure of *mabu* may come out of the *kwi'fo* house in the day to visit a death celebration or to regulate matters to do with markets but when it does it is silent. The idea that power is ambiguous is not unusual in this context and the association of things of the day and those of the night as both necessary and yet terrifying equally so. Nor is the relation of one to the other resolved by their presence in a death celebration. A sort of negative dialectics ensues during the three days of this event. All those elements of the night which had to do with the capacity of the lineage head to use violence (i.e. the elements removed from his house by the *kwi'fo*) are denied as being of any significance for both the successor and the lineage.

Music and the masquerades play another role for the installation of a successor to ancestral title. During a succession ritual, the masquerades that play after the successor has been anointed with a mixture of palm oil and camwood paste, received *ndor* – a necklace of green, succulent leaves (*Basella alba*), an ancestral drinking horn, and seated on his father's stool, are said 'to beat the head' by playing. The people who say this make no comment and it is not easy to interpret what they mean by this but I take it to be that the music continues the work done by the people who have rubbed, clothed and fed (i.e. worked upon) the body of the successor. Noise is physical and it contributes to producing the successor. Throughout the Grassfields, the successor is called the 'chop-chair' in Pidgin English which means the chair eater and the word for successor in Mankon (*ndze nda*) means 'house eater', i.e. to succeed to title is 'to eat the house'. The noises made by the masquerades are therefore physical and convey the idea that they are powerful and will wash over or even penetrate or be absorbed by the body of the successor and change its substance. 'Beating the head' suggests that the music will literally 'beat out' any witchcraft/spirit still inhabiting the body of the successor. Unlike the noise of the night that is threatening, music of the day, on the other hand, works with other materials and objects to feed and smooth the body of the successor, to remove impediments and generally unblock the passage to becoming a notable. The experience conveys a sense of alternative modes of religious practice which depend on a tension existing between more or less material worlds; a blurring of the material and the immaterial in terms of their affect on bodies but also in terms of the more ephemeral and ambiguous their state, the more dangerous this will be. The religiosity of the day in a sense depends on making the ritual practice as material and as concrete as possible in order to lessen the ambiguity and danger of the night which, after all, cannot be seen but will be heard.

Making Contact

My case study of a 'death celebration' serves a purpose in demonstrating the link between sound and making physical contact with ancestors and the world of spirits. When a church choir processed from the Catholic church in Ntualam quarter to sing in the compound of the deceased, the accompanying drummer placed his instrument on top of the grave so the vibrations of his drumming would sink down into the earth. Like a libation, the stamping of feet and the jangling of ankle rattles, church singing and the drumming had to be 'heard' by the deceased. But the word used for the ancestors to 'hear' in Mankon is *edze* which means to eat suggesting that the ancestors are being fed with the music. Smells, noise, music, the jostle of crowds, the stamping of feet, firing of dane guns meld together into an inclusionary feeling of excitement for the living but more significantly perhaps, an answer to the demand of the ancestors that they should not be forgotten and that they should not be left alone. The demands made by the dead on the living suggests that death celebrations are events in which the dead play an active role insisting that their music should be played, dances performed and stories told about them and this will feed them. Also that unresolved conflicts, incompetence or meanness in the performance or absence of significant descendants will be noticed and have an effect whilst an opposite perception of a promise of well-being is heightened by the success of the event.

Whether an anticipated response should be immediate or mediated is of some significance. Anticipation of an ancestral response is not mediated by a petition, by deference or a plea that may or may not be answered. The sound of the living is instead a direct mediation and an expression of a self-confident and demanding relationship. Anthropological studies of African Christianity have also noted a preference for immediacy in the relationship with the deity by comparison to Western Christianity. This provokes discussion on the nature of 'spoken faiths' and how the linking of prophets to God through performance creates a 'religion of talk'. Engelke, for example, uses the phrase 'live and direct' as a point of entry into a Masowe world view that privileges the sound of a performative faith over 'a religion of the book'. Masowe prophets are committed, as he says, to a logic of immateriality; a religion in which things do not matter (Engelke 2005: 119). But the idea that some things are more material than others does not lead to a contrast of text versus objects but rather to more nuanced ideas about what it means to 'hear' the noise of ancestors, ghosts or spirits. The emphasis on speech also tends to correspond with an emphasis on repetition and a stress on regularities, often formulaic and archaic, in the use of religious language whereas noise becomes music as one enters into particular acoustic envelopes. In Engelke's case, people want to talk directly to God and it is the immediacy of the effect that is privileged in the 'live and direct' approach (Engelke 2004: 81). Birgit Meyer has emphasized the need to distinguish between 'Christian' and 'non-Christian' forms of possession in Africa (Meyer 1999a: 205). The boundaries between possession by ancestral spirits and the 'Holy Spirit' connotes shameful aspects of 'custom' that apostolics fight against yet there are of course necessary parallels in the procedural knowledge underlying both. In death celebrations in Bamenda, possession is not the issue but making direct contact with ancestors is. However, in the process, we move even further away from the transcendental notion of contacting a deity to a more immanent notion of a shared place and time where a 'live and direct' approach is a matter of noise. Noise is the attraction that arouses the attention of ancestors and spirits and influences their willingness to inhabit a place or shrine. And, it is the firing of dane guns, the sounds of music, the trampling of dancing feet, rather than the formality of speech, that combines to 'feed' them.

But by overemphasizing the contrast here to the formality of 'ritual speech', there is a danger we could ignore the reality of living next door to a Pentecostal church; that the loudness of the spoken message is part of its efficacy. In both modes of religiosity, it seems, efficacy is a matter of contact or immediacy rather than deference, inaccessibility and hierarchy. Loudness, in both modes (and others) in Bamenda, relate performance to immediacy of contact and a pragmatic view. The distinction between music of the day and noise of the night in a death celebration can perhaps take the point a bit further. In Afro-American gospel singing, the hostility expressed towards the commercialization of the songs was expressed already in the nineteenth century in the distinction between God's story and Devil's music. Yet, with all the contrasts made around this dichotomy in moral terms, they shared in common a focus on singing, on the importance of response and that the words should be heard. And that potentially the music, if it got its message right, could cure, heal or bring about some material effect for individual or community. The various cross-overs from 'gospel' to popular music ('gospel' to 'blues' to 'hot gospel' to 'soul', etc.) rather than being interpreted as a cultural resistance type argument, imply that a more interesting outcome between them can be found through resolving the conflict.

Wealth, Success and the Transmission of Noise

Belonging to a *Bonagen* church in Bamenda is about success. It fits the new breed of charismatic and Pentecostal churches, found particularly in Nigeria, that promote the proposition that a Christian is a success and if s/he is not then there is something wrong. Success as a good Christian is to be experienced in every aspect of life but in particular in financial and material matters, i.e. prosperity. Moreover, success should be superabundant, overflowing and unquestioned and the result of personal conduct, attendance and length of time spent in church. *Bonagen* in Bamenda is fairly typical of the type of Pentacostalism practising what Meyer has described in Ghana, as the 'faith' or 'prosperity gospel' according to which a Christian (through Christ's sacrifice on the cross) is already wealthy and all that he or she must do in order to take possession of health and wealth is to proclaim possession (sometimes called the 'name and claim it' gospel) (Meyer 1999b). Christianity in Africa has always had an association with social success and economic advancement and prosperity to be a sign of divine blessing (Ellis and ter Haar 2004: 138). An undeniable relationship is therefore established between the visible and invisible worlds in the sense that a person in good spiritual health can expect to prosper materially (Ellis and ter Haar 2004: 138). Reasons for failure must therefore have to do with the conditions that block these divine blessings and in the 1990s there were frequent reports of the impact of the global economy and new styles of capitalism that allow intervention in this invisible world and removal of the blockage that hold back success and prosperity as the right of every Christian (cf. Comaroff and Comaroff 1999).

Ellis and ter Haar find these explanations unsatisfactory because they neglect to place current attempts to negotiate with the spirit world to ensure success and prosperity within a longer term history of such mediations (Ellis and ter Haar 2004: 139). In Bamenda, it is certainly the case that Christianity has always been associated with the promise of material prosperity and well-being. Conflicts between chiefs and the missions reported constantly from the 1920s onwards were about something more than promising freedom to young girls from polygamy or men the means to marry but also the promise implied in the act of baptism that cleansed the body and provided access through Europeans and to a new invisible spirit world of unbelievable wealth (Rowlands 2005).

But another invisible world of ancestors exists who are contacted through the sacrifices made by chiefs and elders. Warnier (pers. comm.) describes once being invited by the Fon of Awing (a 'Fondom' on the Bamenda plateau) to come along with him to Bambuluwe lake, to make the annual offering to the ancestors who are supposed to have their village at the bottom of the lake. When they arrived in view of the lake, the Fon and four or five of the notables (including a woman) blew whistles and shook a small church bell. They also shouted. They said they had to inform the ancestors that they were coming and they had to make a noise to wake them up. They sacrificed a sheep by the waterside, butchered it, put camwood and salt on the pieces and threw the pieces into the lake one by one, shouting the name of the quarter to whom the piece was addressed. If the sacrifice was not accepted, i.e. the pieces floated back to the shore and did not sink to the bottom of the lake, the Fon could not hold his annual dance and divination would be required to establish the faults that had led to this rejection. If accepted then the material prosperity and fertility of the 'Fondom' was assured for the following year and the annual dance could be held. In common with *Bonagen* we therefore have the two principles that prosperity is assured as long as the correct procedure is followed and failure is a consequence of blockages that have to be discovered and removed.

In both worlds the role of noise is explicit in making contact between a sensible world and a 'second reality' in Bamenda. Yet in terms of the acoustic envelopes to which they belong, from the beginning noise was involved in reinforcing and contesting these differences in religious belief. The conflict between missions and chiefs in Bamenda in the 1920s had little to do with the political conflicts between colonial and traditional authorities or the role of the European missions as such, but to the fundamental doubt introduced into the process of religious transmission by the challenge of religious service to ancestral authority. Christianity has always had this association with material success in Africa and in Bamenda, as elsewhere, it grew rapidly because it associated acquiring prosperity through education, learning European languages and wearing European clothes. In the early 1990s, in Nigeria the 'faith gospel' became linked with a deliverance theology which argued that wealth and success was still the right of the Christian but these blessings had become blocked by demonic forces. A number of prophets appeared who attracted people to new churches with the promise that they would be able to release them from these constraints. Several of these new style evangelists are immensely rich, have followings in Africa, America and Europe and manage global churches based on their reputation to deliver health and immense riches in return for loyalty and the payment of tithes (cf. Ellis and ter Haar 2004: 137).

Yet in local terms, as in the case of *Bonagen* in Bamenda, it is impossible to imagine the efficacy of the churches apart from the praxeology of speech and sound characteristic of living and dying in Bamenda. What, for analytic purposes, has been distinguished here as noise of the night and music of the day are experienced in a death celebration as part of a continuous sequence of actions that serve to remove any blockages or impediments to the successful transmission of ancestral title. For this not to occur implies anger and conflict in the 'shared symbolic envelope' that would result in misfortunes until resolved by further divination and a renewed attempt to carry out the required ceremony. There are innumerable occasions in almost daily social life when something similar has to occur. In Mankon, 'to speak with one mouth' is the ideal of all family gatherings, social events and church gatherings as well as a prerequisite for the success of death celebrations, annual festival ancestral rites, installing successors and marriage rites. 'To speak with one voice' is not to speak with anger, rather softly while at the same time sharing food or drink from the same containers.

The reason why historically there have been conflicts between churches, chiefs, elders, and women in Bamenda is therefore deeply embedded in struggles to include or exclude each other's practitioners from acoustic envelopes that, in the sense of them belonging to the same 'sonoric bath', provide the basic conditions of a praxeology of speech and sound that is psychically inseparable from a more general sense of well-being. As mentioned earlier, the characteristic of Pentecostal satanic possession and the sound of witchcraft is silence. The person possessed remains silent until the noise of the night or the loudness of singing and shouting torments and provokes the spirit into action at which point the victim will start to yell and shout, or will enter into a trance. Once identified, the healer can intervene to extract the substance or drive out the spirit. The blockages are therefore part of a material but silent reality that can only be apprehended and dealt with by being provoked into action by which it can be identified and made vulnerable to physical intervention and expulsion The music played in a *Bonagen* church uses the same instruments as a 'cry-die', the same people are involved and 'singing' loudly and dressing appropriately are shared in common in both settings. We can see that the contestations between men and women, elders and youths and the struggles for empowerment expressed in the language of removal of blockages and impediments, has constantly been shaped by a praxeology of noise/music which we are only just beginning to grasp a sense of.

Conclusion

In a volume devoted to religious learning, I would argue that we have first to understand the processes of religious transmission as part of a praxeology of noise. There are clearly certain kinds of messages, emotional states and assumptions about the states of social relations that are transmitted through noise/music. The connections between ancestors and living peoples, the revelation of secrets, making contact with invisible worlds and therefore the concepts, attitudes and beliefs that materialize these acts are already predicated in a 'sonoric bath' mode of transmission. I would assume anyway that there is no need to separate learning from transmission. It is more how to get at them both in the same practice.

Finally, I am drawn back to the attractions of Attali writing on the political economy of noise. 'Everywhere we look, the monopolization of the broadcast of messages, the control of noise and the institutionalization of the silence of others assure the durability of power' (Attali 1985: 8). 'I would like to trace the political economy of music as a succession of orders (in other words differences) done violence by noises (in other words, the calling into question of differences) that are prophetic because they create new orders, unstable and changing' (ibid.: 19). In Bamenda, the violence of the night extends to some contemporary examples of state violence (cf. Argenti 2005) which, after all, has a particularly good monopoly of the more threatening kinds of noise. But Attali's point that this is noise that makes people forget is also apposite because it reverses itself in the music of the day when music of the death celebration is intended to reveal secrets and establish communication. How the one bursts through into the other, or not, whether it censors or not, whether it makes people believe in order and harmony or not, makes noise a tool of power.

Acknowledgments

This chapter has benefited greatly from the contribution of Jean-Pierre Warnier. Also the text was much improved by comments from the editors, Mathew Engelke and Chris Pinney.

BIBLIOGRAPHY

Adorno, T. 1982. 'On the Fetish Character of Music and the Regression of Listening'. In *The Essential Frankfurt Reader*, eds. A. Arato and E. Gebhart. New York: Continuum.

——— 2002. *Essays on Music*. Berkeley: University of California Press.

Agence Romande d'Education Chrétienne. 1984. *Venez car tout est prêt!* Lausanne: Agence Romande d'Education chrétienne.

Anzieu, D. 1985. *Le Moi-Peau*. Paris: Dunod.

Appel-Slingbaum, C. 2000. 'The Tradition of Slapping our Daughters'. Retrieved 03/2005 from www.mum.org/slap.htm.

Argenti N. 2005. 'Dancing in the Borderlands: the Forbidden Masquerades of Oku Youth and Women'. In *Makers and Breakers: Children and Youth in Postcolonial Africa*, eds. A. Honwana and F. de Boeck. Oxford: James Currey.

Arnal, W.E. 2000. 'Definition'. In *Guide to the Study of Religion*, eds. W. Braun and R.T. McCutcheon. London and New York: Casell.

Asad, T. 1983. 'Anthropological Conceptions of Religion: Reflections on Geertz'. *Man* (N.S.) 18: 232–59.

——— 1993. *Genealogies of Religion: Discipline and Reasons of Power in Christianity and Islam*. Baltimore: Johns Hopkins University Press.

Astuti, R. 1995. *People of the Sea: Identity and Descent among the Vezo of Madagascar*. Cambridge: Cambridge University Press.

——— 2001. 'Are We All Natural Dualists? A Cognitive Developmental Approach'. *Journal of the Royal Anthropological Institute* 7: 429–47.

Atran, S. 2002. *In Gods We Trust*. New York: Oxford University Press.

Attali, J. 1985. *Noise: the Political Economy of Music*. Minneapolis: University of Minnesota Press.

Austin, J.L. 1965. *How to Do Things with Words*. New York: Oxford University Press.

Badan Pusat Statistik. 1999. 'Tana Toraja dalam angka' [Tana Toraja in figures]. Makale.

———— 2001. 'Tana Toraja dalam angka' [Tana Toraja in figures]. Makale.

Bang, A. 2003. *Sufis and Scholars of The Sea: Family Networks in East Africa, 1860–1925*. London and New York: Routledge.

Barrett, J. 2004. *Why Would Anyone Believe in God?* Walnut Creek: AltaMira Press.

Barth, F. 1975. *Ritual and Knowledge among the Baktaman of New Guinea*. New Haven, CT: Yale University Press.

———— 1987. *Cosmologies in the Making: A Generative Approach to Cultural Variation in Inner New Guinea*. Cambridge: Cambridge University Press.

Bastide, R. 1953. 'Contribution à l'étude de la participation'. *Cahiers Internationaux de Sociologie* XIV(8): 30–40.

———— 1960. *Les Religions Africaines au Brésil*. Paris: PUF.

———— 1970. 'Conclusão de um debate recente: o pensamento obscuro e confuso'. *Revista Tempo Brasileiro* 25: 52–67.

———— 1973. *Estudos Afro-Brasileiros*, São Paulo: Perspectiva.

———— 2000 [1958]. *Le Candomblé da Bahia (Rite Nagô)*, Paris: Plon.

Bateson, G. 1972. 'Style, Grace, and Information in Primitive Art'. In *Steps to an Ecology of Mind*. New York: Ballantine.

Bauman, R. and C.L. Briggs. 1990. 'Poetics and Performance as Critical Perspectives on Language and Social Life'. *Annual Review of Anthropology* 19: 59–88.

Baumann, M. 1993. 'La didactique du catéchisme des adolescents'. Neuchâtel: Université de Neuchâtel. Faculté de théologie protestante. Doctorat de théologie.

Beattie, J. 1964. *Other Cultures*. London: Routledge and Kegan Paul.

Bem, D. 1970. *Beliefs, Attitudes and Human Affairs*. Belont, CA: Brooks and Cole Pub.

Benveniste, É. 1969. *Le vocabulaire des institutions indo-européenes*, Paris: Minuit, 2 vols.

Berliner, D. 2005a. 'The Abuses of Memory: Reflections on the Memory Boom in Anthropology'. *Anthropological Quarterly* 78(1): 183–97.

———— 2005b. 'An "Impossible" Transmission: Youth Religious Memories in Guinea-Conakry'. *American Ethnologist* 32(4): 576–92.

———— 2005c. 'La féminisation de la coutume: femmes possédées et transmission religieuse en pays bulongic (Guinée-Conakry)'. *Cahiers d'Études africaines*, XLV (1), no. 177: 15–38.

Berthoz, A. and G. Jorland (eds). 2004. *L'empathie*. Paris: Odile Jacob.

Beyond the Realms. n.d. Retrieved March 2005 from: http://groups.msn.com/Eeyores100AcresWoods/comingofage.nsnw

Bhran, S. n.d. 'A Women's Coming of Age Ritual, as Seen by a Man'. Retrieved February 2006 from: http://members.tripod.com/~suil_bhran/ritual/mysteries.html.

Bickel, B. and S. Jantz. 2000. *Talking with God*. Eugene, OR: Harvest House.

Bigalke, T.W. 2005. *Tana Toraja: A Social History of an Indonesian People*. Leiden and Singapore: KITVL Press and Singapore University Press.

Binghamton Pagan Community. n.d. 'Menarche ritual'. Retrieved March 2005 from www.homestead.com/barbooch/Menarche.html.

Blackaby, H. and C. King. 2004. *Experiencing God*. Nashville, TN: Broadman/Holman.

Blakemore, S-J. and J. Decety. 2001. 'From the Perception of Action to the Understanding of Intention'. *Nature Reviews: Neuroscience* 2: 561–67.

Bloch, M. (ed.). 1975. *Political Language and Oratory in Traditional Society*. London, New York and San Francisco: Academic Press.

Bloch, M. 1992. *From Prey into Hunter*. Cambridge: Cambridge University Press.

———— 1998. *How We Think They Think: Anthropological Approaches to Cognition, Memory and Literacy*. Boulder, CO. and Oxford: Westview Press.

———— 2002. 'Are Religious Beliefs Counter-Intuitive?' In *Radical Interpretation in Religion*, ed. N.K. Frankenberry. Cambridge: Cambridge University Press (Reprinted in Bloch 2005).

———— 2005. *Essays on Cultural Transmission*. London School of Economics Monographs on Social Anthropology, 75. Oxford: Berg.

———— forthcoming. 'Durkheimian Anthropology and Religion: Going In and Out of Each Other's Bodies'. In *Religion, Anthropology, and Cognitive Science*, eds. H. Whitehouse and J. Laidlaw. Durham, NC: Carolina Academic Press.

Borofsky, R. 1987. *Making History: Pukapukan and Anthropological Construction of Knowledge*. Cambridge: Cambridge University Press.

Bourdieu, P. 1977 [1972]. *Outline of a Theory of Practice*. Cambridge: Cambridge University Press.

Bourguignon, E. 1970. 'Hallucination and Trance: an Anthropologist's Perspective'. In *Origin and Mechanisms of Hallucinations*, ed. W. Keup. New York: Plenum.

Boyer, P. (ed.). 1993. *Cognitive Aspects of Religious Symbolism*. Cambridge: Cambridge University Press.

Boyer, P. 1994. *The Naturalness of Religious Ideas: A Cognitive Theory of Religion*. Berkeley and Los Angeles, University of California Press.

———— 1996. 'What Makes Anthropomorphism Natural: Intuitive Ontology and Cultural Representations'. *Journal of the Royal Anthropological Institute* 2: 83–97.

———— 2000a. 'Evolution of the Modern Mind and the Origins of Culture: Religious Concepts as a Limiting Case'. In *Evolution and the Human Mind: Modularity, Language and Meta-Cognition*, eds. P.C. Carruthers and A. Chamberlain. Cambridge: Cambridge University Press.

———— 2000b. 'Functional Origins of Religious Concepts: Ontological and Strategic Selection in Evolved Minds'. *Journal of the Royal Anthropological Institute* 6: 195–214.

———— 2001a. 'Cultural Inheritance Tracks and Cognitive Predispositions: the Example of Religious Concepts'. In *The Debated Mind: Evolutionary Psychology versus Ethnography*, ed. H. Whitehouse. Oxford and New York: Berg.

———— 2001b. *Religion Explained: The Human Instincts that Fashion Gods, Spirits and Ancestors*, London: Heinemann.

———— 2003. 'Religious Thought and Behaviour as By-Products of Brain Function'. *Trends in Cognitive Sciences* 7(3): 110–24.

Boyer, P. and C. Ramble. 2001. 'Cognitive Templates for Religious Concepts: Cross-Cultural Evidence for Recall of Counter-Intuitive Representations'. *Cognitive Science* 25: 535–64.

Boyer, P. and S. Walker, 2000, 'Intuitive Ontology and Cultural Input in the Acquisition of Religious Concepts'. In *Imagining the Impossible: Magical, Scientific, and Religious Thinking in Children*, eds. K.S. Rosengren, C. Johnson and P.L. Harris. Cambridge: Cambridge University Press.

Braun, W. and R.T. McCutcheon (eds). 2000. *Guide to the Study of Religion*. London and New York: Casell.

Brenner, L. 2000. *Controlling Knowledge: Religion, Power, and Schooling in a West African Muslim Society*. London: Hurst and Company.

Briggs, J. 1998. *Inuit Morality Play: The Emotional Education of a Three-Year-Old*. New Haven, CT: Yale University Press.

Brunner, J. 1973. *Beyond the Information Given: Studies in the Psychology of Knowing*. New York: Norton.

Capone, S. 1999. *La Quête de l'Afrique dans le Candomblé: Pouvoir et Tradition au Brésil*. Paris: Karthala.

Carruthers, M. 1998. *The Craft of Thought: Meditation, Rhetoric, and The Making of Images 400–1200*. Cambridge: Cambridge University Press.

Carruthers, P. and P.K. Smith (eds). 1996. *Theories of Theories of Mind*. Cambridge: Cambridge University Press.

Cavell, S. 1976. *Must We Mean What We Say?* Cambridge: Cambridge University Press.

——— 1995. What Did Derrida Want of Austin? In *Philosophical Passages: Wittgenstein, Emerson, Austin, Derrida*. Oxford: Blackwell.

Centro Redentor. 1986. *Racionalismo Cristão*, 36th ed. Rio de Janeiro: Centro Redentor.

——— 1989. *Prática do Racionalismo Cristão*, 12th ed. Rio de Janeiro: Centro Redentor.

Chapin, M. 1983. 'Curing among the San Blas Kuna'. PhD dissertation, University of Arizona.

Claverie, E. 1990. 'La Vierge, le désordre, la critique: les apparitions de la Vierge à l'âge de la science', *Terrain* 14: 60–75.

——— 2003. *Les guerres de la Vierge: une anthropologie des apparitions*. Paris: Gallimard.

Cole, M. 1996. *Cultural Psychology: the Once and Future Discipline*. Cambridge, MA: Harvard University Press.

Cole, M. and S. Cole. 2001. *The Development of Children*. New York: Worth Publishers.

Cole, M. and S. Scribner. 1974. *Culture and Thought*. New York: John Wiley and Sons.

Collins, J. 2004. 'Ghanaian Christianity and Popular Entertainment: Full Circle'. *History in Africa* 31: 407–23.

Comaroff, J. and J.L. Comaroff. 1999. 'Occult Economies and the Violence of Abstraction: Notes from the South African Postcolony', *American Ethnologist* 26(2): 279–303.

Cossard, G.B. 1970. 'Contribution à l'étude des Candomblés du Brésil: le rite Angola'. PhD dissertation. Université de Paris.

——— 1981. 'A Filha de Santo'. In *Olóòrisà: Escritos sobre a Religião dos Orixás*, ed. C.E.M. de Moura. São Paulo: Ágora.

Costos, D., R. Ackerman and L. Paradis. 2002. 'Recollections of Menarche: Communication between Mothers and Daughters Regarding Menstruation', *Sex Roles: A Journal of Research* 46(1–2): 49–59. Retrieved September 2005 from http://www.findarticles.com.

Coville, E. 1988. 'A Single Word Brings to Life: The Maro Ritual in Tana Toraja (Indonesia)'. PhD dissertation. Chicago: University of Chicago.

—— 2004. 'Words that Renew in Tana Toraja (Indonesia): Unintelligibility, Poetry, and Metadiscourse', Annual Meeting of the American Anthropological Association, Atlanta, 17 December 2004.

Critchley, S., 2005. 'Cavell's "Romanticism" and Cavell's Romanticism'. In *Contending with Cavell*, ed. R. Goodman. Oxford: Oxford University Press.

Crook, N. (ed.). 1996. *The Transmission of Knowledge in South Asia: Essays on Education, Religion, History, and Politics*. Delhi: Oxford University Press.

Crossman, R. 2003. 'Throwing a Menstrual Celebration for Girls', *Daughters* 8(2): 13. Excerpt retrieved March 2006 from www.amazon.com.

Crystal, E. 1974. 'Cooking Pot Politics: a Toraja Village Study', *Indonesia* 18: 119–52.

D'Andrade, R. 1995. *The Development of Cognitive Anthropology*. Cambridge: Cambridge University Press.

Dantas, B.G. 1989. *Vovó Nagô e papai Branco: usos e abusos da África no Brasil*. Rio de Janeiro: Graal.

Davidson, J. and R. Davidson (eds). 1980. *The Psychobiology of Consciousness*. New York: Plenum.

Davies, M. and T. Stone (eds). 1995. *Folk Psychology*. Oxford: Blackwell.

Davis, E. and C. Leonard. 2003. *The Circle of Life: Thirteen Archetypes for Every Woman*. Berkeley: Celestial Arts Publishing. Retrieved March 2005 from: http://www.birth-sex.com

de Certeau, M. 1981. 'Croire: une pratique de la différence'. Universita di Urbino, *Centro Internazionale di Semiotica e di Linguistica* 106: 1–21.

de Lacey, P. 1970. 'A Cross-Cultural Study of Classificatory Ability in Australia'. *Journal of Cross-Cultural Psychology* 1: 293–304.

de Lemos, M. 1969. 'The Development of Conservation in Aboriginal Children'. *International Journal of Psychology* 4: 255–69.

Deeley, P.Q. 2004. 'The Religious Brain: Turning Ideas into Convictions' *Anthropology and Medicine* 11(3): 245–67.

Deleuze, G. 1990. *Pourparliers*. Paris: Minuit.

—— 1999 [1967]. *Nietzsche et la Philosophie*, Paris: PUF.

Deleuze, G. and F. Guattari. 1980. *Mille Plateaux*. Paris: Minuit.

Dianteill, E. 2002. 'Deterritorialization and Reterritorialization of the *Orisha* Religion in Africa and the New World (Nigeria, Cuba and the United States)'. *International Journal of Urban and Regional Research* 26, no. 1: 121–37.

Dillon, R. 1990. *Ranking and Resistance: a Precolonial Cameroonian Polity in Regional Perspective*. Stanford: Stanford University Press.

Dion, M. 1998. *Mémoires de Candomblé: Omindarewa Iyalorisá*. Paris: L'Harmattan.

Donzelli, A. 2003. 'Diversity in Unity: Multiple Strategies of a Unifying Rhetoric. The Case of Resemanticisation of Toraja Rituals: from

"Wasteful Pagan Feasts" into "Modern Auctions" ', *Indonesian Anthropological Journal* 27(72): 38–58.

——— 2004. '"Sang Buku Duang Buku Kada" ("One or Two Words"): Communicative Practices and Linguistic Ideologies in the Toraja Highlands, Eastern Indonesia'. PhD dissertation. Milan: Universtà degli Studi di Milano-Bicocca.

——— 2007. 'Words on the Lips and Meanings in the Stomach: Ideologies of Unintelligibility and Theories of Metaphor in Toraja Ritual Speech'. *Text and Talk* 27(4): 533–57.

Du Bois, J.W. 1986. 'Self-Evidence and Ritual Speech'. In *Evidentiality: The Linguistic Coding of Epistemology*, eds W. Chafe and J. Nichols. Norwood: Ablex.

——— 1993. 'Meaning without Intention: Lessons from Divination'. In *Responsibility and Evidence in Oral Discourse*, eds J. Hill and J. Irvine. Cambridge: Cambridge University Press.

Dubied, P.-L. 1992. *Apprendre Dieu à l'adolescence*. Genève: Labor et Fides.

Dunbar, R. 2003. 'The Social Brain: Mind, Language, and Society in Evolutionary Perspective'. *Annual Review of Anthropology* 32: 163–81.

Durham, W.W. 1991. *Coevolution: Genes, Culture, and Human Diversity*. Stanford: Stanford University Press.

Durkheim, E. 1938. *L'évolution pédagogique en France*, with an introduction by Maurice Halbwachs. Paris: Alcan, 2 vols.

——— 1995 [1912]. *The Elementary Forms of Religious Life*, translated by K.E. Fields. New York: Free Press.

Eickelman, D.F. 1974. *Knowledge and Power in Morocco: The Education of a Twentieth-Century Notable*. Princeton: Princeton University Press.

Elisha, O. 2004. 'Sins of our Soccer Moms: Servant Evangelism and the Spiritual Injuries of Class'. In *Local Actions: Cultural Activism, Power and Public Life in America*, eds. M. Checker and M. Fishman. New York: Columbia University Press.

Ellis, S. and G. ter Haar. 2004. *Worlds of Power*. Oxford: Oxford University Press.

Engelke, M. 2004. 'Text and Performance in an African Church'. *American Ethnologist* 31(1): 76–91.

——— 2005. 'Sticky Subjects and Sticky Objects: the Substance of African Christian Healing'. In *Materiality*, ed. D. Miller. Durham: Duke University Press.

Evans-Pritchard, E. 1937. *Witchcraft, Oracles and Magic among the Azande*. Oxford: Clarendon Press.

Fabian, J. 1983. *Time and the Other: How Anthropology Makes Its Object*. New York: Columbia University Press.

Fardon, R. 1990. 'Localizing Strategies: The Regionalization of Ethnographic Accounts'. In *Localizing Strategies: Regional Traditions of Ethnographic Writing*, ed. R. Fardon. Edinburgh and Washington: Scottish Academic Press and Smithsonian Institution Press.

Favret-Saada, J. 1977. *Les mots, la mort, les sorts*. Paris: Gallimard.

——— 1990. 'Être affecté'. *Gradhiva* 8: 3–9.

Fedele, A. 2006a. 'Sur le chemin de Marie Madeleine: des lectures au pèlerinage', *Quaderns-e* 7 (http://www.icantropologia.org/quaderns-e).

────── 2006b. 'Sacred Blood, Sacred Body: Learning to Honour Menstruation on the Path of Mary Magdalene', *Periferia* 4 (www.periferia.name).

Fellous, M. 2001. *A la recherche de nouveaux rites*. Paris: L'Harmattan.

Fellous, M. and J. Renard. 1993. *Les rites de passage: adolescence*. Paris: Cinétévé-La Sept/Arte-France2-Investimage4.

Ferme, M. 2001. *The Underneath of Things: Violence, History, and the Everyday in Sierra Leone*. Berkeley: University of California Press.

Fichte, H. 1987. *Etnopoesia: antropologia poética das religiões Afro-Brasileiras*, São Paulo: Editora Brasiliense.

Finnegan, R. 1988. *Literacy and Orality: Studies in the Technology of Communication*. Oxford: Blackwell.

Flyvbjerg, B. 2001. *Making Social Science Matter*. Cambridge: Cambridge University Press.

Fodor, J. 1983. *The Modularity of Mind*. Cambridge, MA: MIT Press.

Fortes, M. 1970. 'Social and Psychological Aspects of Education in Taleland'. In *From Child to Adult: Studies in the Anthropology of Education*, ed. J. Middleton. New York: Natural History Press.

Foster, R. 2002. *Prayer*. New York: HarperCollins.

Fox, J.J. (ed.). 1988. *To Speak in Pairs: Essays on the Ritual Languages of Eastern Indonesia*. Cambridge: Cambridge University Press.

Freppel, Ch.-E. 1875. *Catéchisme du diocèse d'Angers*. Angers: Lachèse Belleuvre and Dolbeau.

Fromm, E. and S. Katz. 1990. *Self Hypnosis*. New York: Guilford.

Gallagher, S. 2001. 'The Practice of Mind: Theory, Simulation, or Interaction?' *Journal of Consciousness Studies* 5–7: 83–108.

Gay, J. and M. Cole. 1967. *The New Mathematics and an Old Culture*. New York: Holt, Rinehart and Winston.

Geertz, C. 1966. 'Religion as a Cultural System'. In *Anthropological Approaches to the Study of Religion*, ed. M. Banton. London: Tavistock.

────── 1971. *Islam Observed: Religious Development in Morocco and Indonesia*. Chigaco and London: University of Chicago Press.

────── 1973. *The Interpretation of Cultures*. New York: Basic Books.

────── 1983. *Local Knowledge: Further Essays in Interpretive Anthropology*. New York: Basic Books.

────── 2005. 'Shifting Aims, Moving Targets: on the Anthropology of Religion', *Journal of the Royal Anthropological Institute* 11: 1–15.

George, K.M. 1990. 'Felling a Song with a New Ax: Writing and the Reshaping of Ritual Song Performance in Upland Sulawesi', *Journal of American Folklore* 103(407): 3–23.

Giddens, A. (ed.). 1972. *Durkheim: Selected Writings*. Cambridge: Cambridge University Press.

Goffman, E. 1981. 'Footing'. In *Forms of Talk*. Philadelphia: University of Pennsylvania Press.

Goldman, M. 1984. 'A Possessão e a Construção Ritual da Pessoa no Candomblé'. MA thesis, Universidade Federal do Rio de Janeiro.

————— 1985a. 'A construção ritual da pessoa: a possessão no Candomblé', *Religião e Sociedade* 12(1): 22–54.

————— 1985b. 'O Visível Mundo do Espiritismo', *Anuário Antropológico 1983*: 330–39.

————— 1990. 'Candomblé'. In *Sinais dos Tempos: Diversidade Religiosa no Brasil*, ed. L. Landin, Rio de Janeiro: ISER.

————— 1994. *Razão e diferença: afetividade, racionalidade e relativismo no pensamento de Lévy-Bruhl*. Rio de Janeiro: Universidade Federal do Rio de Janeiro and Grypho Publishers.

Goldwyn, T. (director). 1999. *A Walk on the Moon*. New York: Miramax Films.

Goody, J. 1976. *The Domestication of the Savage Mind*. Cambridge: Cambridge University Press.

Gottlieb, Alma. 2004. *The Afterlife Is Where We Come from: The Culture of Infancy in West Africa*. Chicago: University of Chicago Press.

Greenfield, P. 1966. 'On Culture and Conservation'. In *Studies in Cognitive Growth*, eds. J. Bruner, R. Oliver and P. Greenfield. New York: John Wiley and Sons.

————— 2000. 'Cultural Apprenticeship and Cultural Change'. In *Biology, Brains and Behavior*, eds. S. Parker, J. Langer and M. McKinney. Santa Fe: SAR Press.

————— 2005. 'Culture and Learning'. In *A Companion to Psychological Anthropology: Modernity and Psychocultural Change*, eds. C. Casey and R.B. Edgerton. Oxford: Blackwell.

Guberman, S. and P. Greenfield. 1991. 'Learning and Transfer in Everyday Cognition'. *Cognitive Development* 6: 244–60.

Guthrie, S. 1993. *Faces in the Clouds: A New Theory of Religion*. New York and Oxford: Oxford University Press.

Halbwachs, M. 1994 [1925]. *Les cadres sociaux de la mémoire*. Paris: Editions Albin Michel.

Hann, C.M. 2003. 'Creeds, Cultures and the "Witchery of Music" '. *Journal of the Royal Anthropological Institute* 9(2): 223–41.

Harris, P.L. 2000. *The Work of Imagination*. Oxford: Blackwell.

Hawthorne, N. 1993. 'A Menarche Ritual: Honouring our Daughters' First Bloods', *Sagewoman*, December 31: 79. Retrieved October 2005 from http://proquest.umi.com.

Héritier, F. 1989. *Résumé de cours 1988–1989*. Paris: Collège de France.

Heron, A. 1971. 'Concrete Operations, "G" and Achievement in Zambian Ghildren'. *Journal of Cross-Cultural Psychology* 2: 325–36.

Hervieu-Léger, D. 1997. 'La transmission religieuse en modernité: éléments pour la construction d'un objet de recherche'. *Social Compass* 44(1): 131–43.

Heryanto, A. 1988. 'The Development of "Development" '. *Indonesia* 46: 1–24.

Herzfeld, M. 1991. *A Place in History: Social and Monumental Time in a Cretan Town*. Princeton: Princeton University Press.

————— 1997. *Cultural Intimacy: Social Poetics in the Nation-State*. New York: Routledge.

———— 2004. *The Body Impolitic: Artisans and Artifice in the Global Hierarchy of Value*. Chicago: University of Chicago Press.

Hirschfeld, L.A. 1996. *Race in the Making: Cognition, Culture and the Child's Construction of Human Kinds*. Cambridge, MA: MIT Press.

Hobbs, A. 2005 'Girls Growing Up'. Retrieved March 2006 from www.anitahobbs.com.

Hoffmann, M. 1996. 'Peak Experience'. *On the Issues: the Progressive Woman's Quarterly*, Summer 1996. Retrieved August 2005 from: www.ontheissuesmagazine.com/sum96hoffman.html.

Højbjerg, C.K. 2002a. 'Religious Reflexivity: Essays on Attitudes to Religious Ideas and Practice'. *Social Anthropology* 10(1): 1–10.

————. 2002b. 'Inner Iconoclasm: Forms of Reflexivity in Loma Rituals of Sacrifice'. *Social Anthropology* 10(1): 57–75.

Højbjerg, C.K., P. Rubow and A. Sjorslev. 1999. 'Introductory Paper', Conference on *Religious Reflexivity: Anthropological Approaches to Ambivalent Attitudes to Religious Ideas and Practice*, Institute of Anthropology, University of Copenhagen, 15–17 September 1999.

Holmes, R. 1984. 'In Stevenson's Footsteps'. *Granta magazine*, 10 (on Travel Writing).

Houseman, M. 2000. 'La percezione sociale delle azioni rituali', *Ethnosistemi* 7: 67–74.

———— 2006. 'Relationality'. In *Theorizing Rituals: Classical Topics, Theoretical Approaches, Analytical Concepts, Annotated Bibliography*, eds. J. Kreinath, J. Snoek and M. Stausberg. Leiden: Brill.

Houseman, M. and C. Severi. 1998. *Naven or the Other Self: A Relational Approach to Ritual Action*. Leiden: Brill.

Howell, S. 2001. 'The Mean Reds'. Retrieved March 2006 from http://home.vicnet.net.au/~sincoz/stories01/meanreds.htm.

Hugh-Jones, S. 1994. 'Shamans, Prophets, Priests, and Pastors'. In *Shamanism, History, and the State*, eds. N. Thomas and C. Humphrey. Ann Arbor: University of Michigan Press.

Hume, D. 2000 [1739–40]. *A Treatise of Human Nature: Being an Attempt to Introduce the Experimental Method of Reasoning into Moral Subjects*, edited with an analytical index, by L.A. Selby-Bigge. Oxford: Oxford University Press.

Humphrey, C. and J. Laidlaw. 1994. *The Archetypal Actions of Ritual: A Theory of Ritual Illustrated by the Jain Rite of Worship*. Oxford: Clarendon Press.

Humphrey, N. 2002 [1986]. *The Inner Eye: Social Intelligence in Evolution*. Oxford: Oxford University Press.

Hutchins, E. 1991. 'The Social Organization of Distributed Cognition'. In *Perspectives on Socially Shared Cognition*, eds. L. Resnick, J. Levine and S. Teasley. Washington, DC: American Psychological Association.

Hybells, B. 1998. *Too Busy not to Pray*. Downers Grove, IL: Intervarsity Press.

Jackson, P. 2004. 'Handing Down by Means of Speech: Gesture and Memory in the Study of Religion'. In *Gestures, Rituals and Memory: A Multidisciplinary Approach to Patterned Human Movement across Time*. Symposium at the University of Toronto (Victoria College); 6–8 May

2004. Retrieved July 2006 from http://www.semioticon.com/virtuals/gestures/index.html.

James, W. 2003. *The Ceremonial Animal: A New Portrait of Anthropology*. Oxford: Oxford University Press.

Janzen, J., 1992. *Ngoma: Discourses of Healing in Central and Southern Africa*. Berkeley: University of California Press.

Jeannerod, M. and E. Pacherie. 2004. 'Agency, Simulation and Self-Identification', *Mind and Language* 19(2): 113–46.

Jenkins, T. 1999. *Religion in English Everyday Life*. Oxford and New York: Berghahn.

Jing, J. 1996. *The Temple of Memories: History, Power and Morality in a Chinese Village*. Stanford: Stanford University Press.

Jurkus, P. n.d. *Anthology of Lithuanian Ethnoculture*. Retrieved August 2005 from: http://ausis.gf.vu.lt/eka/customs/youth_ini.html.

Keane, W. 1997a. *Signs of Recognition: Powers and Hazards of Representations in an Indonesian Society*. Berkeley, CA: University of California Press.

———1997b. 'Knowing One's Place: National Language and the Idea of the Local in Eastern Indonesia', *Cultural Anthropology* 12(1): 37–63.

——— 1997c. 'From Fetishism to Sincerity: on Agency, the Speaking Subject, and their Historicity in the Context of Religious Conversion'. *Comparative Studies in Society and History* 39(4): 674–93.

Kierkegaard, S. 1968. *Fear and Trembling*, translated from Danish by W. Lowrie. Princeton: Princeton University Press.

Kipp, R.S. and S. Rodgers (eds). 1987. *Indonesian Religions in Transition*. Tucson: University of Arizona Press.

Koon, S.M. (aka LadyHawke). 2004. 'Girl's/Young Woman's Coming of Age'. Retrieved March 2006 from groups.yahoo.com/group/ChristianWitches.

Kramer, F. 1993 [1987], *The Red Fez: Art and Spirit Possession in Africa*, translated by M. Green. London and New York: Verso.

Kresse, K. 2006. *Knowledge, Islam, and Intellectual Practice in Mombasa: an Ethnography of Swahili Philosophical Discourse*. International African Library. Edinburgh: Edinburgh University Press.

Kuipers, J. 1990. *Power in Performance: the Creation of Textual Authority in Weyewa Ritual Speech*. Philadelphia: University of Pennsylvania Press.

——— 1993. 'Obligation to the Word: Ritual Speech, Performance, and Responsibility among the Weyewa'. In *Responsibility and Evidence in Oral Discourse*, eds. J.H. Hill and J.T. Irvine. Cambridge: Cambridge University Press.

——— 1998. *Language, Identity and Marginality in Indonesia: the Changing Nature of Ritual Speech on the Island of Sumba*. Cambridge: Cambridge University Press.

Kurys, D. (director). 1977. *Diabolo menthe*. France : Films de l'Alma/Alexandre Films.

Lahire, Bernard. 2005. 'Prédispositions naturelles ou dispositions sociales? Quelques raisons de résister à la naturalisation de l'esprit'. In *L'Esprit Sociologique*. Paris: Editions la Découverte.

Lakoff, G. 1987. *Women, Fire and Dangerous Things*. Chicago: University of Chicago Press.

Lalanne, S. and D. de Vinols. 1998. *Faire le catéchisme*. Paris: Droguet et Ardant.

Lambek, M. 1981. *Human Spirits*. Cambridge: Cambridge University Press.

———— 1988. 'Graceful Exits: Spirit Possession as Personal Performance in Mayotte'. *Culture* [since renamed *Anthropologica*] VIII(1): 59–69.

———— 1990. 'Certain Knowledge, Contestable Authority: Power and Practice on the Islamic Periphery'. *American Ethnologist* 17(1): 23–40.

———— 1992. 'Taboo as Cultural Practice among Malagasy Speakers'. *Man* 27: 19–42.

———— 1993. *Knowledge and Practice in Mayotte: Local Discourses of Islam, Sorcery, and Spirit Possession*. Toronto, University of Toronto Press.

———— 2000a. 'Localizing Islamic Performances in Mayotte'. In *Inside and Outside the Mosque: The Anthropology of Muslim Prayer Across the Indian Ocean*, eds D. Parkin and S. Headley. Oxford: Curzon.

———— 2000b. 'The Anthropology of Religion and the Quarrel between Poetry and Philosophy'. *Current Anthropology* 41(3): 309–20.

———— 2002a. *The Weight of the Past: Living with History in Mahajanga, Madagascar*. New York: Palgrave Macmillan.

———— 2002b 'Fantasy in Practice: Projection and Introjection, or the Witch and the Spirit Medium'. In *Beyond Rationalism: Rethinking Magic, Witchcraft and Sorcery*, ed. B. Kapferer. Oxford and New York: Berghahn.

———— 2003. 'Rheumatic Irony: Questions of Agency and Self-Deception as Refracted through the Art of Living with Spirits'. In *Illness and Irony*, eds. M. Lambek and P. Antze. Oxford and New York: Berghahn.

Latour, B. 1990. 'Quand les anges deviennent de bien mauvais messagers'. *Terrain* 14: 76–91.

———— 1996. *Petite réflexion sur le culte moderne des dieux faitiches*. Paris: Synthélabo.

———— 2000. 'Faktura, de la notion de réseaux à celle d'attachement'. In *Ce qui nous relie*, eds. A. Micoud and M. Peroni. La Tour d'Aigues: Éditions de l'Aube.

———— 2002. *Jubiler ou les tourments de la parole religieuse*. Paris: Editions le Seuil.

Lave, J. and E. Wenger. 1991. *Situated Learning: Legitimate Peripheral Participation*. Cambridge: Cambridge University Press.

Lave, J. and S. Chaiklin (eds). 1996. *Understanding Practice: Perspectives on Activity and Context*. Cambridge: Cambridge University Press.

Lawson T.E. and R.N. McCauley. 1990. *Rethinking Religion: Connecting Cognition and Culture*. Cambridge: Cambridge University Press.

Lecourt, E. 1990. 'The Musical Envelope'. In *Psychic Envelopes*, ed. D. Anzieu. London: Karnac Books.

Lenclud, G. 1990. 'Vues de l'esprit, art de l'autre'. *Terrain* 14: 5–19.

Lépine, C. 1978. 'Contribuição ao Estudo da Classificação dos Tipos Psicológicos no Candomblé Ketu de Salvador'. PhD dissertation. Universidade de São Paulo.

———— 2000. 'Os estereótipos da personalidade no Candomblé Nàgô'. In *Candomblé: Tipos Psicológicos nas Religiões Afro-Brasileiras*, ed. C.E.M. de Moura. Rio de Janeiro: Pallas.

Leppert, R. 2002. 'Commentary'. In *Essays on Music*, T. Adorno. Berkeley: University of California Press.

Lévi-Strauss, C., 1963. 'The Sorcerer and His Magic'. In *Structural Anthropology*. New York.

Lévy-Bruhl, L. 1975 [1949]. *The Notebooks on Primitive Mentality*. Oxford: Basil Blackwell.

———— 1979 [1926]. *How Natives Think*. London: Unwin Brothers.

———— 1998 [1949]. *Carnets*. Paris: Presses Universitaires de France.

Lewis, G. 1980. *Day of Shining Red*. Cambridge: Cambridge University Press.

Lewis, I. 1989. *Ecstatic Religion: A Study of Shamanism and Spirit Possession* (2nd edn). London and New York: Routledge.

———— 1996. *Religion in Context: Cults and Charisma* (2nd edn). Cambridge: Cambridge University Press.

Lienhard, J. 1980. 'On "Discernment of Spirits" in the Early Church'. *Theological Studies* 41: 505–29.

Loimeier, R. 2002. 'Je veux etudier sans mendier: the campaign against the Qur'anic schools in Senegal'. In *Social Welfare in Muslim Societies in Africa*, ed. H. Weiss. Stockholm: Nordic Afrikainstitutet.

———— forthcoming. 'Muslim Education in East Africa in the Context of Processes of Globalization'.

Lord, A.B. 1960. *The Singer of Tales*. Cambridge: Cambridge University Press.

Luhrmann, T.M. 1989. *Persuasions of the Witch's Craft: Ritual and Magic in Contemporary England*. Cambridge, MA: Harvard University Press.

———— 2004. 'Metakinesis: How God Becomes Intimate in Contemporary U.S. Christianity'. *American Anthropologist* 106: 518–28.

———— 2005. 'The Art of Hearing God: Absorption, Dissociation and Contemporary American Spirituality'. *Spiritus: a Journal of Christian Spirituality* 5(2): 133–57.

Maggie, Y. 1976. *Guerra de Orixás*, Rio de Janeiro: Zahar.

———— 2001. 'Introdução', in *Guerra de Orixás*, Rio de Janeiro: Zahar, 3rd edn.

Magliocco, S. 2004. *Witching Culture: Folklore and Neo-Paganism in America*. Philadelphia: University of Pennsylvania Press.

Mauss, M. 1923. 'Mentalité Primitive et Participation'. *Bulletin de la Société Française de Philosophie* XXIII, no. 2: 24–29.

McCauley, R.N. 2003. 'Is Religion a Rube Goldberg Device? Or Oh, What a Difference a Theory Makes!' In *Essays in Honor of E. Thomas Lawson*, ed. B. Wilson and T. Light. Leiden: Brill.

McCauley, R.N. and T.E. Lawson. 2002. *Bringing Ritual to Mind: Psychological Foundations of Cultural Forms*. Cambridge: Cambridge University Press.

McCauley, R.N and H. Whitehouse. 2005. 'New Frontiers in the Cognitive Science of Religion'. *Journal of Cognition and Culture* 5(1–2): 1–13.

McGovern, M. 2004. 'Unmasking the State: Developing Modern Political Subjectivities in Twentieth Century Guinea'. PhD dissertation. Emory University.

Medin, D. and S. Atran.1999. *Folkbiology*. Cambridge, MA: MIT Press.

Meslin, M. 1988. *L'expérience humaine du divin: fondements d'une anthropologie religieuse*. Paris: Éditions du Cerne.

Meyer, B. 1999a. *Translating the Devil: Religion and Modernity among the Ewe in Ghana*. Edinburgh: Edinburgh University Press for the International African Institute.

—— 1999b. 'Commodities and the Power of Prayer: Pentecostalist Attitudes towards Consumption in Contemporary Ghana'. In *Globalisation and Identity: Dialectics of Flow and Closure*, eds. B. Meyer and P. Geschiere. Oxford: Blackwell.

Middleton, J. 1970 (ed.). *From Child to Adult: Studies in the Anthropology of Education*. New York: Natural History Press.

Miller, D. 1997. *Reinventing American Protestantism*. Berkeley: University of California Press.

Moingt, J. 1976. *La transmission de la foi*. Paris: Fayard.

Morton, H. 1996. *Becoming a Tongan: An Ethnography of Childhood*. Honolulu: University of Hawaii Press.

Müller, F.M. 1876. *Lectures on the Origin and Growth of Religion*. London: Longmans, Green and Co.

Mystical Mountains. n.d. Retrieved September 2005 from: http://groups.msn.com/ MysticalMountains/sacredmenstruation.msnw

Needham, R. 1972. *Belief, Language, and Experience*, Chicago: University of Chicago Press.

—— 1983. 'Polythetic Classifications, Convergence and Consequences'. In *Against the Tranquility of Axioms*. Berkeley and Los Angeles: University of California Press.

Nehamas, A. 1998. *The Art of Living: Socratic Reflections from Plato to Foucault*. Berkeley, CA: University of California Press.

Nordenskiöld, E. 1938. *An Historical and Ethnological Survey of the Kuna Indians*, Comparative Ethnographical Studies, Vol. 10, Göteborg: Göteborg Ethnological Museum.

Norhala, 1995. 'A Menarche Ritual', *The Hazel Nut* 13. Retrieved February 2006 from http://www.faeriefaith.net/HazelNut/ Issue13.html#Menarche.

Otto, R. 1956 [1918]. *The Idea of the Holy*, translated from German by J.W. Harvey. Oxford: Oxford University Press.

Pals, D.L. 1996. *Seven Theories of Religion*. New York: Oxford University Press.

Parkin, D. 1985a. 'Controlling the U-Turn of Knowledge'. In *Power and Knowledge: Anthropological and Sociological Approaches*, ed. R. Fardon. Edinburgh: Scottish Academic Press.

—— 1985b. 'Being and Selfhood among Intermediary Swahili'. In *Swahili Language and Society*, eds. J. Maw and D. Parkin. Beiträge zur Afrikanistik Band 23. University of Vienna.

—— 1991. *Sacred Void: Spatial Images of Work and Ritual Among the Giriama of Kenya*. Cambridge: Cambridge University Press.

—— 2000. 'Templates, Evocations and the Long-Term Fieldworker'. In *Anthropologists in a Wider World*, eds. P. Dresch, W. James and D. Parkin. Oxford: Berghahn.

Pemberton, J. 1994. *On the Subject of 'Java'*. Ithaca, New York: Cornell University Press.

Pieke, F. 2000. 'Serendipity: Reflections on Fieldwork in China'. In *Anthropologists in a Wider World*, eds. P. Dresch, W. James and D. Parkin. Oxford: Berghahn.

Piette, A. 1997. 'Pour une anthropologie comparée des rituels contemporains'. *Terrain* 29: 139–50.

——— 1999. *La religion de près: l'activité religieuse en train de se faire*. Paris: Métailié.

Pike, S. 2001. *Earthly Bodies, Magical Selves: Contemporary Pagans and the Search for Community*. Berkeley, CA: University of California Press.

——— 2004. *New Age and Neopagan Religions in America*. New York: Columbia University Press.

Pogrebin, L.C. 1994. 'Mother, I Hardly Knew You'. In *Her Face in the Mirror: Jewish Women on Mothers and Daughters*, ed. F. Moskowitz. Boston: Beacon Press. Retrieved March 2006 from http://groups.google.fr/group/shamash.koach.

Pouillon, J. 1979. 'Remarques sur le verbe croire'. In *La fonction symbolique*, eds. P. Smith and M. Izard. Paris: Gallimard.

Price, R. 1983. *First Time: The Historical Vision of an Afro-American People*. Baltimore: Johns Hopkins University Press

Putnam, H. 1992. *Renewing Philosophy*. Harvard: Harvard University Press.

Rappaport, R. 1999. *Ritual and Religion in the Making of Humanity*. Cambridge: Cambridge University Press.

Ray, B.C. 2000. 'Discourse about Difference: Understanding African Ritual Language'. In *A Magic Still Dwells: Comparative Religion in the Postmodern Age*, eds. K.C. Patton and B.C. Ray. Berkeley, CA: University of California Press.

Rayni, J. n.d. 'Crowning at Menarche: Rediscovered Rite of Passage'. Retrieved March 2005 from: www.createyourheartsdesire.com/CrowningAtMenarche.doc.

Reid, S. n.d. 'Boom Boxes and Ribbons'. Excerpt from *Ms Magazine* retrieved October 2005 from www.beliefnet.com.

Richards, A.I. 1956. *Chisungu: A Girls' Initiation Ceremony among the Bemba of Northern Rhodesia*. London: Faber & Faber.

Roberts, S. 1994. 'Blood Sisters: By honouring the fertility cycle, the menstrual-health movement seeks to reclaim an ancient source of female power', *New Age Journal* May/June 1994. Retrieved March 2005 from www.holysmoke.org/fem/fem0426.htm.

Rogoff, B. 1990. *Apprenticeship in Thinking*. New York: Oxford University Press.

Rogoff, B. and J. Lave. 1984. *Everyday Cognition*. Cambridge: Harvard University Press.

Rosa, J.G. 1967. *Grande Sertão: Veredas*. Rio de Janeiro: José Olympio Editora.

Rosenblatt, J. and J. Frame. 1996. 'A Study and Discussion Guide for the Film Period Piece'. Retrieved September 2005 from: http://www.jayrosenblattfilms.com/period_guide.html.

Rowlands, M. 2005. 'A Materialist Approach to Materiality'. In *Materiality*, ed. D. Miller, 72–87. Durham, NC: Duke University Press.

Rudolph, J. 1998. 'Moontime Celebrations'. *New Moon Network: For Adults Who Care About Girls* 5(5): 5–6. Retrieved March 2006 from: www.findarticles.com.

Ruel, M. 1997. *Belief, Ritual, and the Securing of Life: Reflexive Essays on a Bantu Religion.* Leiden: Brill.

Sandarupa, S. 1989. 'Tropes, Symbolism, Rhetorical Structure: Structure of Parallelism and Parallelism of Structure in Toraja'. MA dissertation. University of Chicago.

——— 2004. 'The Exemplary Center: Poetics and Politics of the Kingly Death Ritual in Toraja (South Sulawesi, Indonesia)'. PhD dissertation. University of Chicago.

Sangren, P.S. 2003. 'Separations, Autonomy and Recognition in the Production of Gender Differences: Reflections from Considerations of Myths and Laments'. In *Living with Separation in China: Anthropological Accounts*, ed. C. Stafford. London: Routledge Curzon, pp. 53–84.

Sarró, R. 2002. 'The Iconoclastic Meal: Destroying Objects and Eating Secrets among the Baga of Guinea'. In *Iconoclash: Beyond the Image Wars in Science, Religion, and Art*, eds. B. Latour and P. Weibel. Cambridge and London: MIT Press.

——— 2007a. 'Cómo los pueblos sin religión aprenden que *ya* tenían religión'. In *Identidades, Relaciones y Contextos II*, ed. J. Bestard. Barcelona: Publicaciones de la Universidad de Barcelona.

——— 2007b. 'Hermetic Huts and Modern State: The Politics of Iconoclasm in West Africa'. In *Iconoclasm: Contested Object, Contested Terms*, eds. S. Boldrick and R. Clay. Aldershot: Ashgate.

Satterthwaite, S. nd. 'Older Ladies Talk'. *The Citizen Times*. Retrieved September 2005 from: http://thecitizennews.com/main/archive-050706/op-04_talk_sallie.html.

Schank, R. and R. Abelson. 1977. *Scripts, Plans, Goals and Understanding.* Hillsdale: Erlbaum.

Schleiermacher, F.E. 1994 [1799]. *On Religion: Speeches to its Cultured Despisers*, translated by J. Oman. Westminster: John Knox Press.

Schutz, A., 1964. 'The Well-Informed Citizen'. In *Collected Papers, II*. The Hague: Martinus Nijhoff.

Scribner, S. and M. Cole. 1981. *The Psychology of Literacy.* Cambridge: Harvard University Press.

Segato, R.L. 1995. *Santos e Daimonis: O Politeísmo Afro-Brasileiro e a Tradição Arquetipal*, Brasília, Editora UnB.

Serra, O. 1995. *Águas do Rei.* Petrópolis: Vozes.

Severi, C. 1993a. *La memoria rituale: Follia e Immagine del Bianco in una tradizione sciamanica amerindiana*, La Nuova Italia, Firenze, pp. I–XII, 1–273.

——— 1993b. 'Talking about Souls: on the Pragmatic Construction of Meaning in Cuna Chants'. In *Cognitive Aspects of Religious Symbolism*, ed. P. Boyer. Cambridge: Cambridge University Press.

——— 1997. 'The Kuna Picture-Writing: a Study in Iconography and Memory'. In *The Art of Being Kuna: Layers of Meaning among the Kuna of*

Panama, ed. M. Salvador. Los Angeles: Fowler Museum of the University
of California at Los Angeles.
———— 2001. 'Cosmology, Crisis and Paradox: On the Image of White Spirits
in Kuna Shamanistic Tradition'. In *Disturbing Remains: A Comparative
Inquiry into the Representation of Crisis*, eds. M. Roth and C. Salas. Los
Angeles: Getty Institute for the History of Art and the Humanities
Publications.
———— 2002. 'Memory, Reflexivity and Belief: Reflections on the Ritual Use
of Language'. *Social Anthropology* 10(1): 23–40.
———— 2004a. *Il Percorso e la Voce: Un'antropologia della Memoria*. Turin: Einaudi.
———— 2004b. 'Capturing Imagination: A Cognitive Approach to Cultural
Complexity'. *Journal of the Royal Anthropological Institute* 10(4): 815–38.
———— 2004c. 'Memory between Image and Narrative: an Interdisciplinary
Approach'. *Jahrbuch des Wissenschaftskolleg zu Berlin, 2002–2003*:
334–38.
Shaw, R. 2002. *Memories of the Slave Trade: Ritual and the Historical
Imagination in Sierra Leone*. Chicago: University of Chicago Press.
Sillander, K. 2004. *Acting Authoritatively: How Authority is Expressed through
Social Action among the Bentian of Indonesian Borneo*. Helsinki: University
of Helsinki Press, Swedish School of Social Science.
Silverstein, M. and G. Urban (eds). 1996. *Natural Histories of Discourse*.
Chicago: University of Chicago.
Siregar, S.R. 1979. 'Advice to the Newly Weds: Sipirok Batak Wedding
Speeches – Adat or Art?'. In *Art, Ritual and Society in Indonesia*, eds. E.M.
Bruner and J. Becker. Athens: Ohio University Center for International
Studies (Southeast Asia Series No. 53): 30–61.
Skultans, V. 1974, *Intimacy and Ritual: A Study of Spiritualism, Mediums and
Groups*. London and Boston: Routledge & Kegan Paul.
Smith, J.Z. 1978. *Map is Not Territory: Studies in the History of Religions*,
Leiden: E.J. Brill.
———— 1987. *To Take Place: Toward Theory in Ritual*. Chicago: University of
Chicago Press.
———— 1998. 'Religion, Religions, Religious'. In *Critical Terms for Religious
Studies*, ed. M.C. Taylor. Chicago and London: University of Chicago
Press, pp. 269–84.
———— 2002. 'Manna, Mana Everywhere and /.../.../...'. In *Radical
Interpretation in Religion*, ed. N.K. Frankenberry. Cambridge: Cambridge
University Press.
Smith, P. 1979. 'Aspects de l'organisation des rites'. In *La fonction symbolique:
essais d'anthropologie*, eds. M. Izard and P. Smith. Paris: Gallimard.
———— 1991. 'Rite'. In *Dictionnaire de l'ethnologie et de l'anthropologie*. Paris:
Presses Universitaires de France.
Smith, W.C. 1991 [1962]. *The Meaning and End of Religion*. Minneapolis:
Fortress Press.
Soster-Olmer, K. 2001. 'First Moon Rising: the Making of a Menarche
Ritual', *Mothering* 109. Retrieved March 2006 from:
http://www.mothering.com/community_tools/teen_voices/first-
moon.html.

Sperber, D. 1975. *Rethinking Symbolism*. Cambridge: Cambridge University Press.

———1985. *On Anthropological Knowledge*. Cambridge: Cambridge University Press.

———1994. 'The Modularity of Thought and the Epidemiology of Representations'. In *Domain Specificity in Cognition and Culture*, eds. L. Hirschfield and S. Gelman. Cambridge: Cambridge University Press.

———1996. *Explaining Culture: a Naturalistic Approach*. Oxford: Blackwell Publishers.

———2000. 'Metarepresentations in an Evolutionary Perspective'. In *Metarepresentations: A Multidisciplinary Perspective*, ed. D. Sperber. Oxford: Oxford University Press.

——— forthcoming. 'Modularity and Relevance: How Can a Massively Modular Mind be Flexible and Context-Sensitive?'. In *The Innate Mind: Structure and Content*, eds. P. Carruthers, S. Laurence and S. Stich.

Sperber, D. and D. Wilson. 1995 [1986]. *Relevance: Communication and Cognition*, 2nd edn. Oxford: Blackwell.

Spickard, J.V. 1993. 'For a Sociology of Religious Experience'. In *A Future for Religion? New Paradigms for Social Analysis*, ed. W.H. Swatos. London: Sage.

Spiegel, H. and D. Spiegel. 2004 [1978]. *Trance and Treatment*. New York: Basic Books.

Spindler, G. (ed.). 1997. *Education and Cultural Process: Anthropological Approaches*. Prospect Heights, IL: Waveland Press.

Stafford, C. 1995. *The Roads of Chinese Childhood*. Cambridge: Cambridge University Press.

——— 2000. *Separation and Reunion in Modern China*. Cambridge: Cambridge University Press.

——— 2003. 'Langage et apprentissage des nombres in Chine et a Taiwan'. *Terrain* 40: 65–80.

——— 2007. 'What is Going to Happen Next?' In *Questions of Anthropology*, eds R. Astuti, J. Parry and C. Stafford. London School of Economics Monographs on Social Anthropology, vol. 76. Oxford: Berg.

Stein, D. 1990 *Casting the Circle: a Woman's Book of Ritual*. Freedom, CA: The Crossing Press.

Stevenson, R.L. 1986 [1879]. *Travels with a Donkey*. London: Penguin.

Stobart, H. and R. Howard (eds). 2002. *Knowledge and Learning in the Andes: Ethnographic Perspectives*. Liverpool: Liverpool University Press.

Stoller, P. 1995. *Embodying Colonial Memories: Spirit Possession, Power and the Hauka in West Africa*. New York and London: Routledge.

Strauss, C. 1992. 'What makes Tony Run?' In *Human Motives and Cultural Models*, eds. R. D'Andrade and C. Strauss. Cambridge: Cambridge University Press.

Stringer, M. 1999. 'Rethinking Animism: Thoughts from the Infancy of our Discipline'. *Journal of the Royal Anthropological Institute* 5(4): 541–55.

Stromberg, P.G. 1993. *Language and Self-Transformation: A Study of Christian Conversion Narrative*. Cambridge: Cambridge University Press.

Tambiah, S.J. 1985. *Culture, Thought and Social Action, An Anthropological Perspective*. Cambridge, MA, Harvard University Press.

Tana Toraja Archive. Badan Arsip dan Perpustakaan Daerah Propinsi Sulawesi Selatan di Makassar [Regional Archive and Library of the South Sulawesi Province in Makassar]. Makassar, Sulawesi.

Taussig, M. 1993. *Mimesis and Alterity: a Particular History of the Senses*. New York: Routledge.

——— 2003. 'Viscerality, Faith and Skepticism: Another Theory of Magic'. In *Magic and Modernity: Interfaces of Revelation and Concealment*, eds. B. Meyer and P. Pels. Stanford: Stanford University Press.

Taylor, D. 1988. *Red Flower: Rethinking Menstruation*. Freedom, CA: The Crossing Press.

Taylor, M.C. (ed.). 1998. *Critical Terms for Religious Studies*. Chicago and London: University of Chicago Press.

Tellegen, A. and G. Atkinson. 1974. 'Openness to Absorbing and Self-Altering Experiences ("Absorption"): a Trait Related to Hypnotic Susceptibility'. *Journal of Abnormal Psychology*, 83: 268–77.

Thistle. 2005. 'The Wheel of Life'. Retrieved March 2006 from: http://paganparenting.net.

Thompson, L. n.d. 'Questionnaire about Menstrual Slapping'. Retrieved July 2005 from: http://www.mum.org/slapques.htm.

Thorne, B. 1993. *Gender Play: Girls and Boys in School*. New Brunswick, NJ: Rutdgers University Press.

Tomasello, M., M. Carpenter, J. Call, T. Behne and H. Moll. 2005. 'Understanding and Sharing Intentions: the Origins of Cultural Cognition'. *Behavioural and Brain Sciences* 28: 675–735.

Toren, C. 1998. 'Cannibalism and Compassion: Transformations in Fijian Notions of the Person'. In *Common Worlds and Single Lives: Constituting Knowledge in Pacific Societies*, ed. V. Keck. London: Berg.

——— 1999. 'Compassion for One Another: Constituting Kinship as Intentionality in Fiji'. *Journal of the Royal Anthropological Institute* 5: 265–80.

——— 2001. 'The Child in Mind'. In *The Debated Mind: Evolutionary Psychology versus Ethnography*, ed. H. Whitehouse. London: Berg.

——— 2004. 'Becoming a Christian in Fiji: an Ethnographic Study of Ontogeny'. *Journal of the Royal Anthropological Institute*, 10: 222–40.

Turner, V. 1967. *The Forest of Symbols: Aspects of Ndembu Ritual*. New York: Cornell University Press.

——— 1982. 'Acting in Everyday Life and Everyday Life in Acting'. In *From Ritual to Theatre*. New York: Performing Arts Journal Press.

——— 1986, *The Anthropology of Performance*: New York: Performing Arts Journal Press.

Tversky, A. and D. Kahneman. 1983. 'Extensional vs. Intuitive Reasoning: the Conjunction Fallacy in Probability Judgment'. *Psychological Review* 90: 293–315.

Tylor, E.B. 1903 [1871]. *Primitive Culture: Researches into the Development of Mythology, Philosophy, Religion, Language, Art and Custom*. London: John Murray. 2 vol.

van den End, T. (ed.). 1994. *Sumber-Sumber Zending Tentang Sejarah Gereja Toraja 1901–1961* ['Zending Sources on the History of the Toraja Church 1901–1961']. Jakarta: PT BPK Gunung Mulia.

Van Gennep, A. 1960 [1909]. *The Rites of Passage*, translated by M.B. Vizedom and G.L. Caffee. London: Routledge and Kegan Paul.

Vasconcelos, J. 2003. 'Espíritos Clandestinos: Espiritismo, Pesquisa Psíquica e Antropologia da Religião entre 1850 e 1920'. *Religião e Sociedade* 23(2): 92–126.

———— 2005, 'Langue des esprits et esprit de São Vicente (îles du Cap-Vert)', *Terrain* 44: 109–24.

Virkler, M. and P. Virkler. 1986. *Dialogue with God*. Orlando, FL: Bridge-Logos.

Viveiros de Castro, E. 1999. 'Etnologia Brasileira', in *O que Ler na Ciência Social Brasileira (1970–1995), Vol. 1: Antropologia*, ed. S. Micelli. São Paulo: Sumaré/ANPOCS.

Volkman, T.T.A. and C. Zerner. 1988. 'The Tree of Desire: a Toraja Ritual Poem'. In *To Speak in Pairs: Essays on the Ritual Languages of Eastern Indonesia*, ed. J.J. Fox. Cambridge: Cambridge University Press.

Warnier, J.-P. 2001. 'A Praxeological Approach to Subjectivation in a Material World'. *Journal of Material Culture* 6(1): 5–24.

———— 2006. 'Inside and Ouside: Surfaces and Containers'. In *Handbook of Material Culture*, eds. C. Tilley, W. Keane, S. Kuechler, M. Rowlands and P. Spyer. London: Sage.

———— forthcoming. *The Pot-King: Bodily Conducts, Material Culture and the Technologies of Power*. Amsterdam: Brill.

Warren, R. 2002. *The Purpose Driven Life*. Grand Rapids, MI: Zondervan.

Waterson, R. 1993. 'Taking the Place of Sorrow: the Dynamics of Mortuary Rituals among the Sa'dan Toraja', *Southeast Asian Journal of Social Science* 21: 73–97.

Watson, J.L. 1988. 'The Structure of Chinese Funerary Rites: Elementary Forms, Ritual Sequence, and the Primacy of Performance'. In *Death Ritual in Late Imperial and Modern China*, eds. J.L. Watson and E.S. Rawski. Berkeley, CA: University of California Press.

Weber, M. 1930 [1920]. *The Protestant Ethic and the Spirit of Capitalism*, translated by T. Parsons. London: George Allen & Unwin Ltd.

———— 1948 [1919]. 'Science as a Vocation'. In *From Max Weber: Essays in Sociology*, eds. and translation by H.H. Gerth and C.W. Mills. London: Routledge & Kegan Paul, pp. 129–56.

Whitehead, H. 2000. 'The Hunt for Quesalid: Tracking Levi-Strauss' Shaman'. *Anthropology & Medicine* 7(2):149–68.

Whitehouse, H. 1995. *Inside the Cult: Religious Innovation and Transmission in Papua New Guinea*. Oxford: Oxford University Press.

———— 2000. *Arguments and Icons: Divergent Modes of Religiosity*. Oxford: Oxford University Press.

———— (ed.). 2001. *The Debated Mind: Evolutionary Psychology versus Ethnography*. Oxford and New York: Berg.

———— 2002. 'Religious Reflexivity and Transmissive Frequency'. *Social Anthropology* 10(1): 91–103.

———— 2004. *Modes of Religiosity: A Cognitive Theory of Religious Transmission.* Walnut Creek: AltaMira Press.

———— 2005. 'The Cognitive Foundations of Religiosity'. In *Mind and Religion: Psychological and Cognitive Foundations of Religion*, eds. H. Whitehouse and T. McCauley. Walnut Creek: AltaMira Press.

Whitehouse, H. and J. Laidlaw (eds). 2004. *Ritual and Memory: Toward a Comparative Anthropology of Religion.* Walnut Creek: AltaMira Press.

Whitehouse, H. and T. McCauley (eds). 2005. *Mind and Religion: Psychological and Cognitive Foundations of Religion.* Walnut Creek: AltaMira Press.

Willard, D. 1999. *Hearing God.* Downers Grove, IL: Intervarsity.

Wittgenstein, L. 1958. *Philosophical Investigations.* Oxford: Blackwell.

———— 1961. *Notebooks 1914–16.* Oxford: Blackwell.

———— 1966. *Lectures and Conversations on Aesthetics, Psychology and Religious Belief*, ed. C. Barrett. Oxford: Blackwell.

———— 1969. *On Certainty.* Oxford: Blackwell.

Wolcott, Harry F. 1982. 'The Anthropology of Learning'. *Anthropology & Education Quarterly* 13(2): 83–108.

Wuthnow R. 1998. *After Heaven.* Berkeley, CA: University of California Press.

Zenack, M. 2006. 'First Menstruation Ritual'. Retrieved March 2006 from www.my-articles.com.

Zurbuchen, M. 1987. *The Language of Balinese Shadow Theater.* Princeton, NJ: Princeton University Press.

NOTES ON CONTRIBUTORS

David Berliner is an Assistant Professor of Anthropology at the Université Libre de Bruxelles (Belgium). He holds a Ph.D. in Anthropology from Université Libre de Bruxelles (2002), and has been a doctoral visiting student at Manchester and Oxford, as well as a post-doctoral Fellow at Harvard University (2003–05). He has conducted extensive field research on memory and religious transmission among the Bulongic people of coastal Guinea, as well as on gender, art and material culture. Some of his articles have been published in *American Ethnologist*, *Cahiers d'Études Africaines*, *RES Anthropology and Aesthetics* and *Anthropological Quarterly*. He is now completing a monograph (entitled *Le Silence des Masques*) about his ethnographic research in Guinea-Conakry.

Aurora Donzelli is an Associate Research Fellow at the Institute of Social Sciences in Lisbon and a Research Affiliate at the UCLA Anthropology Department in Los Angeles. She is a linguistic anthropologist and her main areas of research are political and formal speech – with a particular emphasis on honorification and linguistic etiquette, language ideologies, missionization and the emergence of colonial discourse genres. Her recent Ph.D. dissertation, based on extensive fieldwork in the Toraja highlands of Sulawesi (Indonesia), explores communicative practices as a locus for the social reproduction of political theories and moral notions. Her published work deals with code-switching and language ideologies, local theories of action, power and emotions, as well as with evangelization and ritual change in upland Sulawesi. She is currently completing a monograph entitled: *One Word or Two: Language and Politics in the Toraja Highlands*.

Marcio Goldman is Assistant Professor in the Postgraduate Programme of Social Anthropology at the Federal University of Rio de Janeiro (National Museum, Brazil), and a researcher for the Brazilian National Council for Scientific and Technological Development (CNPQ) and for the Estado do Rio Foundation for the Support of Research (FAPERJ). He is the author of *Razão e Diferença: Afetividade, Racionalidade e Relativismo no Pensamento de Lévy-Bruhl* (1994); *Alguma Antropologia* (1999), and *Como Funciona a Democracia: Uma Teoria Etnográfica da Política* (2006). He is presently studying the connections between politics, religion, ethnicity and culture in the town of Ilhéus in southern Bahia (north-eastern Brazil).

Laurence Hérault is a Senior Lecturer in Social Anthropology at the University of Aix-Marseille and a member of the Institute of Mediterranean and European Ethnology (IDEMEC. Aix-en-Provence). Her research interests include rituals, rites of passage, religious apprenticeship in Christianity, and currently process and rituals of 'transsexualization'. She had conducted fieldwork in France and Switzerland. Her publications include *La Grande Communion* (Paris: CTHS 1996) and 'Learning Communion', *Anthropology Today* 15(4), 1999.

Michael Houseman is Director of Studies at the École Pratique des Hautes Etudes (Paris) and a member of the African Worlds Study Centre (CEMAf-Ivry). He has published extensively on ritual and on kinship, and is the co-author (with Carlo Severi) of *Naven or the Other Self* (Brill, 1998).

Michael Lambek is Professor of Anthropology at the London School of Anthropology and the University of Toronto at Scarborough, where he holds a Canada Research Chair. He is the author of *Human Spirits* (1981), *Knowledge and Practice in Mayotte* (1993), *The Weight of the Past: Living with History in Mahajanga, Madagascar* (2002) and editor of a number of collections, including *A Reader in the Anthropology of Religion* (2002) and *Ecology and the Sacred* (2001, with Ellen Messer).

Tanya Luhrmann is Professor in the Department of Anthropology at Stanford University. Her work focuses on the way that social practice affects psychological mechanism, particularly in the domain of what some would call the 'irrational'. She is an anthropologist, and uses primarily ethnographic methods to identify the salient features of the social context. She is the author of three books: *Persuasions of the Witch's Craft* (Harvard, 1989), *The Good Parsi* (Harvard, 1996), and *Of Two Minds* (Knopf, 2000). Her current work looks at the experience of voices and visions both in the new style of American religion and among psychiatric clients, and the way the interpretation of these phenomena may affect the experience of God (on the one hand) and the identification, experience and outcome of psychiatric illness (on the other).

David Parkin has been Professor of Social Anthropology at the University of Oxford since 1996, having beforehand taught at the School of Oriental and African Studies, London. His regional specialization is eastern Africa and the Indian Ocean littoral, with special reference to Swahili speakers and to the Giriama- and Luo-speaking peoples. His recent interests include Islam, healing, cross-cultural semantics, material culture and the relationship between social and biological anthropology. Recent authored and edited publications include *The Sacred Void, Islamic Prayer across the Indian Ocean, The Politics of Cultural Performance, Autorité et pouvoir chez les Swahili* and *Holistic Anthropology* (2007).

Michael Rowlands is Professor of Social Anthropology at University College London, where over the last decades he has played a key role in cementing links between social anthropology and material culture. He is currently the MA tutor for Museum Anthropology as well as the UK coordinator for an EC-funded programme (European Cultural Heritage online) which is committed to place all ethnographic collections in European museums online to form virtual collections. He is also co-ordinator of a Ghetty funded research programme on innovation and change in the Grassfields region of Cameroon. He is currently supervising research on indigenous cultural property and cultural rights in Cameroon, Mali and Taiwan; on illicit trade and perceptions of cultural loss; on craft production and tourism in West Africa; on postcolonial museums and cultural heritage. He has written extensively on a diversity of topics including memory and cultural transmission, material culture, witchcraft and the African state and has recently co-edited the *Handbook of Material Culture* (2006).

Ramon Sarró is a Senior Research Fellow at the Institute of Social Sciences, University of Lisbon. He holds a Ph.D. from London (UCL 1999) and has been the Ioma Evans-Pritchard Junior Research Fellow at St Anne's College, Oxford (2000–02). Since 1992 he has conducted fieldwork on coastal Guinea, mainly on an iconoclastic religious and political movement that took place in 1956 among the Baga-Sitem speaking people and its legacies and memories today. His book *Iconoclasm Done and Undone: the Politics of Religious Change on the Upper Guinea Coast* will be published by the International African Institute in 2008.

Carlo Severi is Director of Research at the CNRS (France) and Director of Studies at the École des Hautes Études en Sciences Sociales (Paris). He has conducted extensive research and published on shamanistic traditions, ritual action and symbolism. He is currently working on the anthropology of memory and the anthropology of images. He is the author of *La Memoria rituale: Follia e immagine del Bianco in una tradizione sciamanica amerindiana* (1993) and of *Il Percorso e la Voce: Una antropologia della memoria* (2004). Both books will be published in French in 2007. He has edited a Special Issue of *L'Homme* on 'Image and Anthropology' (2003) and is the co-author (with Michael Houseman) of *Naven or the Other Self* (Brill, 1998).

Charles Stafford is Professor of Anthropology at the London School of Economics. His research has focused primarily on issues related to learning, cognition and child development, and he has conducted extensive field research in rural Taiwan and China. He is the author of *The Roads of Chinese Childhood* (CUP, 1995) and *Separation and Reunion in Modern China* (CUP, 2000), and the editor of *Living with Separation in China* (RoutledgeCurzon, 2003).

João Vasconcelos is a Senior Research Fellow at the Institute of Social Sciences, University of Lisbon. Since 2000 he has been conducting ethnographic and historical research on Christian Rationalism in Cape Verde and Brazil. He has published extensively on local Catholicism in contemporary Portugal, on Portuguese ethnography and folklore studies, and on the formation of cultural identities.

INDEX

A

Abelson, R., 98
acoustic envelop, 192, 193, 194, 195, 196, 197, 202, 204, 205
acquiring religious knowledge, 10, 14, 47, 58, 72–74, 122, 143, 162
Adorno, T., 194, 195
affection, 35, 137–38
affects, 16, 113, 137–38
African Christianity, 202
Afro-Brazilian Religion, 15, 104–19
Afro-Brazilian Studies, 105–6, 118–19
Agence Romande d'Education Chrétienne, 166, 168, 169
analogical separation, 50
analogical thinking, 116
ancestors, 9, 18, 31, 57, 104, 143, 146, 153–56, 183, 186, 197–206
Angola (in Candomblé), 104–18
animism, 4, 51–57
Anzieu, D., 192, 193
Appel-Slingbaum, C., 34, 35
Argenti N., 206
Arnal, W.E., 5
Asad, T., 3, 73
ashe (force) 110–11, 115
Astrology, 66, 76
Astuti, R., 11
Atkinson, G., 86
Atran, S., 7, 99, 100
Attali, J., 194, 206
attention (in religious acquisition), 8, 122

in African cults, 202
in Chinese religion, 177–88
in Christian catechism, 163–74
Austin, J.L., 14, 67, 68, 69, 70, 71, 72, 73, 81n
authority, 42, 47, 53, 55, 71, 85, 110, 134, 143, 144–55, 152, 195, 199

B

Badan Pusat Statistik, 146, 156
Bang, A., 59
Barrett, J., 8, 84, 185
Barth, F., 7, 27
Bastide, R., 15, 103, 105, 108, 110, 112, 115–17, 119n
Bateson, G., 69, 168, 169
Bauman, R., 157
Baumann, M., 164
Behne, T., 189
belief, 2, 4, 5, 12, 13, 17, 19n, 21–30, 33, 44, 49, 50, 51, 53, 54, 57, 62, 72, 81n, 85, 101, 107, 114, 130, 141, 143, 144, 146, 147, 154, 157n, 163, 164, 176, 177n, 182, 183, 184, 186, 187, 188, 192, 195, 204, 206
Bem, D., 101
Benveniste, É., 2
Berliner, D., 3, 6, 118n, 146
Berthoz, A., 33
Bhran, S., 39
Bible, 1, 14, 85–91, 168–70
Bigalke, T.W., 146

Binghamton Pagan Community, 39
Blakemore, S-J., 33
Bloch, M.,5, 6, 7, 10, 11, 12, 19, 48,
      143, 180, 181, 185, 195
body, 11, 17, 35, 75, 88, 89, 95, 101,
      114, 126, 132, 133, 153, 193,
      196–204
body language, 178 *see also* gesture
body of Christ, 163–75
Born again, 192
Borofsky, R., 7
Bourdieu, P., 74, 180
Bourguignon, E., 86
Boyer, P., 4, 8,–11, 15, 19n, 49, 84, 98,
      122, 180, 181, 185
Braun, W., 19
Brazil, 103–19, 125
Brenner, L., 6
Brickel, 85
bricolage, 107
Briggs, C.L., 157
Briggs, J., 11
Brunner, J., 42

C
Call, J., 189
Cameroon, 191–206
Candomblé, 15, 103–19
Cape Verde, 121–40
Capone, S., 118
Carpenter, M., 189
Carruthers, M., 86
Carruthers, P., 32
Catholicism, 17, 91, 103, 158n
Cavell, S., 69, 70, 71, 81
Centro Redentor, 124, 126, 128, 129,
      131, 133, 139
certainty, 12, 21, 23, 27, 30, 72, 76, 80,
      81n, 130
Chaiklin, S., 11
children, 11, 12, 17, 25, 36, 40, 45,
      48n, 57, 59, 60, 61, 62, 84, 113,
      114, 119n, 125, 131, 133, 134,
      153, 161–76, 178, 184, 189, 196,
      199
China, 12, 17, 18, 177–89
Christian Rationalism, 15, 121–40
Christianity, 55, 85–88, 141, 146, 147,
      148, 157n, 161–76, 194–204
class, 44, 71, 107, 128–39, 158n
Claverie, E.,137, 138, 176n
cognition, 4, 7, 8–18, 84, 98, 122

cognitive accident, 51
cognitive anthropology, 4, 7–10, 11,
      19n, 49, 98–99, 122, 180
cognitive development, 189
cognitive dissonance, 51
Cole, M., 97, 100
Comaroff, Jean, 203
Comaroff, John, 203
conversion, 2, 3, 6, 138, 141, 142, 146,
      148, 155, 159n
conviction, 5, 12, 14, 44, 46, 48, 49–53,
      60, 63, 64, 69, 71–75, 79–80, 86,
      135, 183
cosmology, 15, 103, 107, 107, 110,
      111, 117, 126, 133,183, 184, 192
Cossard, G.B., 108, 109
Costos, D.R., 35, 36, 37
counter-intuitiveness, 8, 180
Coville, E., 157n
Critchley, S., 81
Crook, N., 7
Crossman, R., 38
Crystal, E., 158
cultural transmission, 6, 7, 8, 18, 29,
      84, 122, 143, 179, 180, 192, 203

D
D'Andrade, R., 98
dance, 22, 39, 76, 79, 108,149,
      196–204
Dantas, B.G., 118
Daoist philosophy, 178
Davidson, J. 86
Davidson, R., 86
Davies, M., 32
Davis, E., 38, 43
de Certeau, M., 164, 176n
de Lacey, P., 97
de Lemos, M., 97
de Vinols, D., 163
death, 57, 58, 108, 144, 167, 173, 182,
      184, 192–93, 196–98 *see also*
      death celebration
death celebration, 192–206
Decety, J., 33
Deeley, P.Q., 49
Deleuze, G., 15, 105, 112, 113, 119,
      137
devil, 18, 127, 195, 203
Dianteill, E., 105
Dillon, R., 196
Dion, M., 109

disbelief, 23, 35, 185, 185, 186, 187
divination 51, 188, 204, 205
Donzelli, A., 16, 141, 148, 157n, 158n
doubt, 12, 23–29, 38, 53–54, 70, 183,
   186, 204
Du Bois, J.W., 143
Dubied, P.-L., 176
Dunbar, R., 49
Durham, W.W., 49
Durkheim, E., 4, 5, 6, 50, 51, 96, 106,
   116

E
E. Wenger, 10, 11
Eickelman, D.F., 6
Ellis, S. 203–5
embodied knowledge, 133, 139
embodiment, 139
emotion, 9–11, 18, 32, 33, 34, 36, 37,
   44, 45, 46, 48, 52, 53, 67, 87, 95,
   113, 114, 118, 136, 137, 185,
   187, 188, 200, 206
empathic simulation, 31–48
Engelke, M., 202, 207
episodic memory, 9, 10, 14, 19
Eucharistic, 165–76
Evangelization, 147
Evans-Pritchard, E., 19n, 83, 96
'explaining' vs. 'interpreting' or
   'understanding' religion, 7–18

F
Fabian, J., 147
faith, 21–29, 53, 69, 74, 86, 95, 137,
   161–76, 202–5
falseness, 70–71, 173
Fardon, R., 4
Favret-Saada, J., 137, 176n
fear, 18, 57, 62, 64, 77, 131, 192
Fedele, A., 48
Fellous, M., 39, 45
Ferme, M., 6
Fichte, H., 109
Finnegan, R., 154
flashbulb memory, 13
Flyvbjerg, B., 66
Fortes, M., 6
Fox, J.J., 143
Frame, J., 35
French Philosophical Society, 117
Freppel, Ch.-E., 162, 163
Fromm, E., 86

G
Gallagher, S., 33
Gay, J., 97
Geertz, C., 3, 5, 10, 51, 69, 71, 73
George, K.M., 142, 147, 158
gesture, 42, 50, 108, 127, 145, 169,
   172, 173, 174, 175
Giddens, A., 6
Gnau people, 179–81
God, 14, 18, 21, 52, 54, 56, 57, 58, 64,
   84–102, 140, 161–76, 192
Goddess, 38, 40, 41, 45
gods, 9, 17, 54, 56, 57, 83, 112, 115,
   178, 182–87
Goffman, E., 159n
Goldman, M., 14, 15, 16, 118n, 138
Goldwyn, T., 34
Goody, J., 99
gospel singing, 203
Gottlieb, A., 11
Greenfield, P., 98
Guattari, F., 15, 105, 112–13
Guberman, S., 98
Guthrie, S., 4

H
Halbwachs, M., 6
Hann, C.M., 194
Harris, P.L., 18, 189
Hawthorne, N., 45
healing, 56, 80, 87
hearing and listening, 50, 85, 86, 93,
   144, 178, 193, 195
Heron, A., 97
Hervieu-Léger, D., 7
Heryanto, A.,156
Hirschfeld, L.A., 7
Hobbs, A., 43
Hoffmann, M., 35
Højbjerg, C.K., 3, 12, 24
Holmes, R., 28, 29
Houseman, M., 11, 13, 24, 28, 30n, 31,
   36
Howard, R., 7
Howell, S., 35
Hugh-Jones, S., 65, 68
Hume, D., 23
Humphrey, C., 22, 34, 50
Humphrey, N., 185
Hutchins, E., 98

I
illocutionary, 67, 71, 80
image and imagery, 24–27, 88–100,
    121, 133, 136–39
imagination, 10, 13, 18, 23, 25, 29, 30,
    48, 86, 99, 155, 180, 189
incarnation, 124–26, 166
Indonesia, 141–56
inference, 13, 18, 22, 25, 29, 30, 31, 32,
    37, 41, 42, 46, 98, 99
inferential interpretation, 13, 31–47
initiation, 6, 9, 104, 109–17, 175, 179
insincerity, 69–81
intentionality, 46, 188, 189
internet, 31–43
invisible world, 18, 28, 203, 204, 206
Irony, 68–75
Islam, 50–64, 66, 146, 147, 158n

J
Jackson, P., 19n
James, Wendy, 19n
Janzen, J., 76
Jeannerod, M., 33
Jenkins, T., 54
Jesus Christ, 163, 164, 166, 167, 168, 169
Jing, J., 6
Jorland, G., 33
Jurkus, P., 35

K
Kahneman, D. 98
Kardecism, 16, 124
Katz., S. 86
Keane, W., 142, 143, 144, 154, 155,
    157n, 159n
Kierkegaard, S., 14, 65, 68, 72, 73
Koon, S.M., 43
Kramer, F., 127
Kresse, K., 55
Kuipers, J., 142, 143
Kuna Indians, 24–28
Kurys, D., 34

L
Lahire, B., 10
Laidlaw, J., 9, 22, 34, 50
Lakoff, G., 98
Lalanne, S., 163
Lambek, M., 13, 14, 55, 66, 67, 68, 77,
    81n, 86n, 137, 138, 140n, 157n
Latour, B., 3, 176n

Lave, J., 11, 98
Lawson T.E., 8, 9, 122
Lecourt, E., 192, 193
Lenclud, G., 176
Leonard, C., 38, 43
Lépine, C., 111
Leppert, R., 194, 195
Lévi-Strauss, C., 116, 179
Lévy-Bruhl, L., 15, 83, 84, 93, 95–97,
    102, 116, 117, 137
Lewis, G., 179, 181
Lewis, I., 134, 136
Lienhard, J., 88
literacy, 97, 98, 99, 133
liturgy, 52, 52, 141, 168, 172, 194
Loimeier, R., 54, 59
Lord, A.B., 154
Luhrmann, T.M., 8, 14, 15, 16, 47, 84,
    86, 90

M
Madagascar, 6, 66
madarasa (Qur'anic schools), 54, 55, 57,
    58–60 *see also* school, schooling
Maggie, Y., 118n
magic, 44, 114–15, 124, 136, 169
Magliocco, S., 47, 48n
masquerades, 18, 199, 200
materiality and religion, 9, 22, 77, 95,
    111, 123, 124, 126, 129, 148,
    157n, 191, 192, 196, 201–6
Mauss, M., 15, 116, 118
Mayotte, 66, 75, 76
McCauley, R.N., 8, 9, 122
McCutcheon, R.T., 19
McGovern, M., 4
mechanic memory, 12, 17, 26–27
Medin, D., 100
Mediums, 66, 67, 68, 76, 80, 121–39,
    177, 182, 183, 186
memorizing, 25, 145, 162, 167
memory, 6, 25–29, 86, 98, 166 *see also*
    religious memory, mechanic
    memory, flashbulb memory,
    episodic memory and semantic
    memory
menarche rites, 31–46
menstrual goddess, 38
menstrual slap, 13, 33–48
Meslin, M., 3
methexis (in Plato), 15
Meyer, B., 202, 203, 220, 221

Middleton, J., 7, 215
Miller, D., 84
mimesis, 14, 15, 81n, 141, 142, 144,
    147, 154, 194
mnemonic devices, 26
Moll H., 189
morality, 52, 70, 121, 126, 132–34
Morton, H., 11
Müller, F.M., 4
music, 18, 65, 67, 85, 91, 192–206
Mystical Mountains, 39
mythology, 21, 107, 111

N
Needham, R., 12, 22, 23
Nehamas, A., 66
Neopagan ceremonies 31–48
New Age ceremonies, 31–48
Nigeria, 104, 195, 203, 205
noise, 18, 58, 191–206
non-human entities, 31, 57
Norhala, 39
numeracy, 183–88

O
objectification, 139
objective knowledge, 139
ontology, 103–17, 126, 133
orenda (force), 110
orisha (deity), 103–17
Orthodox Church, 1
Otto, R., 4

P
Pacherie, E., 33
Pals, D.L., 4
Parkin, D., 6, 13, 14, 55, 58
participation, 12, 15, 33, 43, 72, 73,
    83–102, 116–18, 134, 138, 140,
    165–69, 179, 188, 194, 195, 198
    see also methexis
Pemberton, J., 142
Pentecostalism, 18, 191–96, 202, 203,
    205
Pieke, F., 50
Piette, A., 168
Pike, S., 43, 47, 48n
Pogrebin, L.C., 35
prayer, 12, 25, 26, 29, 58, 61–63, 67,
    85–99, 122, 172–73
Price, R., 7
prophet, 5, 55, 87, 202, 205, 206

Putnam, H. 81n

Q
Qur'an, 56, 57, 58, 59, 60–62, 68
Qur'anic school (*see* madarasa)

R
Ramble, C., 180
Rappaport, R., 68, 70, 71, 73, 74
Ray, B.C., 5
Rayni, J., 35
recollection 1, 3, 12, 19n, 25, 29–30
reflexivity, 12, 141, 142, 157
Reformation, 162
Reid, S., 43
relego (in Cicero), 2–3, 19n
religious
    experience, 10, 22, 136–37, 189
    knowledge, 3, 4, 7, 12, 56, 72, 136,
        142, 157n, 162
    memory, 6
    transmission, 3, 7, 8, 9, 10, 11, 12,
        16, 18, 28, 31, 38, 41, 56, 142,
        145, 152, 157, 164, 166, 176,
        191, 192, 194, 204, 206
religo (in Lactantius and Augustine), 3
remembering, 8, 28, 39, 56, 87, 170,
    180, 198
Renard, J., 39
re-semanticisation of rituals, 148
Richards, A.I., 6
ritual
    action, 2, 21, 22, 23–27, 31, 41, 44,
        48, 172, 173, 176
    condensation, 36, 37, 41, 46, 47
    couplets, 143, 144, 154, 155, 159
    economy, 142, 146, 147, 150
    knowledge, 150
    performance, 24, 34, 37, 42, 44, 46,
        47, 48, 67, 145, 148, 179
    speech, 141–56, 157n, 159n
Roberts, S., 43
robustness of religious notions, 3
Rogoff, B., 98
Rosa, J.G., 115
Rosenblatt, J., 35
Rowlands, M., 18, 204
Rudolph, J., 43

S
sacrifice, 53, 67, 77, 104, 113, 114,
    148, 158n, 197, 203, 204

Sandarupa, S.,157
Sangren, P.S., 185
Schank, R., 98
Schleiermacher, F.E. 34, 23
school, schooling, 5, 7, 12, 54, 55, 56, 57, 59–62, 84, 92, 97, 98, 100, 123, 124, 125, 129, 148, 154
Scribner, S., 97
secrecy, 3, 16, 17, 32, 57, 145–46, 152–55
Segato, R.L., 119
selection, 180
semantic
  memory, 9–14, 19n, 25–30
  obscurity, 144
  vs. pragmatic-based phenomena of cultural transmission, 27–29, 33
semantics, 73
serendipity, 50
seriousness, 68–80
Serra, O., 119
Severi, C., 11, 12, 13, 21, 22, 24, 26, 27, 28,30n, 31, 36, 156
shamanism, 24, 51, 65, 86
Shaw, R., 6
Sillander, K., 158
Silverstein, M. and G. Urban, 157n
simulation, 31–48
sincerity, 68–81
Siregar, S.R., 142
Skultans, V., 134
Smith, J.Z., 3, 5, 19n
Smith, P., 22, 23, 23, 32, 42
Smith, P.K, 32
Soster-Olmer, K., 41, 43, 45
sound, 18, 40, 79, 191–202
Sperber, D., 7, 8, 11, 33, 42, 49, 99, 180, 181, 186, 187
Spickard, J.V., 137
Spiegel, D., 86
Spiegel, H., 86
Spindler, G., 7
spirit possession, 51, 66, 68, 73, 75, 80, 103–19, 127, 134, 140n, 186
spiritism, 124, 125, 129, 140n
spiritual knowledge, 16, 122, 135–37
Stafford, C., 11, 17, 18, 177, 183
Stein, D., 42
Stevenson, R.L., 13, 28
Stobart, H., 7
Stoller, P., 6
Stone, T., 32

Strauss, C., 98
Stringer, M., 4
Stromberg, P.G., 121, 137, 138
success, 203–5
Sufism, 62
symbolic
  action, 22
  anthropology, 5
  capital, 144
  envelope, 205
  meaning, 141
symbolism, 22, 24, 37, 46, 182
syncretism, 7, 104, 106

T
Taiwan, 18, 177, 182, 183, 184, 186, 188
Tambiah, S.J., 22
Tana Toraja Archive, 148, 157n
Taussig, M., 68, 81n
Taylor, D., 35
Taylor, M.C., 19n
teacher, 11, 54, 55, 56, 57, 60, 60, 62, 63, 123–25
teaching, 17, 26, 52, 53, 59, 60–62, 88, 95, 109, 142, 162, 163, 164–69, 173, 176, 188
Tellegen, A. 86
ter Haar., G. 203–5
terror (*see* fear)
theory of mind, 32
Thompson, L., 34
Thorne, B., 11
Tomasello, M., 189
Toraja (Indonesia), 141–56
Toren, C., 11
transmission
  of belief, 12, 28
  of faith, 164, 176
  of knowledge, 7, 32, 192
  of relationships, 13, 32
  of ritual behaviour, 31
  of ritual context, 13
  of ritual speech, 145
  see also 'religious transmission' and 'cultural transmission'
truth, 15, 23, 53, 58, 101, 114–16, 136, 162, 164, 166, 186
Turner, V., 6, 22, 81
Tversky, A., 98
Tylor, E.B., 4, 95

U
uncertainty, 24, 25, 41, 53, 64, 73

V
van den End, T., 147, 148
van Gennep, A., 6
Vasconcelos, J., 14, 15, 16, 140n
Vignato, S., 227
Virkler, M., 85
Virkler, P., 85
Viveiros de Castro, E., 48, 106, 118n
vodun (deity), 104
Volkman, T.T.A., 157n

W
Walker, S., 122
Warnier, J.-P., 192, 193, 204, 207
Warren, R., 87
Waterson, R., 158
Watson, J.L., 186
wealth, 158n, 191–205

Weber, M., 5, 136, 137
Whitehead, H., 74
Whitehouse, H., 8, 9, 10, 11, 15, 19n
49, 64, 84, 98, 180, 181
Wilson, D., 139, 181
witchcraft, , 5, 19, 56, 57, 124, 136,
191–207
Wittgenstein, L., 12, 21, 23, 25, 27, 30,
67, 135
worship, 52, 56, 57, 67, 83, 87–95,
161, 178, 180, 183, and music
192–95

Y
youth, 17, 58, 85, 91, 166, 206

Z
Zanzibar, 13, 57, 58, 59, 60, 62, 63
Zenack, M., 43
Zerner, C., 157n
Zurbuchen, M., 154

www.ingramcontent.com/pod-product-compliance
Lightning Source LLC
Chambersburg PA
CBHW072102020426
42334CB00017B/1607